A More
Perfect Union

A More Perfect Union

DOCUMENTS IN U.S. HISTORY

VOLUME I: to 1877

Paul F. Boller, Jr.
Texas Christian University

Ronald Story
University of Massachusetts, Amherst

HOUGHTON MIFFLIN COMPANY • BOSTON

Dallas   Geneva, Illinois   Hopewell, New Jersey   Palo Alto

Cover illustration: The New York Public Library. Astor, Lenox and Tilden Foundations.

Printed in the U.S.A.
Library of Congress Catalog Card Number: 83-81880
ISBN: 0-395-34936-2

ABCDEFGHIJ-MP-89876543

To Martin and Eliza

Contents

Chapter Three   NATIONALISTS AND PARTISANS

Chapter Four   THE AGE OF REFORM

Chapter Five   REBELS, YANKEES, AND FREEDMEN

A STATISTICAL APPENDIX   *after page 211*

Preface

The selections in these volumes represent what the authors believe to be an attractive blend of social and political history, suitable for introductory courses in American history. Three considerations guided our selection of items. First, we looked for famous documents with a lustrous place in the American tradition, regardless of their actual importance. These—the Mayflower Compact, for example, or the Gettysburg Address, or Franklin Roosevelt's first inaugural address—we chose for their great mythic quality, as expressions of fundamental ideals with which students should be familiar. Second, we searched out writings of genuine importance in the sense that they had immediate impact and caused something to happen. Examples from this very large group include the Virginia slave statutes, Tom Paine's *The Crisis,* the Emancipation Proclamation, and Earl Warren's decision in *Brown* v. *Board of Education*—all famous pieces, to be sure, but influential as well. Finally, we included documents that seemed to reflect important attitudes or developments. Into this group fall Thomas Hart Benton's racial views as well as the writings of Upton Sinclair on industrial Chicago and Martin Luther King, Jr., on Vietnam. Here, where the need for selectivity was most apparent, we looked especially for reflective pieces with a measure of fame and influence to carry them. Dorothea Dix's memorial on asylums reflected common attitudes; it also caused something to happen and is by now a well-known statement of reformist compassion.

Familiar documents are intermixed with unexpected ones (Andrew Jackson, say, with T. S. Arthur or Woodrow Wilson with Margaret Sanger). In addition, we did not hesitate to edit severely when the selection seemed too long; this consideration impinged most obviously on book-length works but also on pieces such as John Peter Zenger's account of his trial for libel or Joseph McCarthy's speech on Communist subversion. In some cases, particularly with writings from the colonial era, we have modernized spelling and punctuation. Each document has a lengthy headnote that summarizes the relevant trends of the era, provides a specific setting for the document, and sketches the life of the author. The headnotes are followed by study questions to guide students through the prose and suggest ways of thinking about the selections. The headnotes, and especially the study questions, contain many cross-references to other documents in the collection to provide perspective and encourage comparative analysis.

Each chapter concludes with a Counterpoint, a group of two to five statistical tables dealing with some aspect of American society that is relevant to the era and theme of that chapter's documents. Generally the work of distinguished modern historians, often "classic" studies in their own right, the Counterpoints touch upon issues raised in different ways by the documents—such as the Jacksonian assault on privilege, or difficulties faced by blacks and immigrants in industrial America. They expose the student to statistical as well as documentary or strictly rhetorical evidence. They also add a further flavor of social history to what, given our concern with the famous and influential, is still a predominantly political, constitutional, and diplomatic collection. All Counterpoints have the same type of headnotes, cross-references, and study questions as the main documents. The Statistical Appendix, comprising statistics on population, government, and the economy over the whole life of the nation, is offered in the same spirit—as an alternative way, or in some instances perhaps the only way, of seeing important long-term historical trends. The documents are the creations of particular moments; the Counterpoints provide close-ups of particular eras; the Appendix offers, in its fashion, the whole sweep of American history. The Statistical Appendix thus supplies a foundation over which documents and Counterpoints alike may ultimately be laid.

We would like to thank the following people who reviewed the manuscript for one or both volumes:

John Barnard, Oakland University
Joel A. Carpenter, Wheaton College
James E. Davis, Illinois College
Paul A. Fideler, Lesley College
Sylvia R. Frey, Tulane University
David M. Katzman, University of Kansas, Lawrence
John L. LeBrun, Kent State University, Salem Campus
Robert A. McCaughey, Barnard College, Columbia University
James T. McGowan, Rutgers University, Newark
William M. Wiecek, University of Missouri, Columbia

We also wish to thank the staff of Houghton Mifflin Company for their encouragement and assistance in the preparation of this work.

Paul F. Boller, Jr.
Ronald Story

A More
Perfect Union

Introduction

The two volumes of *A More Perfect Union: Documents in U.S. History* bring together a wide variety of documents illustrating political, social, economic, cultural, constitutional, and intellectual history for use in college courses in American history and culture. Volume I begins with the Mayflower Compact (1620) and ends with a post-Reconstruction speech by Frederick Douglass (1883). Volume II starts with the Reconstruction period and Lincoln's second inaugural address (1865) and continues to the present time, concluding with an essay on high-technology issues (1983).

The documentary readings cover the major themes in American history. In Volume I these include: the strides toward freedom and independence during the colonial period; the growth of nationalism during the early nineteenth century; the sectional conflict at mid-century; and the perennial American racial dilemma. Volume II repeats the last theme and adds these three: the responses to the periodic crises faced by the American economy since the late nineteenth century; the impetus toward humanitarian reform at every period of our national history; and the development of the United States into a superpower in the twentieth century. Both volumes also portray the perpetual tension throughout our history between freedom and security, individual enterprise and social justice, popular democracy and responsible leadership. There is a great deal of political history here; but there is also plenty of social and economic history. In the charters, laws, treaties, speeches, announcements, and reports—together with the end-of-chapter Counterpoint sections, which present statistics covering trends in American life—it is possible to observe American history in the making.

History is a multifaceted enterprise. At its most basic level it is a collection of facts. Historians keep records of treaties, elections, legislative acts, conferences, battles, legal decisions, and other significant happenings so that these are available to lawyers, diplomats, public officials, journalists, and other interested parties to consult. Some collections of documents are little more than reference books. Our volumes are not intended to be used in this way, but they do contain many fundamental records of American history for ready reference: the Declaration of Independence, the Monroe Doctrine, the *Dred Scott* decision, the Emancipation Proclamation, Franklin

Roosevelt's first inaugural address, the Supreme Court decision in *Brown* v. *Board of Education,* and Dwight D. Eisenhower's warning about the military-industrial complex.

But history is more than encyclopedia; history is also story. American history is filled with dramatic events: America's Declaration of Independence in 1776; Mississippi's secession cry in 1860; Lincoln's signing of the Emancipation Proclamation in 1863; Franklin Roosevelt's call for war on Japan after the attack on Pearl Harbor; the Woodstock Festival in 1969; the Watergate crisis in 1972–1974. *A More Perfect Union* is an anthology, not narrative history, so it does not recount any of these stories. Nevertheless, the basic materials from which narrative historians do reconstruct such stories are contained in these volumes: John Peter Zenger's trial in 1735; David Walker's appeal for justice for American blacks in 1829; Woodrow Wilson's impassioned call for war on Germany in 1917; and Richard Nixon's surprise visit to the People's Republic of China in 1972 after years of U.S. hostility toward the Chinese Communists.

Original records are often more fascinating to read than mere summaries of events written by persons who were not on the scene. Who can read David Walker's appeal today and not be deeply moved by what he said about the plight of blacks in the United States in 1829? Or read the description of the treatment of the Cheyenne and not be filled with indignation? Or read Jefferson's first inaugural address and not be filled with hope? Written records form the very substance of narrative history.

History is, however, not merely story, any more than it is merely a collection of facts. It is more than a series of dramatic moments. Life for most people of every era consists largely of habit, ritual, convention, schedule, and routine. And one of the historian's primary tasks is to reconstruct life as it was lived at times and in places enormously different from our own: colonial Massachusetts, antebellum Philadelphia, Chicago at the turn of the century, American society at the time of the Great Depression. *A More Perfect Union* supplies ample materials—statistics as well as documents—for recapturing life in both the near and distant past in this country.

The how and the why behind historical developments are more fascinating than the dates when events occurred. To encourage you to think about the how and the why, the authors have provided questions throughout *A More Perfect Union.* In the introduction to each document, after a general commentary and biographical information where it is appropriate, the last paragraph contains questions to consider. The end-of-chapter Counterpoint sections also have questions pertaining to the tables they contain, and some queries appear in the Statistical Appendix.

We are all culture-bound. We tend to judge other peoples, places, and periods by our own standards, and it is hard for us to comprehend other cultures in their deepest reaches. But if, after mastering the records of a past culture, we succeed in overcoming the parochialism of the present and in penetrating to the central vision of societies quite different from our own, we can become wiser about what human beings have accomplished in other times and places and can be more realistic about our own achievements. The documents in these volumes will enable readers to enter the lives of Americans whose experiences were totally different from their own: people in Pennsylvania in the middle of the eighteenth century, Cherokee Indians in Georgia in the 1830s, chattel slaves in colonial Virginia, emancipated blacks after the Civil War, Chicago stockyard workers in the early twentieth century, and young people at the Woodstock Festival in 1969 at the height of the counterculture movement. Variety, not uniformity, has been the spice of life in America since the very first settlements after Columbus.

But history is more than the study of past cultures. Students who want to understand the American past cannot stop with descriptions of what people did in earlier times; they will want to know why Americans acted as they did, and why, at critical junctures in our history, they took actions laden with momentous consequences for the future. A historian's most challenging task is to find out why social change occurred. Why did colonial Americans decide to strike for independence in 1776? What brought on the Civil War? Why did the United States decide to go to war in 1898, 1917, 1941, and 1950? What caused the Great Depression of the 1930s? What brought about the Great Inflation of the 1970s and 1980s?

Students of history search for factors that cause change. Are technological innovations at the root of historical change, or are new ways of producing and distributing material goods the basic developers? Or is it novelty of outlook—the appearance of new ideas—that transforms society? Undoubtedly, ideas and economic interests are both at work in the historical process. At the same time there is much that is accidental and unexpected in human affairs.

One purpose of *A More Perfect Union* is to stimulate you to think about the tremendous changes that have taken place on the American scene and to try to account for these changes. Original documents form a good basis for such an inquiry. They supply information about why Americans thought and acted as they did at particular points in time. In addition, many records in this anthology explain why Americans behaved as they did at decisive moments. The Declaration of Independence gives reasons why the American people decided on revolution in 1776. *The Federalist*, Number Ten, contains a theory of how societies in general, and American society in particular, operate. The tables showing where eastern college graduates went to teach add insight on the impact and spread of one region's ideas to other areas. Woodrow Wilson's address to Congress on the eve of war with Germany in 1917 contains a theory about the relation of nations to each other.

Past, present, and future are co-implicated in the documents in *A More Perfect Union*. Historical records contain factual data, material for dramatic stories, descriptions of bygone cultures, and suggestions for understanding social change. But they are also filled with guidelines for action. The Declaration of Independence sets forth ideals, goals, and aspirations for the American people to act upon, as well as explanations of actions taken. Thomas Jefferson's first inaugural address and Andrew Jackson's Bank Veto Message do the same. Franklin Roosevelt's first inaugural address in the midst of the Great Depression and his war message to Congress after the attack on Pearl Harbor also combine ideals and actions. The basic documents in these volumes contain prescriptions as well as descriptions: manifestoes, appeals, recommendations, suggestions, and calls to action.

The written word continues, of course, to be the major source for those seeking to understand the American past. But a striking development in historical scholarship during the past twenty years is the extensive use of nonverbal evidence, such as artwork and statistical data, to illuminate the past. These sources can enhance, modify, or explain the written record. Cartoons of Andrew Jackson, for example, tell us something about his popular reputation; photographs from the Great Depression reveal the forces behind the birth of Social Security. But in other cases, nonverbal sources, particularly statistical ones, have a story of their own to tell.

The Counterpoints and Statistical Appendix offer samples of the kind of statistical data that historians are relying on increasingly. The Counterpoint section at the end of each chapter is based upon a series of related tables. These tables concern mainly the American population, economy, and government—obviously important areas in which statistics are abundantly available. The purpose of these Counterpoints is to give you an opportunity to discover how historians draw conclusions from raw data. An introduction alerts you to the principal issues to think about and gives some guidance in reading the tables and extracting their information. You are encouraged to study these tables carefully, and to think about the questions that they raise. The effort will be repaid by an insight into the nature of the historical enterprise, a sense of how historians make sense out of the documents of the past.

At the conclusion of each volume is a Statistical Appendix (the same Statistical Appendix appears in both volumes). The information in this Appendix reveals a great deal about the America of earlier times, just as the Counterpoint tables do. Statistics on population, on changes in wages and consumer prices for different economic sectors, on religious affiliations, and on federal expenditures for defense, debt service, the postal service, and veterans' benefits, all have much to tell about the ways Americans have led their lives. As in the Counterpoints, an introduction to each table explains its relevance and guides the reader toward an understanding of the table's data.

We do not believe numbers will ever supplant words as the basic stuff of historical study. Nevertheless, with the aid of literary records, such figures, stark and ambiguous though they may seem, reveal trends in industry and labor, social and economic problems, and patterns of mobility, to mention only a few possibilities. Quantitative material has become indispensable to fully comprehending the past, and it will become even more significant in the future. Thus, in the two volumes of *A More Perfect Union,* a combination of numbers and original words is presented to give depth to the images of America's past and to shed light on its future.

"The First Day at Jamestown." The first English colony along the Atlantic coast, established in 1607. (Library of Congress)

CHAPTER ONE

Puritans and Planters

1. Separatist Beginnings
THE MAYFLOWER COMPACT (1620)

The Mayflower Compact has been called the first American constitution. It was a covenant or agreement drawn up by a group of Separatists, a small group of religious extremists who had separated from the Church of England because they did not think it was "pure" enough in its religious observances. Like all Puritans, the Separatists disliked the elaborate ceremonies of the Church of England; they favored plain and simple church services centered on the Bible. They also rejected the hierarchical structure of the Anglican church, with its archbishops and bishops. For them the congregation, organized by devout people who had experienced conversion, was the center of religious authority. The congregation had the power to choose its own ministers and deacons and to adopt rules and regulations for governing the church. Regarded with hostility by the government and with suspicion by their neighbors, the Separatists left England in 1608 and the following year formed a "community of saints" in Holland. But they did not feel at home among the Dutch, and they decided to move to the American wilderness, where they could organize their own Congregational churches and worship God as they pleased.

In September 1620, thirty-five "Pilgrims" (called that because of their many wanderings in search of a place to live) sailed for the New World on the *Mayflower*. They had received a grant from the Virginia Company, a joint-stock corporation of British investors, to establish a settlement in "northern Virginia" and financial aid from some London merchants. Sixty-seven additional emigrants, not all of whom were Puritans, were aboard the *Mayflower* —they were along to help make the colony profitable for the London investors. Arriving off Cape Cod in November, before landing, the Pilgrim leaders sought to retain their authority over the settlers and unify them for the difficult tasks lying ahead by drawing up the Mayflower Compact.

Although the compact professed allegiance to the king of England, it was actually an extension of the Separatists' church covenant to matters of civil government. Since the Pilgrims who settled at Plymouth never managed to obtain a royal charter for their colony, the Mayflower Compact itself served as their constitution until Plymouth was absorbed by Massachusetts Bay Colony in 1691. It thus became a precedent for the formation of new governments in America.

Questions to consider. What objectives other than religious ones did the Pilgrims set forth in the compact? Examine the list of people who signed it. What does this list reveal about the representation of the 102 settlers, their status, and their view of women? Of what significance is the use of the title *Mr.* before some of the names? What does the compact tell you about the Pilgrims' belief in self-government?

"The Signing of the Compact." Scene in the cabin of the *Mayflower*, November 21, 1620. This reproduction of a painting found in Plymouth, Massachusetts, shows the Pilgrims signing the agreement they had drawn up for establishing a government before going ashore. The Pilgrims had obtained a grant from the Virginia Company to settle in Virginia. The voyage across the Atlantic, however, was rough, and when the *Mayflower* reached the harbor of Cape Cod in New England the Pilgrims decided to land there instead of going on to Virginia. Since Cape Cod was not within the area controlled by the Virginia Company, they were able to devise a government of their own for Plymouth Plantation. (Library of Congress)

THE MAYFLOWER COMPACT (1620)

In the Name of God, Amen. We, whose names are underwritten, the Loyal Subjects of our dread Sovereign Lord King *James*, by the Grace of God, of *Great Britain, France,* and *Ireland,* King, *Defender of the Faith,* &c. Having undertaken for the Glory of God, and Advancement of the Christian Faith, and the Honour of our King and Country, a Voyage to plant the first colony in the northern Parts of Virginia; Do by these Presents, solemnly and mutually in the Presence of God and one another, covenant and combine ourselves together into a civil Body Politick, for our better Ordering and Preservation, and Furtherance of the Ends aforesaid; and by Virtue hereof do enact, constitute, and frame, such just and equal Laws, Ordinances, Acts, Constitutions, and Offices, from time to time, as shall be thought most meet and convenient for the general Good of the Colony; unto which we promise all due Submission and Obedience. In WITNESS whereof we have hereunto subscribed our names at *Cape Cod* the eleventh of *November,* in the Reign of our Sovereign Lord King *James* of *England, France,* and *Ireland,* the eighteenth and of *Scotland,* the fifty-fourth. *Anno Domini,* 1620.

Mr. John Carver
Mr. William Bradford
Mr. Edward Winslow
Mr. William Brewster
Isaac Allerton
Miles Standish
John Alden
John Turner
Francis Eaton
James Chilton
John Craxton
John Billington
Joses Fletcher
John Goodman
Mr. Samuel Fuller
Mr. Christopher Martin
Mr. William Mullins
Mr. William White
Mr. Richard Warren
John Howland

Mr. Stephen Hopkins
Digery Priest
Thomas Williams
Gilbert Winslow
Edmund Margesson
Peter Brown
Richard Bitteridge
George Soule
Edward Tilly
John Tilly
Francis Cooke
Thomas Rogers
Thomas Tinker
John Ridgate
Edward Fuller
Richard Clark
Richard Gardiner
Mr. John Allerton
Thomas English
Edward Doten
Edward Liester

From Benjamin Perley Poore, ed., *The Federal and State Constitutions, Colonial Charters, and Other Organic Laws of the United States* (2 v., Government Printing Office, Washington, D.C., 1878), I: 931.

2. The Puritan Vision
John Winthrop,
A MODEL OF CHRISTIAN CHARITY (1630)

In 1630 began the Great Migration of Puritans to America. That summer, under the direction of John Winthrop, a fleet of seventeen ships carrying about one thousand men and women crossed the Atlantic to Massachusetts Bay. A few months later, the settlers founded a colony on the site of the present city of Boston. Within a few years Massachusetts Bay Colony was the largest of all the English colonies on the American mainland.

John Winthrop, a college-educated squire from Groton Manor, Suffolk, had been elected governor of the new colony even before the settlers left England. Though not a clergyman, he was a devout Puritan. During the passage he delivered a lecture called "A Model of Christian Charity" to his coreligionists on the flagship *Arbella*. In it he reminded them of their Puritan ideals and outlined the religious and social purposes by which he expected them to organize their settlement in the New World. He wanted Massachusetts Bay Colony to be a model "Christian commonwealth," that is, a kind of "city upon a hill" for the rest of the world to admire and perhaps imitate. The settlers, he said, had a special commission from God to establish such a community in the New World. The new colony was to be dedicated to the glory of God rather than to worldly success. The "care of the public," he declared, "must oversway all private respects," and the settlers must strive at all times "to do justly, to love mercy, to walk humbly with our God."

For almost two decades Winthrop dominated Massachusetts Bay Colony. John Cotton, Boston's leading clergyman, called him "a brother . . . who has been to us a mother," but he was a father as well. He was convinced he was destined to rule and was an exacting parent. Born to wealth in Suffolk in 1588, he was educated at Trinity College, Cambridge, became prominent in the legal profession, and served as justice of the peace and lord of Groton Manor before heading the expedition to America. A strong leader who opposed both religious dissent and popular rule in Massachusetts, Winthrop served as governor for twelve years; when not governor he served as deputy governor and member of the governing council. He regarded democracy as "the meanest and worst form of government," and most people agreed with him in those days. When criticized for highhandedness, he managed to convince his critics that "liberty" meant not the right to do as one pleased but, rather, emancipation from selfish desires and obedience to the moral law. A journal he kept from the inception of the colony until his death in 1649 is a rich source for the early history of Massachusetts Bay Colony.

Questions to consider. In his lecture to the settlers, Winthrop spoke of the "law of the Gospel." In what ways did he make the Bible the basis of his plans for Massachusetts Bay Colony? How close were relations between church and state to be in the new settlement? Which was to come first: the individual or the community? What principles of behavior did he consider essential to the success of the enterprise? What did he mean by his statement that the Puritans were operating under a "special overruling providence"? What did he think would be the fate of the colonists if they failed to carry out the high purposes he had outlined for them?

A MODEL OF CHRISTIAN CHARITY (1630)

This law of the Gospel propounds likewise a difference of seasons and occasions. There is a time when a Christian must sell all and give to the poor as they did in the apostles' times; there is a time also when a Christian, though they give not all yet, must give beyond their ability, as they of Macedonia (II Cor. 8). Likewise, community of perils calls for extraordinary liberality, and so doth community in some special service for the church. Lastly, when there is no other means whereby our Christian brother may be relieved in this distress, we must help him beyond our ability, rather than tempt God in putting him upon help by miraculous or extraordinary means.

1. For the persons, we are a company professing ourselves fellow members of Christ, in which respect only, though we were absent from each other many miles, and had our employments as far distant, yet we ought to account ourselves knit together by this bond of love, and live in the exercise of it, if we would have comfort of our being in Christ.

2. For the work we have in hand, it is by mutual consent, through a special overruling providence and a more than an ordinary approbation of the churches of Christ, to seek out a place of cohabitation and consortship, under a due form of government both civil and ecclesiastical. In such cases as this, the care of the public must oversway all private respects by which not only conscience but mere civil policy doth bind us; for it is a true rule that particular estates cannot subsist in the ruin of the public.

3. The end is to improve our lives to do more service to the Lord, the comfort and increase of the body of Christ whereof we are members, that ourselves and posterity may be the better preserved from the common corruptions of this evil world, to serve the Lord and work out our salvation under the power and purity of His holy ordinances.

4. For the means whereby this must be effected, they are twofold: a conformity with the work and the end we aim at; these we seek are extraordinary, therefore we must not content ourselves with usual ordinary means. Whatsoever we did or ought to have done when we lived in England, the same must we do, and more also where we go. That which the most in their churches

From *The Winthrop Papers* (5 v., Massachusetts Historical Society, Boston, 1931), II: 282-295. Reprinted by permission.

John Winthrop, second governor of Massachusetts. This engraving (undated) shows Winthrop in the prime of life. He was forty-two when he succeeded Matthew Cradock as governor of Massachusetts in 1629. The following year he came to America on the *Arbella* in a fleet of seventeen ships carrying close to one thousand men and women. He settled at Charleston first and began building a house there, but soon changed his mind and moved to Boston, where he spent the rest of his life. Winthrop's term as governor was one year and he was re-elected three times. But when John Cotton, prominent Boston clergyman, announced that competent magistrates ought to be re-elected continually, the freemen showed their independence by choosing someone else in 1634. They turned to Winthrop again, however, in 1642, and from 1645 to 1649, the year of his death, he was re-elected annually. (Library of Congress)

maintain as a truth in profession only, we must bring into familiar and constant practice: as in this duty of love we must love brotherly without dissimulation; we must love one another with a pure heart fervently, we must bear one another's burdens, we must not look only on our own things but also on the things of our brethren. Neither must we think that the Lord will bear with such failings at our hands as He doth from those among whom we have lived. . . .

Thus stands the cause between God and us; we are entered into covenant with Him for this work; we have taken out a commission, the Lord hath given us leave to draw our own articles. We have professed to enterprise these actions upon these and these ends; we have hereupon besought Him of favor and blessing. Now if the Lord shall please to hear us and bring us in peace to the place we desire, then hath He ratified this covenant and sealed our Commission, [and] will expect a strict performance of the articles contained in it. But if we shall neglect the observation of these articles which are the ends we have propounded, and dissembling with our God, shall fall to embrace this present world and prosecute our carnal intentions, seeking great things for ourselves and our posterity, the Lord will surely break out in wrath against us, be revenged of such a perjured people, and make us know the price of the breach of such a covenant.

Now the only way to avoid this shipwreck and to provide for our posterity is to follow the counsel of Micah: to do justly, to love mercy, to walk humbly with our God. For this end, we must be knit together in this work as one man. We must entertain each other in brotherly affection; we must be willing to abridge ourselves of our superfluities for the supply of others' necessities; we must uphold a familiar commerce together in all meekness, gentleness, patience and liberality. We must delight in each other, make others' condition our own, rejoice together, mourn together, labor and suffer together: always having before our eyes our commission and community in the work, our community as members of the same body. So shall we keep the unity of the spirit in the bond of peace, the Lord will be our God and delight to dwell among us, as His own people, and will command a blessing upon us in all our ways, so that we shall see much more of His wisdom, power, goodness, and truth than formerly we have been acquainted with. We shall find that the God of Israel is among us, when ten of us shall be able to resist a thousand of our enemies, when He shall make us a praise and glory, that men shall say of succeeding plantations: "The Lord make it like that of New England." For we must consider that we shall be as a city upon a hill, the eyes of all people are upon us. So that if we shall deal falsely with our God in this work we have undertaken, and so cause Him to withdraw His present help from us, we shall be made a story and a by-word through the world: we shall open the mouths of enemies to speak evil of the ways of God and all professors for God's sake; we shall shame the faces of many of God's worthy servants, and cause their prayers to be turned into curses upon us, till we be consumed out of the good land whither we are going.

And to shut up this discourse with that exhortation of Moses, that faithful servant of the Lord, in his last farewell to Israel (Deut. 30): Beloved, there is now set before us life and good, death and evil, in that we are commanded this day to love the Lord our God, and to love one another, to walk in His ways and to keep His commandments and His ordinance and His laws and the articles of our covenant with Him, that we may live and be multiplied, and that the Lord our God may bless us in the land whither we go to possess it: but if our hearts shall turn away so that we will not obey, but shall be seduced and worship . . . other gods, our pleasures and profits, and serve them, it is propounded unto us this day, we shall surely perish out of the good land whither we pass over this vast sea to possess it.

> Therefore, let us choose life,
> that we, and our seed,
> may live; by obeying His
> voice and cleaving to Him,
> for He is our life and
> our prosperity.

3. A Gathering of Individuals

Roger Williams,

THE BLOODY TENENT OF PERSECUTION (1644)

Massachusetts Bay Colony was not a theocracy; ministers, though important there, could not serve as magistrates, nor could magistrates be ministers. Yet in Massachusetts the Puritans made the Congregational church the official state church, supported it by taxation, and prohibited people who did not share their views from worshipping as they pleased in the colony. In 1631, a devout young Puritan preacher named Roger Williams arrived in Boston and from almost the beginning began challenging the Puritan establishment. Williams favored separation of church and state; he thought religion was corrupted when it got involved in politics. He also championed religious liberty; authentic religion, he insisted, flourishes only when people can practice it freely without government coercion.

To the consternation of John Winthrop and other Massachusetts leaders, Williams began attracting support for his views among some of the people in the colony. In 1635 they put him on trial, convicted him of spreading "dangerous opinions," and banished him from the colony. In January 1636 Williams and some of his followers fled into the wilderness. They made their way southward and finally reached the shores of Narragansett Bay, where they founded Providence Plantation. In 1640 the inhabitants of Providence drew up a "Plantation Agreement" for governing their town, emphasizing "liberty of conscience" and the settlement of disputes by peaceful arbitration. Eventually Providence joined with other settlements in the area to form the colony of Rhode Island, for which Williams secured a charter in 1644. Williams wrote many eloquent tracts setting forth his views on religious liberty and freedom of conscience; and in Rhode Island, where he held office for many years, there was religious freedom for Catholics and Jews as well as for Protestants of all denominations. In 1644 he published a book presenting his opinions entitled *The Bloody Tenent (Tenet) of Persecution for the Cause of Conscience*, the conclusion of which appears below.

Williams, the son of a tailor, was born in London around 1603. He studied theology at Cambridge University and served as chaplain to a Puritan noble before coming to America. In Massachusetts he angered the authorities by both his political and his religious heresies. Not only did he espouse a democratic form of government ("The sovereign, original, and foundation of civil powers lies in the people"), he also insisted that the colonists were not entitled to the land on which they settled until they bought it from the Indians. In Rhode Island Williams purchased land from the Indians; he also made a study of their language and published a book about it. And he engaged Massachusetts's John Cotton in a lively controversy about religious liberty. When Cotton blasted Williams's *Bloody Tenent of Persecution for the Cause of Conscience* with a book entitled *The Bloody Tenent Washed and Made White in the Blood of the Lamb* (1647), Williams responded with *The Bloody Tenent Yet More Bloody by Mr. Cotton's Endeavor to Wash it White in the Blood of the Lamb* (1652). Williams's fight against religious repression continued until his death in 1683.

Questions to consider. Two questions come at once to mind in reading the following summary of the major points made in Williams's book. What were his main arguments against religious uniformity? How far did his toleration of religious diversity extend? Toleration today rests largely in indifference. Can it be said that Williams's toleration of differing religious beliefs and practices grew out of a lukewarm faith?

THE BLOODY TENENT OF PERSECUTION (1644)
(TWELVE CONCLUSIONS)

First, that the blood of so many hundred thousand souls of Protestants and Papists, spilt in the wars of present and former ages, for their respective consciences, is not required nor accepted by Jesus Christ the Prince of Peace.

Secondly, pregnant scriptures and arguments are throughout the work proposed against the doctrine of persecution for cause of conscience.

Thirdly, satisfactory answers are given to scriptures, and objections produced by Mr. Calvin, Beza [French theologian, 1519-1605], Mr. Cotton, and the ministers of the New English churches and others former and later, tending to prove the doctrine of persecution for cause of conscience.

Fourthly, the doctrine of persecution for cause of conscience is proved guilty of all the blood of the souls crying for vengeance under the altar.

Fifthly, all civil states with their officers of justice in their respective constitutions and administrations are proved essentially civil, and therefore not judges, governors or defenders of the spiritual or Christian state and worship.

Sixthly, it is the will and command of God that (since the coming of his Son the Lord Jesus) a permission of the most paganish, Jewish, Turkish, or anti-christian consciences and worships, be granted to all men in all nations and countries: and they are only to be fought against with that sword which is only (in soul matters) able to conquer, to wit, the sword of God's spirit, the Word of God.

Seventhly, the state of the land of Israel, the kings and people thereof in peace and war, is proved figurative and ceremonial, and no pattern nor precedent for any kingdom or civil state in the world to follow.

Eighthly, God requireth not an uniformity of religion to be enacted and enforced in any civil state; which enforced uniformity (sooner or later) is the

From Roger Williams, *The Bloody Tenent of Persecution* (London?, 1644), 3-4.

Landing of Roger Williams. This wood engraving shows Williams, who was banished from Massachusetts Bay Colony for advocating religious liberty, being greeted by a group of Indians when he reached the shores of Naragansett Bay in the winter of 1636. Williams was on good terms with native Americans from the beginning. He and his associates purchased land from them and founded a settlement at the head of Naragansett Bay which they called Providence Plantation. Under Williams an agreement similar in form to the Mayflower Compact was drawn up providing for the colony's government and giving people the right to worship as they pleased. (Library of Congress)

greatest occasion of civil war, ravishing of conscience, persecution of Christ Jesus in his servants, and of the hypocrisy and destruction of millions of souls.

Ninthly, in holding an enforced uniformity of religion in a civil state, we must necessarily disclaim our desires and hopes of the Jews' conversion to Christ.

Tenthly, an enforced uniformity of religion throughout a nation or civil state confounds the civil and religious, denies the principles of Christianity and civility, and that Jesus Christ is come in the flesh.

Eleventhly, the permission of other consciences and worships than a state professeth only can (according to God) procure a firm and lasting peace (good assurance being taken according to the wisdom of the civil state for uniformity of civil obedience from all sorts).

Twelfthly, lastly, true civility and Christianity may both flourish in a state or kingdom, notwithstanding the permission of divers and contrary consciences, either of Jew or Gentile.

4. First Rights and Privileges
THE VIRGINIA ORDINANCE OF 1621

The first representative body in the New World was the Virginia Assembly—or House of Burgesses. This development came about when the Virginia Company directors decided to allow more freedom in order to attract more colonists. The directors scrapped the colony's military and communal organization when the little settlement at Jamestown, established in 1607, failed to produce a profit and came close to collapsing due to disease and starvation. The company directors distributed land to the settlers, arranged to transport craftsmen and indentured servants, as well as women, to the colony, and authorized the election of a general assembly to help govern the colony. On July 30, 1619, twenty-two burgesses, chosen by the settlers, met for the first time with the governor and the council, appointed by the company.

The document authorizing the House of Burgesses has been lost, but the "ordinance" of 1621 is believed to reproduce the provisions of 1619. Largely the work of Sir Edwin Sandys, one of the leading directors of the Virginia Company, the ordinance provided for a Council of State, appointed by the company, as well as for an assembly elected by the people. The Virginia Assembly had the power to "make, ordain, and enact such general Laws and Orders, for the Behoof of the said Colony, and the good Government thereof, as shall, from time to time, appear necessary or requisite," subject to the company's approval. The new governmental arrangements, together with the discovery that tobacco could be a lucrative crop, soon made Virginia a thriving enterprise, and these arrangements were continued after Virginia became a royal colony in 1624.

Questions to consider. In examining the ordinance's description of the two councils for governing Virginia, it is helpful to consider the following questions: How large was the Council of State? How was it chosen? What responsibilities did it possess? How did the responsibilities of the General Assembly compare in importance with those of the Council of State? Who possessed the ultimate authority in Virginia?

THE VIRGINIA ORDINANCE OF 1621

An ordinance and Constitution of the Treasurer, Council, and Company in England, for a Council of State and General Assembly. Dated July 24, 1621.

To all People, to whom these Presents shall come, be seen, or heard the Treasurer, Council, and Company of Adventurers and Planters for the city of *London* for the first colony of *Virginia*, send Greeting. . . .

We . . . the said Treasurer, Council, and Company, by Authority directed to us from his Majesty under the Great Seal, upon mature Deliberation, do hereby order and declare, that, from henceforward, there shall be TWO SUPREME COUNCILS in *Virginia*, for the better Government of the said Colony aforesaid.

The one of which Councils, to be called THE COUNCIL OF STATE (and whose Office shall chiefly be assisting, with their Care, Advise, and Circumspection, to the said Governor) shall be chosen, nominated, placed and displaced, from time to time, by Us, the said Treasurer, Council, and Company, and our Successors: Which Council of State shall consist, for the present, only of these Persons, as are here inserted, *viz.* Sir *Francis Wyat*, Governor of *Virginia*, Captain *Francis West*, Sir *George Yeardley*, Knight, Sir *William Neuce*, Knight Marshal of *Virginia*, Mr. *George Sandys*, Treasurer, Mr. *George Thorpe*, Deputy of the College, Captain *Thomas Neuce*, Deputy for the Company, Mr. *Pawlet*, Mr. *Leech*, Captain *Nathaniel Powel*, Mr. *Harwood*, Mr. *Samuel Macock*, Mr. *Christopher Davison*, Secretary, *Doctor Pots*, Physician to the Company, Mr. *Roger Smith*, Mr. *John Berkley*, Mr. *John Rolfe*, Mr. *Ralph Hamer*, Mr. *John Pountis*, Mr. *Michael Lapworth*. Which said Counsellors and Council we earnestly pray and desire, and in his Majesty's Name strictly charge and command, that (all Factions, Partialities, and sinister Respect laid aside) they bend their Care and Endeavors to assist the said Governor; first and principally in the Advancement of the Honour and Service of God, and the Enlargement of his Kingdom amongst the Heathen People; and next, in erecting of the said Colony in due obedience to his Majesty, and all lawful Authority from his Majesty's Directions; and lastly, in maintaining the said People in Justice and *Christian* Conversation amongst themselves, and in Strength and Ability to withstand their Enemies. And this Council, to be always, or for the most Part, residing about or near the Governor.

The other Council, more generally to be called by the Governor, once yearly, and no oftener, but for very extraordinary and important occasions, shall consist, for the present, of the said Council of State, and of two Burgesses out of every Town, Hundred, or other particular Plantation, to be respectively chosen by the Inhabitants; Which Council shall be called THE GENERAL ASSEMBLY, wherein (as also in the said Council of State) all Matter shall be decided, determined, and ordered, by the greater Part of the Voices then present; reserving to the Governor always a Negative Voice. And this General Assembly shall have free Power to treat, consult, and conclude, as well of all emergent Occasions concerning the Public Weal of the said Colony and every

From F. N. Thorpe, ed., *The Federal and State Constitutions* (7 v., Government Printing Office, Washington, D.C., 1909), VII: 3810-3812.

First meeting of the Assembly in Virginia, August 1619.
During the early years in Jamestown, the laws governing
the colonists were extremely harsh. But in 1618 the Virginia
Company placed the colony under English common law.
This meant that trial by jury, free speech, and freedom
from imprisonment except for specified crimes were guaranteed to the Virginians. The company also provided for a
representative assembly with power to make new laws,
subject to the consent of the company directors. On July
30, 1619, twenty-two "burgesses," chosen by the settlers,
met for the first time with the governor and council, appointed by the company. (Library of Congress)

Part thereof, as also to make, ordain, and enact such general Laws and Orders, for the Behoof of the said Colony, and the good Government thereof, as shall, from time to time, appear necessary or requisite. . . .

Whereas in all other Things, we require the said General Assembly, as also the said Council of State, to imitate and follow the Policy of the Form of Government—Laws, Customs, and Manner of Trial, and other administration of Justice, used in the Realm of *England*, as near as may be, even as ourselves, by his Majesty's Letters Patent, are required.

Provided, that no Law or Ordinance, made in the said General Assembly, shall be or continue in Force or Validity, unless the same shall be solemnly ratified and confirmed, in a General Quarter Court of the said Company here in England and so ratified, be returned to them under our Seal; It being our Intent to afford the like Measure also unto the said Colony, that after the Government of the said Colony shall once have been well framed, and settled accordingly, which is to be done by Us, as by Authority derived from his Majesty, and the same shall have been so by Us declared, no Orders of Court afterwards shall bind the said Colony, unless they be ratified in like Manner in the General Assemblies. IN WITNESS whereof we have here unto set our Common Seal, the 24th of *July* 1621, and in the Year of the Reign of our Sovereign Lord, JAMES, King of *England*, &c.

5. The Underside of Privilege
VIRGINIA SLAVERY LEGISLATION (1630–1691)

In 1619 a Dutch trader brought twenty "Negars" from Africa and sold them in Jamestown. For a long time, however, black slavery, though common in Spanish and Portuguese colonies in the New World, was not important in Virginia. For many years white indentured servants from England performed most of the labor in the colony; after three decades there were still only about three hundred blacks in the English colonies. By the end of the seventeenth century, however, transporting Africans to America had become a profitable business for English and American merchants, and the slave trade had grown to enormous proportions.

In Virginia the planters used blacks as cheap labor on their plantations and also employed them as household servants, coachmen, porters, and skilled workers. Their status was indeterminate at first, and they may have been treated somewhat like indentured servants for some time. As tobacco became important, however, and the number of blacks working on plantations soared, the position of blacks declined rapidly. The Virginia Assembly began enacting laws governing their behavior and regulating their relations with whites. The statutes, some of which are reproduced here, do not show whether racial prejudice and discrimination preceded slavery, followed it, or, more likely, accompanied it. But they do dramatize the fact that in Virginia, as elsewhere, the expansion of freedom and self-government for whites could go hand in hand with the exploitation and oppression of blacks.

Questions to consider. How strictly did the Virginia lawmakers attempt to control the behavior of blacks in the colony? How severe were the punishments provided for offenders against the law? What penalties were provided for the "casual killing" of slaves? What appeared to be the greatest fear of the Virginia lawmakers?

VIRGINIA SLAVERY LEGISLATION (1630–1691)

[1630]   September 17th, 1630. Hugh David to be soundly whipped, before an assembly of Negroes and others for abusing himself to the dishonor of God and shame of Christians, by defiling his body in lying with a negro; which fault he is to acknowledge next Sabbath day.

[1640]   Robert Sweet to do penance in church according to laws of England, for getting a negro woman with child and the woman whipt.

[1661]   *Be it enacted* That in case any English servant shall run away in company with any negroes who are incapable of making satisfaction by addition of time, *Be it enacted* that the English so running away in company with them shall serve for the time of the said negroes absence as they are to do for their own by a former act.

[1668]   Whereas some doubts, have arisen whether negro women set free were still to be accompted tithable according to a former act, *It is declared by this grand assembly* that negro women, though permitted to enjoy their Freedom yet ought not in all respects to be admitted to a full fruition of the exemptions and impunities of the England, and are still liable to payment of taxes.

[1669]   *An act about the casual killing of slaves.*

Whereas the only law in force for the punishment of refractory servants resisting their master, mistress or overseer cannot be inflicted upon negroes, nor the obstinacy of many of them by other than violent means supprest, *Be it enacted and declared by this grand assembly*, if any slave resist his master (or other by his master's order correcting him) and by the extremity of the correction should chance to die, that his death shall not be accompted Felony, but the master (or that other person appointed by the master to punish him) be acquit from molestation, since it cannot be presumed that prepensed malice (which alone makes murder Felony) should induce any man to destroy his own estate.

[1680]   Act X. *An act for preventing Negro Insurrections.*

It is hereby enacted by the authority aforesaid, that from and after the publication of this law, it shall not be lawful for any negro or other slave to carry or arm himself with any club, staff, gun, sword, or any other weapon of defence or offence, nor to go to depart from his master's ground without a certificate from his master, mistress or overseer, and such permission not to be granted but upon particular and necessary occasions; and every negro or slave so offending not having a certificate as aforesaid shall be sent to the next constable, who is hereby enjoined and required to give the said negro twenty

From William Hening, ed., *The Laws of Virginia, 1619-1792* (13 v., Samuel Pleasants, Richmond, 1809-1823).

Cutaway sectional view of a slave ship. During the seventeenth and eighteenth centuries thousands of slaves were brought to the colonies from Africa. The voyage across the Atlantic was horrendous. Some slave-traders tried to avoid overcrowding, but most of them packed as many slaves as they could into the holds of their ships to maximize profits. In most ships there was a "slave deck," or shelf, in the middle of the hold, for carrying additional slaves. Some ships even had two slave decks. Every so often small groups of slaves were taken on deck and forced to dance to restore their blood circulation. Nets along the sides of the ships kept them from jumping overboard. When they refused to eat, funnels were forced down their throats and "slabber juice," a mixture of palm oil, horse beans, and flour, was poured down the funnel. (Library of Congress)

lashes on his bare back well laid on, and so sent home to his said master, mistress or overseer. *And it is further enacted by the authority aforesaid* that if any negro or other slave shall presume to lift up his hand in opposition against any christian, shall for every such offense, upon due proof made thereof by the oath of the party before a magistrate, have and receive thirty lashes on his bare back well laid on.

[1691]   Act XVI. *An act for suppressing outlying Slaves.*

It is hereby enacted, that in all such cases upon intelligence of any such negroes, mulattoes, or other slaves lying out, two of their majesties' justices of the peace of that county, whereof one to be of the quorum, where such negroes, mulattoes or other slave shall be, shall be impowered and commanded, and are hereby impowered and commanded, to issue out their warrants directed to the sheriff of the same county to apprehend such negroes, mulattoes, and other slaves, which said sheriff is hereby likewise required upon all such occasions to raise such and so many forces from time to time as he shall think convenient and necessary for the effectual apprehending such negroes, mulattoes and other slaves, and in case any negroes, mulattoes or other slave or slaves lying out as aforesaid shall resist, run away, or refuse to deliver and surrender him or themselves to any person or persons that shall be by lawful authority employed to apprehend and take such negroes, mulattoes or other slaves that in such cases it shall and may be lawful for such person and persons to kill and destroy such negroes, mulattoes, and other slave or slaves by gun or any other ways whatsoever.

6. An Imperial Presence
THE NAVIGATION ACT OF 1660

Although the British government gave the colonies a great deal of political liberty, it placed many restrictions on their economic activities. The mercantilist theory, which shaped British policies, held that trade and commerce within the British Empire should be carried on chiefly to benefit the mother country. "I conceive, no foreign plantation should be undertaken or prosecuted," wrote a British mercantilist in 1663, "but in such countries that may increase the wealth and trade of this nation, either in furnishing us, with what we are otherwise forced to purchase from strangers, or else by increasing such commodities, as are vendible abroad; which may both increase our shipping, and profitably employ our people." During the seventeenth century Parliament passed several Laws of Trade and Navigation regulating American economic life. These laws made the colonies' welfare subordinate to Great Britain's: the colonies were to send such raw materials as sugar, cotton, and tobacco to Britain, purchase manufactured goods in England rather than in Europe, and confine their trade to English and American ships manned largely by English crews. The objective was economic self-sufficiency: a self-sufficient British Empire would export more goods than it imported, and other nations would have to pay for British goods with precious metals. Gold and silver, according to mercantilism, constituted the real wealth of a nation.

The Navigation Act of 1660 systematized various regulatory laws passed by Parliament during the preceding fifteen years and made clear the aim of British policy: to advance the interests of English merchants, traders, producers, and shipbuilders and to make Britain, not the colonies, wealthy. There were, to be sure, some benefits for Americans. The British government paid bounties to producers of naval stores and indigo in America and saw to it that American tobacco had a preferential position in England. The British navy, moreover, protected the colonies as well as the mother country. But there were disadvantages as well as advantages. Mercantilism hurt the northern colonies, which concentrated on trade, more than it did the southern colonies, which engaged primarily in agriculture, and American enterprisers, eager to forge ahead on their own, found British policies increasingly irksome.

At first the trade laws were only loosely enforced. For many years Britain was engaged in wars with France and failed to crack down on Americans who ignored the laws. But after winning the French and Indian War in 1760 and taking over Canada from France by treaty in 1763, Britain turned its attention to American economic activities. When Britain began to enact legislation (such as the Sugar Act of 1764 and the Stamp Act of

1765) to raise money in America, the reaction in the colonies was violent. Americans denied that Britain had the right to regulate their economy and began calling for economic as well as political liberty for themselves. British economic measures after the French and Indian War drove American merchants increasingly into protest, evasion of the law, resistance, and, in the end, outright rebellion.

Questions to consider. The Navigation Act passed by Parliament in 1660 is extremely wordy, but its intention is clear enough. What basic objective did it proclaim at the outset? What restrictions did it place on ships engaged in trade between Britain and its colonies? On merchants engaged in such trade? On the crews of vessels transporting goods to and from Britain? On goods brought to Britain from foreign countries? What regulations did the act provide for the import of fish and fish products into Great Britain? On sugar, tobacco, cotton, and other goods produced in the American colonies? What penalties did the act prescribe for violations of its provisions?

THE NAVIGATION ACT OF 1660

For the increase of shipping and encouragement of the navigation of this nation, wherein, under the good providence of God, the wealth, safety and strength of this kingdom is so much concerned; be it enacted by the King's most excellent majesty, and by the lords and commons in this present parliament assembled, and by the authority thereof, That from and after the first day of *December* one thousand six hundred and sixty, and from thenceforward, no goods or commodities whatsoever shall be imported into or exported out of any lands, islands, plantations or territories to his Majesty belonging or in his possession, or which may hereafter belong unto or be in the possession of his Majesty, his heirs and successors, in *Asia, Africa* or *America*, in any other ship or ships, vessel or vessels whatsoever, but in such ships or vessels as do truly and without fraud belong only to the people of *England* or *Ireland*, dominion of *Wales* or town of *Berwick* upon *Tweed** or are of the build of and belonging to any the said lands, islands, plantations or territories, as the proprietors and right owners thereof, and whereof the master and three fourths of the mariners at least are *English;* under the penalty of the forfeiture and loss of all the goods and commodities which shall be imported into or exported out of any the aforesaid places in any other ship or vessel, as also of the ship or vessel. . . .

From Danby Pickering, *The Statutes at Large from the Magna Charta to the End of the Eleventh Parliament of Great Britain, anno 1761* (46 v., J. Bentham, Cambridge, 1806), VII: 452.

*Berwick upon Tweed, a seaport and market town in northeastern England, was for many years involved in the border wars between England and Scotland and changed hands many times. After it was ceded to England in 1482, it became customary to mention it after Wales in proclamations and Parliamentary acts—Eds.

II. And be it enacted, That no alien or person not born within the allegiance of our sovereign lord the King, his heirs and successors, or naturalized, or made a free denizen, shall from and after the first day of *February*, 1661, exercise the trade or occupation of a merchant or factor in any the said places; upon pain of the forfeiture and loss of all his goods and chattels . . . and all governors of the said lands, islands, plantations or territories, and every of them, are hereby strictly required and commanded, and all who hereafter shall be made governors of any such islands, plantations or territories, by his Majesty, his heirs or successors, shall before their entrance into their government take a solemn oath, to do their utmost, that every the aforementioned clauses, and all the matters and things therein contained, shall be punctually and *bona fide* observed according to the true intent and meaning thereof; and upon complaint and proof made before his Majesty, his heirs or successors, or such as shall be by him or them thereunto authorized and appointed, that any the said governors have been willingly and wittingly negligent in doing their duty accordingly, that the said governor so offending shall be removed from his government.

III. And it is further enacted. . . . That no goods or commodities whatsoever of the growth, production or manufacture of *Africa*, *Asia* or *America*, or of any part thereof, or which are described or laid down in the usual maps or cards of those places, be imported into *England*, *Ireland* or *Wales*, islands of *Guernsey* and *Jersey* [in the English Channel], or town of *Berwick* upon *Tweed*, in any other ship or ships, vessel or vessels whatsoever, but in such as do truly and without fraud belong only to the people of *England* or *Ireland*, dominion of *Wales*, or town of *Berwick* upon *Tweed* or of the lands, islands, plantations or territories in *Asia*, *Africa* or *America* to his Majesty belonging, as the proprietors and right owners thereof, and whereof the master, and three fourths at least of the mariners are *English*: (2) under the penalty of the forfeiture of all such goods and commodities, and of the ship or vessel in which they were imported. . . .

IV. And it is further enacted. . . . That no goods or commodities that are of foreign growth, production or manufacture, and which are to be brought into *England*, *Ireland*, *Wales*, the islands of *Guernsey* and *Jersey*, or town of *Berwick* upon *Tweed*, in *English*-built shipping, or other shipping belonging to some of the aforesaid places, and navigated by *English* mariners, as aforesaid, shall be shipped or brought from any other place of places, country or countries, but only from those of the said growth, production or manufacture, or from those ports where the said goods and commodities can only, or are, or usually have been, first shipped for transportation, and from none other places or countries; under the penalty of the forfeiture of all such of the aforesaid goods as shall be imported from any other place or country contrary to the true intent and meaning hereof, as also of the ship in which they were imported. . . .

V. And it is further enacted. . . . That any sort of ling, stock-fish, pilchard, or any other kind of dried or salted fish, usually fished for and caught by the people of *England*, *Ireland*, *Wales*, or town of *Berwick* upon *Tweed*; or any sort of cod-fish or herring, or any oil or blubber made or that shall be made of any kind of fish whatsoever, or any whale-fins or whale-bones, which shall be imported into *England, Ireland, Wales,* or town of *Berwick* upon *Tweed,* not having been caught in vessels truly and properly belonging thereunto as proprietors and right owners thereof, and the said fish cured saved and dried, and the oil and blubber aforesaid (which shall be accounted and pay as oil) not made by the people thereof, and shall be imported into *England, Ireland,* or *Wales,* or town of *Berwick* upon *Tweed,* shall pay double aliens custom. . . .

XVIII. And it is further enacted. . . . That from and after the first day of *April,* 1661, no sugars, tobacco, cotton wool, indigoes, ginger, fustick, or other dying wood, of the growth, production or manufacture of any *English* plantations in *America, Asia* or *Africa,* shall be shipped, carried, conveyed or transported from any of the said *English* plantations to any land . . . other than to such other *English* plantations as do belong to his Majesty. . . .

COUNTERPOINT
Andover: Land Division, Estate Values, and Geographical Mobility in Colonial America

What happened to the land and the people when a group of colonists founded a town? The three tables that follow concern Andover, settled by Massachusetts Bay colonists in the 1640s. Philip Greven has analyzed the division of land for this town, the estate values for four generations of male inhabitants, and records of those men who, in successive generations, remained in the town or moved away. Remember, as you look at these tables, that land represented wealth in the colonial era.

Table 1.1 shows the successive divisions of upland, meadow, and swamp land among the original handful of families in the town. The first column indicates the size of each family's house lot. In this first division — or portioning out of land — the family with a 4-acre house lot received 4 acres of upland area, 6 acres of meadow land, and 4 acres of swamp land. The family acquiring a house lot of 20 acres received 20 acres of upland, 30 acres of meadow, and 20 acres of swamp. The upland was divided three more times and the meadow land two more times as families grew. The swamp land was evidently not in demand — or had all been portioned out. Thus, by 1662, families with the smallest house lot had a total of 122 acres, while those with 20-acre lots owned 610 acres. Look at the total column. What does this say about the community? Were there any destitute, landless families? Was there an effort made to be equitable in the distribution of the various types of land? Compare these totals with those of New Jersey inhabitants a century later in Table 2.1 (page 77). "Massachusetts Bay settlers used land division as a concrete means of carrying out the Puritan ideals and objectives embodied in the Mayflower Compact and John Winthrop." Do you agree with this statement?

Table 1.2 lists the estate values for four generations of Andover men. In the first generation, all but two men were worth between 200 and 600 pounds. By the time of the fourth generation, however, less than half were so wealthy. At the same time, nearly 12 percent possessed at least 2,000 pounds, while another 11 percent were poor, worth only from 0 to 99 pounds. What do the figures tell you about the original distribution of land/wealth? About the gradual change over time in wealth patterns? Can you suggest some reasons for the change? What do you suppose happened to the land in families with eight children? With one child? Would population growth have changed wealth patterns?

Table 1.3 gets away from land and wealth and shows movement — whether resident males remained in Andover during three generations. Although nearly 80 percent of second-generation men living in Andover remained there, more than half of the fourth generation moved out of town. Why do you think so many men left Andover? We can see that migration was an early tendency in American settlement patterns. Our mobility was not created by the invention of the train, automobile, and airplane. The desire to move to locales where there was religious toleration —as Roger Williams (Document 3) did—was not the only reason behind the settlement of new areas of America. Have the tables suggested another reason to you?

TABLE 1.1 **Allotment of Land (in Acres) in Andover During Successive Divisions to 1662**

Acreage of house lot	Upland divisions				Meadow divisions		Swamp division	Total acreage in 1662
	First	Second	Third	Fourth	First	Second		
4	4	4	16	80	6	4	4	122
5	5	5	20	100	7.5	5	5	152.5
6	6	6	24	120	9	6	6	183
7	7	7	28	140	10.5	7	7	213.5
8	8	8	32	160	12	8	8	244
10	10	10	40	200	15	10	10	305
12	12	12	48	240	18	12	12	366
15	15	15	60	300	22.5	15	15	457.5
20	20	20	80	400	30	20	20	610

Source: From Philip J. Greven, Jr., *Four Generations: Population, Land, and Family in Colonial Andover, Massachusetts.* Copyright © 1970 by Cornell University. Used by permission of the publisher, Cornell University Press.

TABLE 1.2 **Values of Estates for Four Generations of Andover Men**

Value (in £)	First generation		Second generation		Third generation		Fourth generation	
	No.	%	No.	%	No.	%	No.	%
0-99	0	0.0	3	8.6	3	4.0	10	10.8
100-199	1	6.7	6	17.1	4	5.3	11	11.8
200-399	8	53.3	12	34.3	16	21.1	27	29.0
400-599	5	33.3	5	14.3	9	11.8	13	14.0
600-799	1	6.7	1	2.9	15	19.7	9	9.7
800-999	0	0.0	3	8.6	5	6.6	5	5.4
1,000-1,999	0	0.0	2	5.7	15	19.7	7	7.5
2,000 and over	0	0.0	3	8.6	9	11.8	11	11.8
Total	15	100.0	35	100.1	76	100.0	93	100.0

Source: From Philip J. Greven, Jr., *Four Generations: Population, Land, and Family in Colonial Andover, Massachusetts.* Copyright © 1970 by Cornell University. Used by permission of the publisher, Cornell University Press.

TABLE 1.3   Geographical Mobility for Three Generations of Andover Men

Generation	Men living to age 21	Men living in Andover		Men moving	
		No.	%	No.	%
Second	129	101	78.3	28	21.7
Third	287	175	61.0	112	39.0
Fourth	398	174	43.7	224	56.3

Source: From Philip J. Greven, Jr., *Four Generations: Population, Land, and Family in Colonial Andover, Massachusetts.* Copyright © 1970 by Cornell University. Used by permission of the publisher, Cornell University Press.

George Washington taking charge of the Continental Army in Cambridge, Massachusetts. (Library of Congress)

CHAPTER TWO

Strides Toward Freedom

7. A Right to Criticize
JOHN PETER ZENGER'S LIBEL TRIAL (1735)

In 1735 came the first great battle over freedom of the press in America. Two years earlier, John Peter Zenger, publisher of the outspoken *New-York Weekly Journal,* began printing articles satirizing corruption and highhandedness in the administration of William Cosby, the new royal governor of New York, and he also distributed song sheets praising those who would "boldly despise the haughty knaves who keep us in awe." In 1734 Cosby arranged for Zenger to be arrested, charged with seditious libel, and thrown in prison. He also ordered copies of the *New-York Weekly Journal* burned in public. When Zengers's case came before the court in 1735, Andrew Hamilton, a prominent Philadelphian who was the most skillful lawyer in America, agreed to defend him. According to English law, a printed attack on a public official, even if true, was considered libelous; and the judge ruled that the fact that Zenger had criticized the New York governor was enough to convict him. But Hamilton argued that no one should be punished for telling the truth; Zenger, he pointed out, had told the truth and should not be convicted of libel. In "a free government," he insisted, the rulers should "not be able to stop the people's mouths when they feel themselves oppressed." Liberty, he added, is the "only bulwark against lawless power." Hamilton was so eloquent in his plea that in the end the jury voted "not guilty" and spectators in the courtroom cheered the verdict.

After his release, Zenger printed a complete account of the trial in his paper (some of which appears below) and also arranged to have it printed separately as a pamphlet. The report of the trial aroused great interest in Britain as well as in America and went through many editions. Hamilton's plea to the jury on behalf of "speaking and writing the truth" was one of the landmarks in the struggle for a free press in America. Though other royal judges did not accept the principle enunciated by Hamilton, the decision in the Zenger case did set an important precedent against judicial tyranny in libel suits. New York Gouverneur Morris, statesman and diplomat, called it "the morning star of that liberty which subsequently revolutionized America."

Zenger did not speak on his own behalf during the trial. But he had planned, if found guilty, to make a speech reminding the jurors that he and his parents had "fled from a country where oppression, tyranny, and arbitrary power had ruined almost all the people." Zenger, who was born in Germany in 1697, came to America, along with many other German immigrants, when he was twelve years old and was indentured to William Bradford, "the pioneer printer of the middle colonies." In 1726 he set up a printing shop of his own, publishing tracts and pamphlets mainly of a religious nature, and in 1730 he published the first arithmetic text in New

York. A few years after his famous trial he became public printer for the colony of New York and a little later for New Jersey as well. He died in 1746.

Questions to consider. In the following exchange between the prosecuting attorney and Hamilton, Zenger's lawyer, why did Hamilton place such emphasis on the word *false?* What complaint did he make about his effort to present evidence to the court on behalf of his client? What did he mean by saying that "the suppression of evidence ought always to be taken for the strongest evidence"? Why did he think Zenger's case was so important? Do you consider his final appeal to the jury a convincing one?

JOHN PETER ZENGER'S LIBEL TRIAL (1735)

MR. ATTORNEY. . . . The case before the court is whether Mr. Zenger is guilty of libeling His Excellency the Governor of New York, and indeed the whole administration of the government. Mr. Hamilton has confessed the printing and publishing, and I think nothing is plainer than that the words in the information [indictment] are scandalous, and tend to sedition, and to disquiet the minds of the people of this province. And if such papers are not libels, I think it may be said there can be no such thing as a libel.

MR. HAMILTON. May it please Your Honor, I cannot agree with Mr. Attorney. For though I freely acknowledge that there are such things as libels, yet I must insist, at the same time, that what my client is charged with is not a libel. And I observed just now that Mr. Attorney, in defining a libel, made use of the words "scandalous, seditious, and tend to disquiet the people." But (whether with design or not I will not say) he omitted the word "false."

MR. ATTORNEY. I think I did not omit the word "false." But it has been said already that it may be a libel, notwithstanding it may be true.

MR. HAMILTON. In this I must still differ with Mr. Attorney; for I depend upon it, we are to be tried upon this information now before the court and jury, and to which we have pleaded not guilty, and by it we are charged with printing and publishing a certain false, malicious, seditious, and scandalous libel. This word "false" must have some meaning, or else how came it there? . . .

MR. CHIEF JUSTICE. You cannot be admitted, Mr. Hamilton, to give the truth of a libel in evidence. A libel is not to be justified; for it is nevertheless a libel that it is true. . . .

MR. HAMILTON. I thank Your Honor. Then, gentlemen of the jury, it is to you we must now appeal, for witnesses, to the truth of the facts we have offered, and are denied the liberty to prove. And let it not seem strange that I apply myself to you in this manner. I am warranted so to do both by law and reason.

The law supposes you to be summoned out of the neighborhood where the fact [crime] is alleged to be committed; and the reason of your being taken

---

From J. P. Zenger, *The Tryal of J. P. Z. of New York* (London, 1738), 10-17.

Andrew Hamilton's defense of Zenger. This reproduction
of a drawing by Kendrick in Ellis Youth's *History of the
United States* shows the aged Philadelphia lawyer Andrew
Hamilton in the courtroom pleading the case of John Peter
Zenger, publisher of the *New-York Weekly Journal*. Zenger
had printed some articles in his paper criticizing Governor
Cosby, who then had him arrested and charged with false
and scandalous libel. In August 1735, in a stunning decision,
the jury rendered a verdict of "not guilty" for the printer.
(Library of Congress)

out of the neighborhood is because you are supposed to have the best knowledge of the fact that is to be tried. And were you to find a verdict against my client, you must take upon you to say the papers referred to in the information, and which we acknowledge we printed and published, are false, scandalous, and seditious. But of this I can have no apprehension. You are citizens of New York; you are really what the law supposes you to be, honest and lawful men. And, according to my brief, the facts which we offer to prove were not committed in a corner; they are notoriously known to be true; and therefore in your justice lies our safety. And as we are denied the liberty of giving evidence to prove the truth of what we have published, I will beg leave to lay it down, as a standing rule in such cases, that the suppressing of evidence ought always to be taken for the strongest evidence; and I hope it will have weight with you. . . .

I hope to be pardoned, sir, for my zeal upon this occasion. It is an old and wise caution that when our neighbor's house is on fire, we ought to take care of our own. For though, blessed be God, I live in a government [Pennsylvania] where liberty is well understood, and freely enjoyed, yet experience has shown us all (I'm sure it has to me) that a bad precedent in one government is soon set up for an authority in another. And therefore I cannot but think it mine, and every honest man's duty, that (while we pay all due obedience to men in authority) we ought at the same time to be upon our guard against power, wherever we apprehend that it may affect ourselves or our fellow subjects.

I am truly very unequal to such an undertaking on many accounts. And you see I labor under the weight of many years, and am borne down with great infirmities of body. Yet old and weak as I am, I should think it my duty, if required, to go to the utmost part of the land, where my service could be of any use, in assist—to quench the flame of prosecutions upon informations, set on foot by the government, to deprive a people of the right of remonstrating (and complaining too) of the arbitrary attempts of men in power. Men who injure and oppress the people under their administration provoke them to cry out and complain; and then make that very complaint the foundation for new oppressions and prosecutions. I wish I could say there were no instances of this kind.

But to conclude. The question before the court and you, gentlemen of the jury, is not of small nor private concern. It is not the cause of a poor printer, nor of New York alone, which you are now trying. No! It may, in its consequence, affect every freeman that lives under a British government on the main[land] of America. It is the best cause. It is the cause of liberty. And I make no doubt but your upright conduct, this day, will not only entitle you to the love and esteem of your fellow citizens; but every man who prefers freedom to a life of slavery will bless and honor you, as men who have baffled the attempt of tyranny, and, by an impartial and uncorrupt verdict, have laid a noble foundation for securing to ourselves, our posterity, and our neighbors, that to which nature and the laws of our country have given us a right—the liberty both of exposing and opposing arbitrary power (in these parts of the world, at least) by speaking and writing truth. . . .

8. The Great Awakening
Jonathan Edwards,
SINNERS IN THE HANDS OF AN ANGRY GOD (1741)

Jonathan Edwards was upset by the "extraordinary dullness in religion" he observed around him. During the first part of the eighteenth century, as the population of the colonies increased and Americans developed a thriving trade with other parts of the world, they became increasingly worldly in their outlook. It wasn't that they abandoned religion; what they abandoned was the stern, harsh religion that Edwards considered essential to salvation. Edwards, like John Winthrop, was a devout Puritan. He believed human beings were incorrigible sinners, filled with greed, pride, and lust, and that a just God had condemned them to eternal damnation for their transgressions. But God was merciful as well as just. Because Jesus had atoned for man's sins by dying on the cross, God agreed to shed his grace on some men and women and elect them for salvation. The individual who was chosen for salvation experienced God's grace while being converted. For Edwards the conversion experience was the greatest event in a person's life. After conversion, the individual dedicated himself to the glory of God and possessed a new strength to resist temptation.

In his sermons, Edwards, pastor of the Congregational church in Northampton, Massachusetts, tried to impress on people the awful fate that awaited them unless they acknowledged their sinfulness and threw themselves upon the mercy of God. During the last part of 1734 Edwards delivered a series of sermons that moved his congregation deeply. In them he gave such vivid descriptions of human depravity and the torments awaiting the unredeemed in the next world that people in the congregation wept, groaned, and begged for mercy. Edwards's sermons produced scores of conversions. During the winter and spring over three hundred people were converted and admitted to full membership in the church. "This town," wrote Edwards joyfully, "never was so full of Love, nor so full of Joy, nor so full of distress as it has lately been." The religious revival that Edwards led in Northampton was only one of many revivals sweeping America at this time — in New England, in the Middle Colonies, and in the South. The Great Awakening, as the revivalist movement was called, affected the Presbyterians as well as the Congregationalists, and also swept through other denominations, keeping the churches in turmoil from about 1734 to 1756. The Great Awakening did produce a renewed interest in religion, but not always in Edwards's austere Puritanism. Edwards led revivals only in New England. George Whitefield, an English associate of John Wesley, the founder of Methodism, came to America, toured the colonies, and led revivals wherever he went. He helped make the Great

Awakening an intercolonial movement. It was the first movement in which all the colonies participated before the American Revolution.

Edwards, who was born in East Windsor, Connecticut, in 1703, was a precocious lad. He wrote a treatise on spiders at age twelve and entered Yale College at age thirteen. The son of a Congregational minister, he experienced conversion as a young man, dedicated his life to the church, and pursued theological studies at Yale after graduation. In 1726 he became associate pastor of the Congregational church in Northampton, and in 1729 he was appointed pastor. For twenty-one years he labored hard in Northampton, studying, writing, and preaching; he also launched his ambitious plan for publishing treatises on all of the great Puritan doctrines. He wrote, too, a psychological analysis of the conversion experience, based on his study of the revivals that took place in Northampton and elsewhere. He delivered his famous sermon, "Sinners in the Hands of an Angry God" in Enfield, Connecticut, in 1741. In 1750 he took his family to Stockbridge. There he spent the rest of his life, preaching and serving as missionary to the Indians. In 1758 he was appointed president of the College of New Jersey (Princeton), but he died of smallpox before beginning his duties there.

Questions to consider. Edwards was not a spellbinder like Whitefield. He delivered his sermons in a quiet, though impassioned, tone of voice and looked at the back wall of the church, not the congregation, while preaching. How, then was he able, in a sermon like "Sinners in the Hands of an Angry God," to arouse the rapt attention of the people? In what ways did he set forth the sovereignty of God, a prime doctrine of the Puritans? Do you think there is any inconsistency in his belief that only a few people (the elect) are saved and his insistence that everybody strive for salvation? Can you think of any contemporary examples of people who share Edwards's outlook? In what ways could the Great Awakening have fostered anti-establishment, anti-imperial attitudes among the American colonists?

SINNERS IN THE HANDS OF AN ANGRY GOD (1741)

. . . This that you have heard is the case of every one of you that are out of Christ. That world of misery, that lake of burning brimstone, is extended abroad under you. There is the dreadful pit of the glowing flames of the wrath of God; there is hell's wide gaping mouth open; and you have nothing to stand upon, nor any thing to take hold of; there is nothing between you and hell but the air; 'tis only the power and mere pleasure of God that holds you up.

You probably are not sensible of this; you find you are kept out of hell, but don't see the hand of God in it, but look at other things, as the good state of

From Samuel Austin, ed., *The Works of President Edwards* (6 v., Isaiah Thomas, Worcester, 1808), II, 72-79.

your bodily constitution, your care of your own life, and the means you use for your own preservation. But indeed these things are nothing; if God should withdraw his hand, they would avail no more to keep you from falling, than the thin air to hold up a person that is suspended in it.

Your wickedness makes you as it were heavy as lead, and to tend downwards with great weight and pressure towards hell; and, if God should let you go, you would immediately sink, and swiftly descend and plunge into the bottomless gulf; and your healthy constitution, and your own care and prudence, and best contrivance, and all your righteousness, would have no more influence to uphold you and keep you out of hell, than a spider's web would have to stop a falling rock. Were it not that so is the sovereign pleasure of God, the earth would not bear you one moment; for you are a burden to it; the creation groans with you; the creature is made subject to the bondage of your corruption, not willingly; the sun don't willingly shine upon you, to give you light to serve sin and Satan; the earth don't willingly yield her increase to satisfy your lusts, nor is it willingly a stage for your wickedness to be acted upon; the air don't willingly serve you for breath to maintain the flame of life in your vitals, while you spend your life in the service of God's enemies. God's creatures are good, and were made for men to serve God with, and don't willingly subserve to any other purpose, and groan when they are abused to purposes so directly contrary to their nature and end. And the world would spue you out, were it not for the sovereign hand of him who hath subjected it in hope. There are the black clouds of God's wrath now hanging directly over your heads, full of the dreadful storm, and big with thunder; and, were it not for the restraining hand of God, it would immediately burst forth upon you. The sovereign pleasure of God for the present stays his rough wind; otherwise it would come with fury, and your destruction would come like a whirlwind, and you would be like the chaff of the summer threshing-floor.

The wrath of God is like great waters that are dammed for the present; they increase more and more, and rise higher and higher, till an outlet is given; and the longer the stream is stopt, the more rapid and mighty is its course when once it is let loose. 'Tis true, that judgment against your evil works has not been executed hitherto; the floods of God's vengeance have been withheld; but your guilt in the mean time is constantly increasing, and you are every day treasuring up more wrath; the waters are continually rising, and waxing more and more mighty; and there is nothing but the mere pleasure of God that holds the waters back that are unwilling to be stopt, and press hard to go forward. If God should only withdraw his hand from the floodgate, it would immediately fly open, and the fiery floods of the fierceness and wrath of God would rush forth with inconceivable fury, and would come upon you with omnipotent power; and if your strength were ten thousand times greater than it is, yea ten thousand times greater than the strength of the stoutest, sturdiest, devil in hell, it would be nothing to withstand or endure it.

The bow of God's wrath is bent, and the arrow made ready on the string; and justice bends the arrow at your heart, and strains the bow; and it is nothing but the mere pleasure of God, and that of an angry God, without any promise or obligation at all, that keeps the arrow one moment from being made drunk with your blood.

Thus are all you that never passed under a great change of heart, by the mighty power of the spirit of God upon your souls; all that were never born again, and made new creatures, and raised from being dead in sin, to a state of new, and before altogether unexperienced light and life. However you may have reformed your life in many things, and may have had religious affections, and may keep up a form of religion in your families and closets, and in the house of God, and may be strict in it, you are thus in the hands of an angry God; 'tis nothing but his mere pleasure that keeps you from being this moment swallowed up in everlasting destruction.

However unconvinced you may now be of the truth of what you hear, by and by you will be fully convinced of it. Those that are gone from being in the like circumstances with you, see that it was so with them; for destruction came suddenly upon most of them, when they expected nothing of it, and while they were saying, peace and safety. Now they see, that those things that they depended on for peace and safety, were nothing but thin air and empty shadows.

The God that holds you over the pit of hell, much as one holds a spider or some lothsom insect over the fire, abhors you, and is dreadfully provoked; his wrath towards you burns like fire; he looks upon you as worthy of nothing else but to be cast into the fire; he is of purer eyes than to bear to have you in his sight; you are ten thousand times so abominable in his eyes as the most hateful venomous serpent is in ours. You have offended him infinitely more than ever a stubborn rebel did his prince; and yet 'tis nothing but his hand that holds you from falling into the fire every moment. 'Tis to be ascribed to nothing else, that you did not go to hell the last night; that you was suffered to awake again in this world, after you closed your eyes to sleep. And there is no other reason to be given why you have not dropt into hell since you arose in the morning, but that God's hand has held you up. There is no other reason to be given why you haven't gone to hell since you have sat here in the House of God, provoking his pure eyes by your sinful wicked manner of attending his solemn worship; yea, there is nothing else that is to be given as a reason why you don't this very moment drop down into hell.

O Sinner! Consider the fearful danger you are in. 'Tis a great furnace of wrath, a wide and bottomless pit, full of the fire of wrath, that you are held over in the hand of that God, whose wrath is provoked and incensed as much against you as against many of the damned in hell. You hang by a slender thread, with the flames of divine wrath flashing about it, and ready every moment to singe it, and burn it asunder; and you have no interest in any mediator, and nothing to lay hold of to save yourself, nothing to keep off the flames of wrath, nothing of your own, nothing that you ever have done, nothing that you can do, to induce God to spare you one moment. . . .

How dreadful is the state of those that are daily and hourly in danger of this great wrath, and infinite misery! But this is the dismal case of every soul in this congregation that has not been born again, however moral and strict, sober and religious they may otherwise be. Oh that you would consider it, whether you be young or old! There is reason to think, that there are many in this congregation, now hearing this discourse, that will actually be the subjects of this very misery to all eternity. We know not who they are, or in what seats they sit, or what thoughts they now have. It may be they are now at ease, and hear all these things without much disturbance, and are now flattering themselves that they shall escape. If we knew that there was one person, and but one, in the whole congregation, that was to be the subject of this misery, what an awful thing would it be to think of! If we knew who it was, what an awful sight would it be to see such a person! How might all the rest of the congregation lift up a lamentable and bitter cry over him! But alas! instead of one, how many is it likely will remember this discourse in hell? And it would be a wonder if some that are now present should not be in hell in a very short time, before this year is out; and it would be no wonder if some person that now sits here in some seat of this meeting-house, in health, and quiet and secure, should be there before to-morrow morning. . . .

9. Multiplicity and Abundance
Gottlieb Mittelberger,
JOURNEY TO PENNSYLVANIA (1756)

Between 1749 and 1754 more than thirty thousand Germans came to Pennsylvania. Soon they came to constitute about one-third of the colony's population. Most Germans coming to America at this time were indentured servants; that is, they were contracted to work for a master for a certain period of time before striking off on their own. They were also known as "redemptioners." To pay for the trip across the Atlantic they sold their labor for a period of two to seven years. On reaching America they "redeemed" themselves by working for a farmer or merchant until they had paid off the debt they had contracted. Slaves were scarce in Pennsylvania, and there was a great demand for redemptioners to work as farm laborers, skilled craftsmen, and domestic servants. Unfortunately, there was much skullduggery in the redemption system. Although redemptioners from England received written contracts or indentures specifying the service they owed, German immigrants received only verbal assurances from shipmasters and merchants as to their future obligations. Once they reached America their labor was auctioned off to the highest bidder, they had nothing to say about their terms of service, and they were often cruelly exploited.

Gottlieb Mittelberger, a native of Württemberg, arrived in Philadelphia late in 1750. He was one of about five hundred passengers aboard the ship *Osgood*. Mittelberger settled in a German community not far from Philadelphia and became organist and schoolmaster there. But less than four years later he returned to Germany, where he spent the rest of his life. In 1756 he published a little volume entitled *Journey to Pennsylvania* describing life in the New World. He filled his book with statistics, geographical information, and anecdotes, but he also had much to say about conditions among German immigrants like himself in America.

Mittelberger was especially critical of "Newlanders" (agents of shipmasters charged with recruiting redemptioners) who traveled about Germany exaggerating the opportunities for immigrants in the "New Land." Not only was Mittelberger distressed by the exploitation of the redemptioners, he was also bothered by the disregard for rank in Pennsylvania, by the laxity in religion, and by the free and easy manners of the back-country Pennsylvanians whom he encountered. Immigrants from Germany belonged to a variety of religious sects, and in Pennsylvania they were free to practice their religion as they pleased. Mittelberger was struck by the bounteous freedom which the colony offered its inhabitants, but feared it might jeopardize social stability. Mittelberger's book did not stop the flow of Germans to America. Though conditions in America were not as glorious as the Newlanders portrayed them, life was still considerably better there than in Germany, which was ravaged by war, famine, and poverty.

Questions to consider. In the following extract from *Journey to Pennsylvania* Mittelberger recorded his observations of religious and economic life in Pennsylvania in the early 1750s. What impressed him the most about religion in the colony? Did he entirely approve of it? How much economic freedom did he find in the colony? How much opportunity to get ahead did he think existed there? What comments did he make on the size of America as compared with that of Europe? Do you think his overall impression of America was a favorable one?

JOURNEY TO PENNSYLVANIA (1756)

In Pennsylvania there exist so many varieties of doctrines and sects that it is impossible to name them all. Many people do not reveal their own particular beliefs to anyone. Furthermore there are many hundreds of adults who not only are unbaptized, but who do not even want baptism. Many others pay no attention to the Sacraments and to the Holy Bible, or even to God and His Word. Some do not even believe in the existence of a true God or Devil, Heaven or Hell, Salvation or Damnation, the Resurrection of the Dead, the Last Judgment and Eternal Life, but think that everything visible is of merely natural origin. For in Pennsylvania not only is everyone allowed to believe what he wishes; he is also at liberty to express these beliefs publicly and freely.

Thus when young people not raised in the fundamentals of religion must go into service for many years with such freethinkers and unbelievers and are not permitted by these people to attend any church or school, especially when they live far away from them, then such innocent souls do not reach a true knowledge of the Divine and are brought up like heathen or Indians. . . .

To come back to Pennsylvania again. It offers people more freedom than the other English colonies, since all religious sects are tolerated there. One can encounter Lutherans, members of the Reformed Church, Catholics, Quakers, Mennonites or Anabaptists, Herrenhüter or Moravian Brothers, Pietists, Seventh-Day Adventists, Dunkers, Presbyterians, New-born, Freemasons, Separatists, Freethinkers, Jews, Mohammedans, Pagans, Negroes, and Indians. But the Evangelicals and the Reformed constitute the majority. There are several hundred unbaptized people who don't even wish to be baptized. Many pray neither in the morning nor in the evening, nor before or after meals. In the homes of such people are not to be found any devotional books, much less a Bible. It is possible to meet in one house, among one family, members of four or five or six different sects.

Reprinted by permission of the publishers from *Journey to Pennsylvania* by Gottlieb Mittelberger, trans. & ed. by Oscar Handlin, Cambridge, Mass.: The Belknap Press of Harvard University Press, Copyright © 1960 by the President and Fellows of Harvard College.

Freedom in Pennsylvania extends so far that everyone's property—commercial, real estate, and personal possessions—is exempt from any interference or taxation. For owning a hundred morgen [Dutch unit of land] one is assessed an annual tax of not more than one English shilling. This is called ground-rent or quit-rent. One shilling is worth approximately eighteen kreuzer in German money. What is peculiar is that single men and women must pay two to five shillings annually, in proportion to their earnings, the reason for this being that they have none but themselves to look after. In Philadelphia the money raised in this way is used to purchase lights by which the streets of the city are illuminated every night. . . .

In Pennsylvania no profession or craft needs to constitute itself into a guild. Everyone may engage in any commercial or speculative ventures, according to choice and ability. And if someone wishes or is able to carry on ten occupations at one and the same time, then nobody is allowed to prevent it. And if, for example, a lad learns his skill or craft as an apprentice or even on his own, he can then pass for a master and may marry whenever he chooses. It is an admirable thing that young people born in this new country are easily taught, clever, and skillful. For many of them have only to look at and examine a work of skill or art a few times before being able to imitate it perfectly. Whereas in Germany it would take most people several years of study to do the same. But in America many have the ability to produce even the most elaborate objects in a short span of time. When these young people have attended school for half a year, they are generally able to read anything.

The province of Pennsylvania is a healthy one; for the most part it has good soil, good air and water, lots of high mountains, and lots of flat land. There are many woods, and where these are not inhabited, there is natural forest through which flow many small and large rivers. The land is also very fertile, and all kinds of grain flourish.

The province is well populated, inhabited far and wide, and various new towns have been founded here and there, namely Philadelphia, Germantown, Lancaster, Reading, Bethlehem, and New Frankfort. Many churches have also been built in this region, but it takes a great many people two, three, four, five, and up to ten hours to get to church. But everyone, men and women, ride to church on horseback, even though they could walk the distance in half an hour. This is also customary at weddings and funerals. At times at such formal country weddings or funerals, it is possible to count up to four hundred or five hundred persons on horseback. One can easily imagine that on such occasions, just as at Holy Communion, nobody appears in black crepe or in a black cloak. . . .

Concerning the size of America, people in Pennsylvania say that this part of the world is supposed to be far larger than Europe, and that it would be impossible to explore it completely on account of the lack of roads, and because of the forests, and the rivers, great and small. Pennsylvania is not an island, as some simpletons in Germany believe it to be. I took the opportunity of talking about the size of this part of the world with an English traveler, who had been with the savages far inland. He told me that he had been with the Indians in the country, trading for skins and furs, more than 700 miles from Philadelphia, that is a journey of 233 Swabian [Swabia = German duchy] hours. He had spoken about this topic with a very aged Indian who gave him to understand in English that he and his brother had at one time traveled straight across the country and through the bush toward the setting sun, starting out from the very place where the meeting with the English traveler took place. And according to their calculations they had journeyed 1,600 English miles. But when they realized that they had no hope of reaching the end of the country they had turned back again. . . .

In the province of Pennsylvania three principal roads have been constructed, all of which lead from Philadelphia into the country as far as it is inhabited. The first runs from Philadelphia to the right hand by the Delaware to New Frankfort; the second or middle road runs toward Germantown, Reading, and Tulpehocken, extending across the Blue Mountains; the third road runs to the left toward Lancaster and Bethlehem, where there is a monastery and convent full of Dunker Brethren and Sisters. The men do not shave their beards; many among them have beards half an ell [an old English unit of length] in length. They wear cowls like the Capuchin monks, in winter of the same cloth or at least the same color, in summer, however, of fine white linen. The Sisters dress in the same manner. These people are not baptized until they are grown up and can testify to their faith, when it is done by dunking in deep water. They keep Saturdays instead of Sundays as holidays. Their convent Sisters, however, frequently bring forth living fruit with much patience.

10. Colonial Wisdom
Benjamin Franklin,
THE WAY TO WEALTH (1758)

Benjamin Franklin was an amazingly versatile man: printer, journalist, editor, educator, satirist, reformer, scientist, inventor, and public servant. He also knew how to make money. His printing business did so well that he was able to retire from active work while in his forties and devote the rest of his life to public service, humanitarian causes, and science and invention. In *Poor Richard's Alamanac,* an annual journal containing weather and astronomical information that he published from 1733 to 1758, he scattered mottoes, epigrams, and proverbs throughout every issue making the point that diligence, temperance, moderation, and thrift were prime essentials to worldly success.

The Way to Wealth, which Franklin printed in 1758, is a compilation of the best of the sayings from *Poor Richard's Almanac.* All had a similar theme: if you want to succeed in life you must work hard, shun excess, and use your time carefully. Some of the mottoes were invented by Franklin himself, but most of them came from a wide variety of sources, ancient and modern, and were put by him into homespun language which he thought would appeal to his readers. Some of them are still familiar: "Early to bed, and early to rise, makes a man healthy, wealthy, and wise"; "God helps them that help themselves"; "One today is worth two tomorrows." Others are no longer popular, but the point they make is familiar enough: "Keep thy shop and thy shop will keep thee"; "Beware of little expenses; a small leak will sink a great ship"; "Dost thou love life, then do not squander time, for that's the stuff life is made of."

In *The Way to Wealth* Franklin puts all of these mottoes into the mouth of Father Abraham, who preaches the gospel of thrift and industry to a large crowd of people. The tone of the discourse appears to be deadly serious, even stuffy, throughout. But when Father Abraham finishes, Franklin tells us, tongue in cheek, the people "approved the Doctrine and immediately practiced the contrary, just as if it had been a common Sermon." Still, when he was a young man, Franklin lived very much by the rules he sets forth in his book, and he thought other people could get ahead in life the way he did if they also practiced these virtues.

Franklin surely knew something about rising in the world. Born in Boston in 1706, the son of a candlemaker, he was apprenticed to his brother, a printer, at the age of twelve. At seventeen, having mastered the trade, Franklin ran away to Philadelphia and soon established a thriving printing establishment of his own. Not only did he become famous as a writer and publisher; he also became active in civic affairs (he founded a fire department, a library, and a scientific society in Philadelphia) and in politics (he represented the colonies in England from 1757 to 1775 and served as minister to France during the war for independence). For his pioneering work in the field of electricity he was as famous in Europe as in America. In his *Autobiography,* which he wrote for his son in 1777, he dwelt on his early years, in order, he said, to make it "of more general use to young readers, as exemplifying strongly the effects of prudent and imprudent conduct in the commencement of a life of business." He continued active until his death in 1790, becoming president of the executive council of Pennsylvania at the age of seventy-nine and representing his state in the Constitutional Convention, which met in Philadelphia in 1787.

Questions to consider. What did Franklin say about his "Brother Authors" at the beginning of *The Way to Wealth?* What did he mean by "solid Pudding"? How does Father Abraham respond to the people's complaints about taxes? What does he consider the "greatest Prodigality?" How much truth is there in his contention that industrious people "shall never starve"? What is his attitude toward leisure? Why does he link frugality so closely with diligence? How do the goals presented by Franklin compare with those outlined by John Winthrop on the *Arbella* (Document 2)? How much validity do you think there is in Father Abraham's outlook on life? In what way is *The Way to Wealth* one of the first do-it-yourself books printed in America?

THE WAY TO WEALTH (1758)

I have heard that nothing gives an Author so great Pleasure, as to find his Works respectfully quoted by other learned Authors. This Pleasure I have seldom enjoyed; for tho' I have been, if I may say it without Vanity, an *eminent Author* of Almanacks annually now a full Quarter of a Century, my Brother Authors in the same Way, for what Reason I know not, have ever been very sparing in their Applauses, and no other Author has taken the least Notice of me, so that did not my Writings produce me some solid *Pudding*, the great Deficiency of *Praise* would have quite discouraged me.

I concluded at length, that the People were the best Judges of my Merit; for they buy my Works; and besides, in my Rambles, where I am not personally known, I have frequently heard one or other of my Adages repeated, with, *as Poor Richard says,* at the End on 't; this gave me some Satisfaction, as it showed not only that my Instructions were regarded, but discovered likewise some Respect for my Authority; and I own, that to encourage the Practice of remembering and repeating those wise Sentences, I have sometimes *quoted myself* with great Gravity.

From Albert Henry Smyth, ed., *The Writings of Benjamin Franklin* (9 v., Haskell House, New York, 1907), III: 407-418.

Judge, then how much I must have been gratified by an Incident I am going to relate to you. I stopt my Horse lately where a great Number of People were collected at a Vendue of Merchant Goods. The House of Sale not being come, they were conversing on the Badness of the Times and one of the Company call'd to a plain clean old Man, with white Locks, "Pray, Father Abraham, what think you of the Times? Won't these heavy Taxes quite ruin the Country? How shall we be ever able to pay them? What would you advise us to?" Father *Abraham* stood up, and reply'd, "If you'd have my Advice, I'll give it you in short, for *A Word to the Wise is enough, and many Words won't fill a Bushel*, as *Poor Richard* says." They join'd in desiring him to speak his Mind, and gathering round him he proceeded as follows:

"Friends," says he, "and Neighbours, the Taxes are indeed very heavy. *Poor Richard* says, *the greatest Prodigality;* since as he elsewhere tells us, and if those laid on by the Government were the only Ones we had to pay, we might more easily discharge them; but we have many others, and much more grievous to some of us. We are taxed twice as much by our Idleness, three times as much by our *Pride*, and four times as much by our *Folly;* and from these Taxes the Commissioners cannot ease or deliver us by allowing an Abatement. However let us hearken to good Advice, and something may be done for us; *God helps them that help themselves*, as *Poor Richard says*, in his Almanack of 1733.

It would be thought a hard Government that should tax its People one-tenth Part of their *Time*, to be employed in its Service. But *Idleness* taxes many of us much more, if we reckon all that is spent in absolute *Sloth*, or doing of nothing, with that which is spent in idle Employment or Amusements that amount to nothing. *Sloth*, by bringing on Diseases, absolutely shortens life. *Sloth, like Rust, consumes faster than Labour wears; while the used key is always bright*, as Poor Richard says. *But dost thou love Life, then do not squander Time, for that's the stuff Life is made of*, as Poor Richard says. How much more than is necessary do we spend in sleep, forgetting that *The sleeping Fox catches no Poultry*, and that *There will be sleeping enough in the Grave*, as *Poor Richard* says.

If Time be of all Things the most precious, wasting Time must be, as *Poor Richard* says, *the greatest Prodigality;* since, as he elsewhere tells us, *Lost Time is never found again; and what we call Time enough, always proves little enough:* Let us then up and be doing, and doing to the Purpose; so by Diligence shall we do more with less Perplexity. *Sloth makes all Things difficult, but Industry all easy*, as *Poor Richard* says; and *He that riseth late must trot all Day, and shall scarce overtake his Business at Night; while Laziness travels so slowly, that Poverty soon overtakes him*, as we read in *Poor Richard*, who adds, *Drive thy Business, let not that drive thee;* and *Early to Bed, and early to rise, makes a Man healthy, wealthy, and wise.*

So what signifies *wishing* and *hoping* for better Times. We may make these Times better, if we bestir ourselves. *Industry need not wish*, as *Poor Richard* says, *and he that lives upon Hope will die fasting. There are no Gains without Pains; then Help Hands, for I have no Lands*, or if I have, they are smartly taxed. And, as *Poor Richard* likewise observes, *He that hath a Trade hath an Estate; and he that hath a Calling, hath an Office of Profit and*

Honour; but then the *Trade* must be worked at, and the *Calling* well followed, or neither the *Estate* nor the *Office* will enable us to pay our Taxes. If we are industrious, we shall never starve; for, as *Poor Richard* says, *At the working Man's House Hunger looks in, but dares not enter.* Nor will the Bailiff or the Constable enter, for *Industry pays Debts, while Despair encreaseth them,* says *Poor Richard.* What though you have found no Treasure, nor has any rich Relation left you a Legacy, *Diligence is the Mother of Good-luck* as *Poor Richard* says *and God gives all Things to Industry. Then plough deep, while sluggards sleep, and you shall have Corn to sell and to keep,* says *Poor Dick.* Work while it is called To-day, for you know not how much you may be hindered To-morrow, which makes *Poor Richard* say, *One to-day is worth two To-morrows,* and farther *Have you somewhat to do To-morrow, do it To-day.* If you were a Servant, would you not be ashamed that a good Master should catch you idle? Are you then your own Master, *be ashamed to catch yourself idle,* as *Poor Dick* says. When there is so much to be done for yourself, your Family, your Country, and your gracious King, be up by Peep of Day; *Let not the Sun look down and say, Inglorious here he lies.* Handle your Tools with Mittens; remember that *The Cat in Gloves catches no Mice,* as *Poor Richard* says. 'Tis true there is much to be done, and perhaps you are weak-handed, but stick to it steadily; and you will see great Effects, for *Constant Dripping wears away Stones,* and by *Diligence and Patience the Mouse ate in two the Cable;* and *Little Strokes fell great Oaks,* as *Poor Richard* says in his Almanack, the Year I cannot just now remember.

Methinks I hear some of you say, *Must a Man afford himself no Leisure?* I will tell thee, my friend, what *Poor Richard* says, *Employ thy Time well, if thou meanest to gain Leisure; and, since thou art not sure of a Minute, throw not away an Hour.* Leisure, is Time for doing something useful; this Leisure the diligent Man will obtain, but the lazy Man never; so that, as *Poor Richard* says, *A Life of Leisure and a Life of Laziness are two Things.* Do you imagine that Sloth will afford you more Comfort than Labour? No, for as *Poor Richard* says, *Trouble springs from Idleness, and grievous Toil from needless Ease. Many without Labour, would live by their Wits only, but they break for want of Stock.* Whereas Industry gives Comfort, and Plenty, and Respect: *Fly Pleasures, and they'll follow you. The diligent Spinner has a large Shift; and now I have a Sheep and a Cow, every-Body bids me good Morrow;* all which is well said by *Poor Richard.* . . .

So much for Industry, my Friends, and Attention to one's own Business; but to these we must add *Frugality,* if we would make our *Industry* more certainly successful. A Man may, if he knows not how to save as he gets, *keep his Nose all his Life to the Grindstone,* and die not worth a *Groat* at last. *A fat Kitchen makes a lean Will,* as *Poor Richard* says; and

> *Many Estates are spent in the Getting,*
> *Since Women for Tea forsook Spinning and Knitting,*
> *And Men for Punch forsook Hewing and Splitting.*

If you would be wealthy, says he, in another Almanack, *think of Saving as well as of Getting: The Indies have not made Spain rich, because her Outgoes are greater than her Incomes.*

Poor Richard, 1733.

A N

Almanack

For the Year of Chrift

1733,

Being the Firft after LEAP YEAR:

And makes fince the Creation	Years
By the Account of the Eastern *Greeks*	7241
By the Latin Church, when ☉ ent. ♈	6932
By the Computation of *W. W.*	5742
By the *Roman* Chronology	5682
By the *Jewish* Rabbies	5494

Wherein is contained

The Lunations, Eclipfes, Judgment of the Weather, Spring Tides, Planets Motions & mutual Afpects, Sun and Moon's Rifing and Setting, Length of Days, Time of High Water, Fairs, Courts, and obfervable Days.

Fitted to the Latitude of Forty Degrees, and a Meridian of Five Hours Weft from *London*, but may without fenfible Error, ferve all the adjacent Places, even from *Newfoundland* to *South-Carolina*.

By *RICHARD SAUNDERS*, Philom.

PHILADELPHIA:
Printed and fold by *B. FRANKLIN*, at the New Printing-Office near the Market.

Poor Richard, 1733. An Almanac. Just about every colonial household acquired an almanac: a little paperbound book published at the end of each year containing weather forecasts, recipes, jokes, poems, and proverbs. Franklin entered the field in December 1732 with *Poor Richard, 1733*, which sold for five-pence a copy. *Poor Richard* was an immediate success; soon it was doing better than all the other almanacs being sold, in great measure because of the character, Richard Saunders, which Franklin created. Poor Richard entertained his readers with pithy maxims, homely little poems, and witty remarks. He also regaled them with stories about his quarrels with his wife Bridget. (Library of Congress)

Away then with your expensive Follies, and you will not then have so much Cause to complain of hard Times, heavy Taxes, and chargeable Families; for, as *Poor Dick* says,

> *Women and Wine, Game and Deceit,*
> *Make the Wealth small and the Wants great.*

And farther, *What maintains one Vice, would bring up two Children.* You may think perhaps that a *little* Tea, or a *little* Punch now and then, Diet a *little* more costly, Clothes a *little* finer, and a *little* Entertainment now and then, can be no great Matter; but remember what *Poor Richard* says, *Many a Little makes a Mickle*; and farther, *Beware of little Expences; A small Leak will sink a great Ship*; and again, *Who Dainties love, shall Beggars prove*; and moreover, *Fools make Feasts, and wise Men eat them.*

Here you are all got together at this Vendue of *Fineries* and *Knicknacks*. You call them *Goods*; but if you do not take Care, they will prove *Evils* to some of you. You expect they will be sold *cheap*, and perhaps they may for less than they cost; but if you have no Occasion for them, they must be *dear* to you. Remember what *Poor Richard* says; *Buy what thou hast no Need of, and ere long thou shalt sell thy Necessaries.* And again, *At a great Pennyworth pause a while:* He means, that perhaps the Cheapness is *apparent* only, and not *Real*; or the bargain, by straitening thee in thy Business, may do thee more Harm than Good. For in another Place he says, *Many have been ruined by buying good Pennyworths.* Again, *Poor Richard* says, *'tis foolish to lay out Money in a Purchase of Repentance*; and yet this Folly is practised every Day at Vendues, for want of minding the Almanack. *Wise Men*, as *Poor Dick* says, *learn by others' Harms, Fools scarcely by their own; but felix quem faciunt aliena pericula cautum.* Many a one, for the Sake of Finery on the Back, have gone with a hungry Belly, and half-starved their Families. *Silks and Satins, Scarlet and Velvets*, as *Poor Richard* says, *put out the Kitchen Fire.*

These are not the *Necessaries* of Life; they can scarcely be called the *Conveniences*; and yet only because they look pretty, how many *want* to *have* them! The *artificial* Wants of Mankind thus become more numerous than the *Natural*; and, as *Poor Dick* says, *for one poor Person, there are an hundred indigent.* By these, and other Extravagancies, the Genteel are reduced to poverty, and forced to borrow of those whom they formerly despised, but who through Industry and Frugality have maintained their Standing; in which Case it appears plainly, that *A Ploughman on his Legs is higher than a Gentleman on his Knees*, as *Poor Richard* says. Perhaps they have had a small Estate left them, which they knew not the Getting of; they think, *'tis Day, and will never be Night*; that a little to be spent out of *so much*, is not worth minding; *A Child and a Fool*, as *Poor Richard* says, *imagine Twenty shillings and Twenty Years can never be spent* but, *always taking out of the Meal-tub, and never putting in, soon comes to the Bottom*; as *Poor Dick* says, *When the Well's dry, they know the Worth of Water.* But this they might have known before, if they had taken his Advice; *If you would know the Value of Money, go and try to borrow some; for, he that goes a borrowing goes a sorrowing*; and indeed so does he that lends to such People, when he goes *to get it in again. Poor Dick* farther advises, and says,

> *Fond Pride of Dress is sure a very Curse;*
> *E'er Fancy you consult, consult your Purse.*

And again, *Pride as as loud a Beggar as Want, and a great deal more saucy.* When you have bought one fine Thing, you must buy ten more, that your Appearance may be all of a Piece; but *Poor Dick* says, *'Tis easier to suppress the first Desire, than to satisfy all that follow it.* And 'tis as truly Folly for the Poor to ape the Rich, as for the Frog to swell in order to equal the ox.

> *Great Estates may venture more,*
> *But little Boats should keep near shore.*

'Tis, however, a Folly soon punished; for *Pride that dines on Vanity, sups on Contempt,* as *Poor Richard* says. And in another Place, *Pride breakfasted with Plenty, dined with Poverty, and supped with Infamy.* And after all, of what Use is this *Pride of Appearance,* for which so much is risked so much is suffered? It cannot promote Health, or ease Pain; it makes no Increase of Merit in the Person, it creates Envy, it hastens Misfortune.

> *What is a Butterfly? At best*
> *He's but a Caterpillar drest.*
> *The gaudy Fop's his Picture just.*

as *Poor Richard* says.

   But what Madness must it be to *run in Debt* for these Super-Fluities! We are offered, by the Terms of this Vendue, *Six Months' Credit;* and that perhaps has induced some of us to attend it, because we cannot spare the ready Money, and hope now to be fine without it. But, ah, think what you do when you run in Debt; *you give to another Power over your Liberty.* If you cannot pay at the Time, you will be ashamed to see your Creditor; you will be in Fear when you speak to him; you will make poor pitiful sneaking Excuses, and by Degrees come to lose your Veracity, and sink into base downright lying; for, as *Poor Richard* says, *The second Vice is Lying, the first is running in Debt.* And again, to the same Purpose, *Lying rides upon Debt's Back.* Whereas a free-born *Englishman* ought not to be ashamed or afraid to see or speak to any Man living. But Poverty often deprives a Man of all Spirit and Virtue: *'Tis hard for an empty Bag to stand upright,* as *Poor Richard* truly says."

11. A Shattered Empire
THE DECLARATION OF INDEPENDENCE (1776)

On June 7, 1776, Richard Henry Lee, delegate from Virginia to the Second Continental Congress meeting in Philadelphia, proposed a resolution calling for independence from Great Britain. Three days later Congress appointed a committee of five to prepare a statement giving reasons for independence. The committee appointed a subcommittee, consisting of John Adams and Thomas Jefferson, to draft such a statement. The subcommittee met, according to Adams, and Jefferson suggested that Adams write up a statement. "I will not," said Adams emphatically. "You should do it," said Jefferson. "Oh, no," persisted Adams. "Why will you not?" asked Jefferson. "You ought to do it." "I will not," said Adams stubbornly. "Why?" cried Jefferson. "Reasons enough," said Adams. "What can be your reasons?" Jefferson wanted to know. Explained Adams: "Reason first—you are a Virginian, and a Virginian ought to appear at the head of this business. Reason second—I am obnoxious, suspected, and unpopular. You are very much otherwise. Reason third—you can write ten times better than I can." "Well," said Jefferson, "if you are decided, I will do as well as I can." In the end, Jefferson wrote the Great Declaration, minor changes being made by Adams and Franklin, and after the Continental Congress made some additional changes in it, the delegates voted to adopt it on July 4. Two days earlier Congress had accepted Lee's resolution for independence. But July 4, not July 2, soon became the great day for patriotic celebrations.

Jefferson's "peculiar felicity of expression," according to John Adams, made him the ideal choice for writing the Declaration. In simple, lucid, logical language, Jefferson explained to the world what he thought the American people were fighting for: to establish a government based, not on force and fraud, but on the freely given consent of the people and dedicated to safeguarding the basic rights of all citizens. Jefferson's Declaration made it clear that the American Revolution was more than a fight for independence. "Take away from the Declaration of Independence its self-evident truths," said Adams, "and you rob the North American Revolution of all its moral principles, and proclaim it a foul and unnatural rebellion." After the United States achieved its independence in 1783, the Declaration continued to inspire countless reformers seeking to make their country a better place in which to live: abolitionists, feminists, farmers, and working people. The Declaration also influenced reformers and revolutionaries in other parts of the world—Europe, Asia, and Africa—during the nineteenth and twentieth centuries.

Questions to consider. In 1858, when Massachusetts lawyer Rufus Choate contemptuously dismissed the Declaration as a collection of "glittering generalities," Ralph Waldo Emerson exclaimed indignantly: "Glittering generalities! Say, rather, blazing ubiquities!" Do you agree with Choate or with Emerson? What are the main generalities set forth in the first two paragraphs of the Declaration? How valid do you think Jefferson's assertions are about equality, "unalienable rights," and the right of the people to "alter or abolish" their governments? How much prudence do you think the Founding Fathers exercised in their decision to fight for independence? What were Jefferson's major charges against King George III? Do you think he was successful in his attempt to make a long list of abuses and usurpations by the king? Was he fair in blaming the king for all of these abuses and usurpations? Why did he attack the king and avoid any mention of Parliament? What did he say about the English people and why? Do you find any inconsistencies or omissions in the Declaration? Would you sign the Declaration of Independence today?

THE DECLARATION OF INDEPENDENCE (1776)

When in the Course of human events, it becomes necessary for one people to dissolve the political bands which have connected them with another, and to assume among the Powers of the earth, the separate and equal station to which the Laws of Nature and of Nature's God entitle them, a decent respect to the opinions of mankind requires that they should declare the causes which impel them to the separation.

We hold these truths to be self-evident, that all men are created equal, that they are endowed by their Creator with certain unalienable Rights, that among these are Life, Liberty and the pursuit of Happiness. That to secure these rights, Governments are instituted among Men, deriving their just powers from the consent of the governed. That whenever any Form of Government becomes destructive of these ends, it is the Right of the People to alter or to abolish it, and to institute new Government, laying its foundation on such principles and organizing its powers in such form, as to them shall seem most likely to effect their Safety and Happiness. Prudence, indeed, will dictate that Governments long established should not be changed for light and transient causes; and accordingly all experience hath shown, that mankind are more disposed to suffer, while evils are sufferable, than to right themselves by abolishing the forms to which they are accustomed. But when a long train of abuses and usurpations, pursuing invariably the same Object evinces a design to reduce them under absolute Despotism, it is their right, it is their duty, to throw off such Government, and to provide new Guards for their future security.—Such has been the patient sufferance of these Colonies; and such is now the necessity which constrains them to alter their former Systems of Government. The history of the present King of Great Britain is a history of repeated injuries and

From F. N. Thorpe, ed., *The Federal and State Constitutions* (7 v., Government Printing Office, Washington, D.C., 1909), I: 3.

usurpations, all having in direct object the establishment of an absolute Tyranny over these States. To prove this, let Facts be submitted to a candid world.

He has refused his Assent to Laws, the most wholesome and necessary for the public good.

He has forbidden his Governors to pass Laws of immediate and pressing importance, unless suspended in their operation till his Assent should be obtained; and when so suspended, he has utterly neglected to attend to them.

He has refused to pass other Laws for the accommodation of large districts of people, unless those people would relinquish the rights of Representation in the Legislature, a right inestimable to them and formidable to tyrants only.

He has called together legislative bodies at places unusual, uncomfortable, and distant from the depository of their Public Records, for the sole purpose of fatiguing them into compliance with his measures.

He has dissolved Representative Houses repeatedly, for opposing with manly firmness his invasions on the rights of the people.

He has refused for a long time, after such dissolutions, to cause others to be elected; whereby the Legislative Powers, incapable of Annihilation, have returned to the People at large for their exercise; the State remaining in the mean time exposed to all the dangers of invasion from without, and convulsions within.

He has endeavoured to prevent the population of these States; for that purpose obstructing the Laws of Naturalization of Foreigners; refusing to pass others to encourage their migration hither, and raising the conditions of new Appropriations of Lands.

He has obstructed the Administration of Justice, by refusing his Assent to Laws for establishing Judiciary Powers.

He has made Judges dependent on his Will alone, for the tenure of their offices, and the amount and payment of their salaries.

He has erected a multitude of New Offices, and sent hither swarms of Officers to harass our People, and eat out their substance.

He has kept among us, in times of peace, Standing Armies without the Consent of our legislature.

He has affected to render the Military independent of and superior to the Civil Power.

He has combined with others to subject us to a jurisdiction foreign to our constitution, and unacknowledged by our laws; giving his Assent to their acts of pretended legislation:

For quartering large bodies of armed troops among us:

For protecting them, by a mock Trial, from Punishment for any Murders which they should commit on the Inhabitants of these States:

For cutting off our Trade with all parts of the world:

For imposing taxes on us without our Consent:

For depriving us in many cases, of the benefits of Trial by Jury:

For transporting us beyond Seas to be tried for pretended offences:

For abolishing the free System of English Laws in a neighbouring Province, establishing therein an Arbitrary government, and enlarging its Boundaries so as to render it at once an example and fit instrument for introducing the same absolute rule into these Colonies:

Committee of Congress drafting the Declaration of Independence. In this engraving after an 1851 painting, we see the five men who made up the committee appointed by Congress in June 1776 to draw up a statement of the reasons why the Americans had decided to fight for independence from Britain: Thomas Jefferson, John Adams, Benjamin Franklin, Roger Sherman, and Robert Livingston. The committee of five appointed a subcommittee consisting of Jefferson and Adams to draft such a statement, and Jefferson ended up writing most of it. Except for a paragraph blaming King George III for the slave trade, which the delegates voted to excise, the Great Declaration remains pretty much as Jefferson originally wrote it. (Library of Congress)

For taking away our Charters, abolishing our most valuable Laws, and altering fundamentally the Forms of our Governments:

For suspending our own Legislature, and declaring themselves invested with Power to legislate for us in all cases whatsoever.

He has abdicated Government here, by declaring us out of his Protection and waging War against us.

He has plundered our seas, ravaged our Coasts, burnt our towns, and destroyed the lives of our people.

He is at this time transporting large armies of foreign mercenaries to compleat the works of death, desolation and tyranny, already begun with circumstances of Cruelty & perfidy scarcely paralleled in the most barbarous ages, and totally unworthy the Head of a civilized nation.

He has constrained our fellow Citizens taken Captive on the high Seas to bear Arms against their Country, to become the executioners of their friends and Brethren, or to fall themselves by their Hands.

He has excited domestic insurrections amongst us, and has endeavoured to bring on the inhabitants of our frontiers, the merciless Indian Savages, whose known rule of warfare, is an undistinguished destruction of all ages, sexes and conditions.

In every state of these Oppressions We have Petitioned for Redress in the most humble terms: Our repeated Petitions have been answered only by repeated injury. A Prince, whose character is thus marked by every act which may define a Tyrant, is unfit to be the ruler of a free People.

Nor have We been wanting in attention to our British brethren. We have warned them from time to time of attempts by their legislature to extend an unwarrantable jurisdiction over us. We have reminded them of the circumstances of our emigration and settlement here. We have appealed to their native justice and magnanimity, and we have conjured them by the ties of our common kindred to disavow these usurpations, which, would inevitably interrupt our connections and correspondence. They too have been deaf to the voice of justice and of consanguinity. We must, therefore, acquiesce in the necessity, which denounces our Separation, and hold them, as we hold the rest of mankind, Enemies in War, in Peace Friends.

We, therefore, the Representatives of the united States of America, in General Congress, Assembled, appealing to the Supreme Judge of the world for the rectitude of our intentions, do, in the Name, and by Authority of the good People of these Colonies, solemnly publish and declare, That these United Colonies are, and of Right ought to be Free and Independent States; that they are Absolved from all Allegiance to the British Crown, and that all political connection between them and the State of Great Britain, is and ought to be totally dissolved; and that as Free and Independent States, they have full Power to levy War, conclude Peace, contract Alliances, establish Commerce, and to do all other Acts and Things which Independent States may of right do. And for the support of this Declaration, with a firm reliance on the Protection of Divine Providence, we mutually pledge to each other our Lives, our Fortunes and our sacred Honor.

12. Ideology and Agitation
Thomas Paine,
THE CRISIS, NUMBER ONE (1776)

On December 18, 1776, George Washington wrote his brother discouragedly: "Between you and me, I think our affairs are in a very bad situation. . . . If every nerve is not strained up to the utmost to recruit the new army with all possible expedition, I think the game is up." A few days later Thomas Paine published the first number of *The Crisis,* a pamphlet calling attention to the heartbreaking difficulties the Americans faced in their struggle with Britain and appealing for renewed dedication to the Revolutionary cause. Paine said he wrote in "a passion of patriotism." His essay quickly "rallied and reanimated" the people, according to one observer, and before long "hope succeeded to despair, cheerfulness to gloom, and firmness to irresolution." In twelve more issues of *The Crisis* Paine continued his impassioned fight against apathy, indifference, and defeatism in American ranks. He also wrote additional numbers about American problems after the Yorktown victory in 1781.

Paine, a British corset maker and excise officer, was an ardent supporter of the American cause from almost the beginning. Shortly after arriving in Philadelphia in November 1774, he became editor of the *Pennsylvania Magazine,* discovered he had great gifts as a journalist, and in January 1776 published a little pamphlet entitled *Common Sense* urging Americans to convert their resistance to British oppression into a fight for national independence. Before long thousands of copies of his pamphlet were circulating in the colonies and Washington arranged to have passages from it read to his troops. The first best-seller in history, *Common Sense* persuaded many Americans who were wavering that separation from Britain was both possible and desirable.

Paine pioneered in a new kind of journalism. He avoided the elegant and ornate kind of writing fashionable in aristocratic circles and wrote simply, naturally, and forcefully. He used homely metaphors, introduced everday words and phrases into his essays, translated foreign phrases for his readers, interspersed his logical arguments with lively anecdotes, and brought a sense of immediacy to his writings by including personal, on-the-spot reports. He was, in short, writing for the plain people from whom he himself had come. His influence on the thinking of countless people was enormous.

Paine, born in England of Quaker parents in 1737, lived in obscurity until he came to America in 1774. He became editor of the *Pennsylvania Magazine* and quickly identified himself with the American cause. After the American Revolution he went to France, supported the revolution that broke out there in 1789, and published *The Rights of Man* (1791-1792), a work defending the principles of the French Revolution. He also wrote *The Age of Reason* (1793-1795), criticizing both atheism and orthodox Christianity and calling for a religion based on reason. Though sympathetic to the French Revolution, Paine opposed the execution of King Louis XVI and was appalled by the Reign of Terror that accompanied the Revolution. In the end he was thrown in prison and sentenced to the guillotine; but he was saved by the intervention of the American minister in France, James Monroe. In 1802 he returned to America; but his attacks on George Washington while in France and his religious radicalism made him an outcast. He died in New York, lonely, poverty-stricken, and largely forgotten, in 1809.

Questions to consider. Paine is eminently quotable. Do you find any passages in the essay below that seem especially eloquent? Do you think Paine's appeal rests on substance as well as style? How did he attempt to whip up enthusiasm for the American cause despite reverses on the battlefield? Do you think his handling of Tories, that is, Americans who were sympathetic to Britain, was effective? Do you think he was just to the Loyalists? What about his treatment of King George III and General William Howe, an English general? Do you think his appeals to God were likely to impress religious people in America? What parts of the essay do you think George Washington chose to have read to his troops?

THE CRISIS, NUMBER ONE (1776)

These are the times that try men's souls. The summer soldier and the sunshine patriot will, in this crisis, shrink from the service of his country; but he that stands it NOW, deserves the love and thanks of man and woman. Tyranny, like hell, is not easily conquered; yet we have this consolation with us, that the harder the conflict, the more glorious the triumph. What we obtain too cheap, we esteem too lightly: 'Tis dearness only that gives every thing its value. Heaven knows how to put a proper price upon its goods; and it would be strange indeed, if so celestial an article as FREEDOM should not be highly rated. Britain, with an army to enforce her tyranny, has declared that she has a right (*not only to* TAX) but "*to* BIND *us in* ALL CASES WHATSOEVER," and if being *bound in that manner*, is not slavery, then is there not such a thing as slavery upon earth. Even the expression is impious, for so unlimited a power can belong only to GOD. . . .

I have as little superstition in me as any man living, but my secret opinion has ever been, and still is, that God Almighty will not give up a people to military destruction, or leave them unsupportedly to perish, who had so earnestly and so repeatedly sought to avoid the calamities of war, by every

From Daniel E. Wheeler, ed., *Life and Writings of Thomas Paine* (10 v., V. Parke and Co., New York, 1915), III: 1-16.

decent method which wisdom could invent. Neither have I so much of the infidel in me, as to suppose that HE has relinquished the government of the world, and given us up to the care of devils; and as I do not, I cannot see on what grounds the king of Britain can look up to Heaven for help against us: A common murderer, a highwayman, or a house-breaker has a good a pretence as he. . . .

I shall not now attempt to give all the particulars of our retreat to the Delaware; suffice it for the present to say, that both officers and men, though greatly harassed and fatigued, frequently without rest, covering, or provision, the inevitable consequences of a long retreat, bore it with a manly and a martial spirit. All their wishes were one, which was, that the country would turn out and help them to drive the enemy back. Voltaire has remarked that King William never appeared to full advantage but in difficulties and in action; the same remark may be made on General Washington, for the character fits him. There is a natural firmness in some minds which cannot be unlocked by trifles, but which, when unlocked, discovers a cabinet of fortitude; and I reckon it among those kind of public blessings, which we do not immediately see, that GOD hath blest him with uninterrupted health, and given him a mind that can even flourish upon care.

I shall conclude this paper with some miscellaneous remarks on the state of our affairs; and shall begin with asking the following question, Why is it that the enemy have left the New-England provinces, and made these middle ones the seat of war? The answer is easy: New-England is not infested with tories, and we are. I have been tender in raising the cry against these men, and used numberless arguments to shew them their danger, but it will not do to sacrifice a world to either their folly or their baseness. The period is now arrived, in which either they or we must change our sentiments, or one or both must fall. And what is a tory? Good GOD! what is he? I should not be afraid to go with an hundred whigs against a thousand tories, were they to attempt to get into arms. Every tory is a coward, for a servile, slavish, self-interested fear is the foundation of toryism; and a man under such influence, though he may be cruel, never can be brave.

But, before the line of irrecoverable separation be drawn between us, let us reason the matter together: Your conduct is an invitation to the enemy, yet not one in a thousand of you has heart enough to join him. Howe is as much deceived by you as the American cause is injured by you. He expects you will all take up arms, and flock to his standard with muskets on your shoulders. Your opinions are of no use to him, unless you support him personally, for 'tis soldiers, and not tories, that he wants.

I once felt all that kind of anger, which a man ought to feel, against the mean principles that are held by the tories: A noted one, who kept a tavern at Amboy, was standing at his door, with as pretty a child in his hand, about eight or nine years old, as most I ever saw, and after speaking his mind as freely as he thought was prudent, finished with this unfatherly expression, "*Well! give me peace in my day.*" Not a man lives on the continent but fully believes that a separation must some time or other finally take place, and a generous parent should have said, "*If there must be trouble, let it be in my day that my child may have peace;*" and this single reflection, well applied, is sufficient to awaken every man to duty. Not a place upon earth might be so happy as America. Her situation is remote from all the wrangling world, and she has nothing to do but to trade with them. A man may easily distinguish in himself between temper and principle, and I am' as confident, as I am that GOD governs the world, that America will never be happy till she gets clear of foreign dominion. Wars, without ceasing, will break out till that period arrives, and the continent must in the end be conqueror; for though the flame of liberty may sometimes cease to shine, the coal never can expire. . . .

Not all the treasures of the world, so far as I believe, could have induced me to support an offensive war, for I think it murder; but if a thief break into my house, burn and destroy my property, and kill or threaten to kill me, or those that are in it, and to *"bind me in all cases whatsoever,"* to his absolute will, am I to suffer it? What signifies it to me, whether he who does it, is a king or a common man; my countryman or not my countryman? whether it is done by an individual villain, or an army of them? If we reason to the root of things we shall find no difference; neither can any just cause be assigned why we should punish in the one case and pardon in the other. Let them call me rebel, and welcome. I feel no concern from it; but I should suffer the misery of devils, were I to make a whore of my soul by swearing allegiance to one whose character is that of a sottish, stupid, stubborn, worthless, brutish man. I conceive likewise a horid idea in receiving mercy from a being, who at the last day shall be shrieking to the rocks and mountains to cover him, and fleeing with terror from the orphan, the widow, and the slain of America.

There are cases which cannot be overdone by language, and this is one. There are persons too who see not the full extent of the evil which threatens them, they solace themselves with hopes that the enemy, if they succeed, will be merciful. It is the madness of folly to expect mercy from those who have refused to do justice; and even mercy, where conquest is the object, is only a trick of war: The cunning of the fox is as murderous as the violence of the wolf; and we ought to guard equally against both. Howe's first object is partly by threats and partly by promise, to terrify or seduce the people to deliver up their arms, and receive mercy. The ministry recommended the same plan to Gage, and this is what the tories call making their peace: *"a peace which passeth all understanding"* indeed! A peace which would be the immediate forerunner of a worse ruin than any we have yet thought of. Ye men of Pennsylvania, do reason upon these things! Were the back counties to give up their arms, they would fall an easy prey to the Indians, who are all alarmed. This perhaps is what some tories would not be sorry for. Were the home counties to deliver up their arms, they would be exposed to the resentment of the back counties, who would then have it in their power to chastise their defection at pleasure. And were any one state to give up its arms, THAT state must be garrisoned by all Howe's army of Britons and Hessians to preserve it from the anger of the rest. Mutual fear is a principal link in the chain of mutual love, and woe be to that state that breaks the compact. Howe is mercifully inviting you to barbarous destruction, and men must be either rogues or fools that will not see it. I dwell not upon the powers of imagination; I bring reason to your ears; and in language as plain as A, B, C, hold up truth to your eyes.

I thank GOD that I fear not. I see no real cause for fear. I know our situation well, and can see the way out of it. While our army was collected, Howe dared not risk a battle, and it is no credit to him that he decamped from the White Plains, and waited a mean opportunity to ravage the defenceless Jerseys; but it is great credit to us, that, with a handful of men, we sustained an orderly retreat for near an hundred miles, brought off our ammunition, all our field-pieces, the greatest part of our stores, and had four rivers to pass. None can say that our retreat was precipitate, for we were near three weeks in performing it, that the country might have time to come in. Twice we marched back to meet the enemy and remained out till dark. The sign of fear was not seen in our camp, and had not some of the cowardly and disaffected inhabitants spread false alarms through the country, the Jerseys had never been ravaged. Once more we are again collected and collecting; our new army at both ends of the continent is recruiting fast, and we shall be able to open the next campaign with sixty thousand men, well armed and cloathed. This is our situation, and who will may know it. By perseverance and fortitude we have the prospect of a glorious issue; by cowardice and submission, the sad choice of a variety of evils—a ravaged country—a depopulated city—habitations without safety, and slavery without hope—our homes turned into barracks and bawdy-houses for Hessians, and a future race to provide for whose fathers we shall doubt of. Look on this picture and weep over it! and if there yet remains one thoughtless wretch who believes it not, let him suffer it unlamented.

13. Securing Liberty
James Madison,
THE FEDERALIST, NUMBER TEN (1787)

In May 1787 delegates from every state except Rhode Island met in Philadelphia to revise the Articles of Confederation. But they disregarded their instructions; by mid-September they had drawn up an entirely new frame of government for the nation that had achieved its independence in 1783. The Constitutional Convention was a distinguished gathering; the states sent their ablest men to Philadelphia. George Washington was there; so were Benjamin Franklin, Alexander Hamilton, and James Madison. For many weeks the delegates labored mightily to construct a constitution that would "form a more perfect union" without jeopardizing liberty. In September they completed their work and submitted the Constitution to the states for ratification. At once a great debate commenced. In countless essays, editorials, pamphlets, and handbills the American people discussed the merits and defects of the new instrument of government offered for their consideration. The most famous of all the commentaries on the Constitution appeared in *The Federalist*.

The Federalist Papers consist of eighty-five essays appearing in various New York newspapers between October 1787 and August 1788. Hamilton, who had taken part in the Constitutional Convention, wrote the major portion of them; but James Madison, whose diligence in Philadelphia won him the nickname "Father of the Constitution," wrote a sizable number as well. John Jay, author of the New York State Constitution of 1777, also wrote a few. The essays, which were soon published in book form, discussed the weakness of the Confederation, the powers assigned to the federal government in the new Constitution, and the organization of these powers into legislative, executive, and judicial branches of government, and the safeguards that were built into the Constitution to prevent oppression. Thomas Jefferson, who was in Paris at the time as minister to France, wrote to say he read the *Papers* with "care, pleasure, and improvement" and called them the "best commentary on the principles of government which was ever written."

The immediate impact of *The Federalist Papers* was probably not great. Most of the states had completed ratification before many of the essays were published. But the essays may have helped persuade New York and Virginia to ratify the Constitution; and their long-range influence has been profound. Since their first appearance the *Papers* have become a classic of political science. Scholars, legislators, judges, and Supreme Court justices have looked to them time and again for clues to understanding the Constitution that was accepted by the states in 1788. After the Declaration of Independence and the Constitution they are the nation's most important political statement. *The Federalist,* Number Ten, written by Madison, is perhaps the most famous. In it, Madison points out the inevitability of conflicts of interest (particularly economic interest) in free societies and insists that representative government can keep these conflicts from getting out of hand and endangering both private rights and the public good.

James Madison, son of a Virginia planter, was born in Port Conway, Virginia, in 1751, and attended the College of New Jersey (now Princeton). In 1776 he helped frame Virginia's constitution and declaration of rights. Between 1780 and 1783 he was a member of the Continental Congress; after the Revolution he served in Virginia's House of Delegates, where he sponsored legislation to disestablish the Anglican church and provide for religious freedom. As a member of Virginia's delegation to the Philadelphia convention in 1787 he played a major role in shaping the Constitution that was finally adopted; he also took notes on the debates which are our main source for information about what was discussed at the convention. As a member of the First Congress under Washington he sponsored legislation establishing the State, Treasury, and War Departments and also introduced the first ten amendments to the Constitution (the Bill of Rights) into the House of Representatives. For eight years he served as Thomas Jefferson's secretary of state and succeeded him as president in 1809. His own presidency was a stormy one. Though a man of peace he presided over the controversial War of 1812 with Britain ("Mr. Madison's War"), which ended with a treaty settling none of the outstanding disputes between the two countries. While he was president the Republican party gradually accepted the economic program once sponsored by Hamilton and opposed by Jefferson: a second Bank of the United States, a protective tariff, and a large funded debt. In 1817, Madison retired to his estate at Montpelier to manage his farm, pursue his studies, advise James Monroe, his successor in the White House, and warn against disunion. He died in 1836 at the age of eighty-five.

Questions to consider. In the extract from *The Federalist,* Number Ten, presented below, Madison's argument is carefully organized and closely reasoned and shows great insight into the workings of social groups. Madison began by singling out factions as the chief problem confronting free nations like the United States. How did he define *faction*? He said there are two ways to prevent factions from forming. What are they? Why did he reject both of them? What did he mean by saying that the "latent causes of faction" are found in human nature? Do you think he was right in his statement that "the most common and durable source of factions has been the various and unequal distribution of property"? What examples did he give of various propertied interests? Do you agree with his assertion that the "principal task of legislation" is to regulate these interests and see to it that they are "subservient to the public good"? Madison believed there is no real problem in dealing with factions that represent minority interests. The real problem, he said, is with factions that include the majority of the people; majority factions, he feared, would pose a threat both to private rights and the public good. Madison did not think a "pure democracy" could handle the "mischief of faction." Why not? How did he distinguish a republic from a democracy? Why did he think a republican form of government, such as outlined in the U.S. Constitution, could deal effectively with the problem of factions?

THE FEDERALIST, NUMBER TEN (1787)

Among the numerous advantages promised by a well-constructed Union, none deserves to be more accurately developed than its tendency to break and control the violence of faction. The friend of popular governments never finds himself so much alarmed for their character and fate as when he contemplates their propensity to this dangerous vice. He will not fail, therefore, to set a due value on any plan which, without violating the principles to which he is attached, provides a proper cure for it. The instability, injustice, and confusion introduced into the public councils have, in truth, been the mortal diseases under which popular governments have everywhere perished, as they continue to be the favorite and fruitful topics from which the adversaries to liberty derive their most specious declamations. The valuable improvements made by the American constitutions on the popular models, both ancient and modern, cannot certainly be too much admired; but it would be an unwarrantable partiality to contend that they have as effectually obviated the danger on this side, as was wished and expected. Complaints are everywhere heard from our most considerate and virtuous citizens, equally the friends of public and private faith and of public and personal liberty, that our governments are too unstable, that the public good is disregarded in the conflicts of rival parties, and that measures are too often decided, not according to the rules of justice and the rights of the minor party, but by the superior force of an interested and overbearing majority. However anxiously we may wish that these complaints had no foundation, the evidence of known facts will not permit us to deny that they are in some degree true. It will be found, indeed, on a candid review of our situation, that some of the distresses under which we labor have been errone-ously charged on the operation of our governments; but it will be found, at the same time, that other causes will not alone account for many of our heaviest misfortunes; and, particularly, for that prevailing and increasing distrust of public engagements and alarm for private rights which are echoed from one end of the continent to the other. These must be chiefly, if not wholly, effects of the unsteadiness and injustice with which a factious spirit has tainted our public administrations.

By a faction I understand a number of citizens, whether amounting to a majority or minority of the whole, who are united and actuated by some common impulse of passion, or of interest, adverse to the rights of other citizens, or to the permanent and aggregate interests of the community.

From *The Federalist* (Colonial Press, New York, 1901), 44-51.

There are two methods of curing the mischiefs of faction: the one, by removing its causes; the other, by controlling its effects.

There are again two methods of removing the causes of faction: the one, by destroying the liberty which is essential to its existence; the other, by giving to every citizen the same opinions, the same passions, and the same interests.

It could never be more truly said than of the first remedy that it was worse than the disease. Liberty is to faction what air is to fire, an ailment without which it instantly expires. But it could not be a less folly to abolish liberty, which is essential to political life, because it nourishes faction than it would be to wish the annihilation of air, which is essential to animal life, because it imparts to fire its destructive agency.

The second expedient is as impracticable as the first would be unwise. As long as the reason of man continues fallible, and he is at liberty to exercise it, different opinions will be formed. As long as the connection subsists between his reason and his self-love, his opinions and his passions will have a reciprocal influence on each other; and the former will be objects to which the latter will attach themselves. The diversity in the faculties of men, from which the rights of property originate, is not less an insuperable obstacle to a uniformity of interests. The protection of these faculties is the first object of government. From the protection of different and unequal faculties of acquiring property, the possession of different degrees and kinds of property immediately results; and from the influence of these on the sentiments and views of the respective proprietors ensues a division of the society into different interests and parties.

The latent causes of faction are thus sown in the nature of men; and we see them everywhere brought into different degrees of activity, according to the different circumstances of civil society. A zeal for different opinions concerning religion, concerning government, and many other points, as well of speculation as of practice; an attachment to different leaders ambitiously contending for pre-eminence and power; or to persons of other descriptions whose fortunes have been interesting to the human passions, have, in turn, divided mankind into parties, inflamed them with mutual animosity, and rendered them much more disposed to vex and oppress each other than to co-operate for their common good. So strong is this propensity of mankind to fall into mutual animosities that where no substantial occasion presents itself the most frivolous and fanciful distinctions have been sufficient to kindle their unfriendly passions and excite their most violent conflicts. But the most common and durable source of factions has been the various and unequal distribution of property. Those who hold and those who are without property have ever formed distinct interests in society. Those who are creditors, and those who are debtors, fall under a like discrimination. A landed interest, a manufacturing interest, a mercantile interest, a moneyed interest, with many lesser interests, grow up of necessity in civilized nations, and divide them into different classes, actuated by different sentiments and views. The regulation of these various and interfering interests forms the principal task of modern legislation and involves the spirit of party and faction in the necessary and ordinary operations of the government.

No man is allowed to be a judge in his own cause, because his interest would certainly bias his judgment, and, not improbably, corrupt his integrity.

Washington presiding over the Constitutional Convention.
In May 1787, the Constitutional Convention, made up of
delegates from every state except Rhode Island, met in
Philadelphia to revise the Articles of Confederation. The
states sent some of their ablest men to Philadelphia: George
Washington, James Madison (who played such an important role there that he was called the "Father of the Constitution"), George Mason (author of the Virginia Bill of
Rights), Alexander Hamilton, and Benjamin Franklin. Absent were Thomas Jefferson and John Adams, who were on
missions abroad, and Samuel Adams and Patrick Henry,
who opposed changing the Articles of Confederation. Very
early in their deliberations the delegates decided to scrap
the Articles and draft an entirely new framework of government. (Library of Congress)

With equal, nay with greater reason, a body of men are unfit to be both judges and parties at the same time; yet what are many of the most important acts of legislation but so many judicial determinations, not indeed concerning the rights of single persons, but concerning the rights of large bodies of citizens? And what are the different classes of legislators but advocates and parties to the causes which they determine? Is a law proposed concerning private debts? It is a question to which the creditors are parties on one side and the debtors on the other. Justice ought to hold the balance between them. Yet the parties are, and must be, themselves the judges; and the most numerous party, or in other words, the most powerful faction must be expected to prevail. Shall domestic manufactures be encouraged, and in what degree, by restrictions on foreign manufactures? are questions which would be differently decided by the landed and the manufacturing classes, and probably by neither with a sole regard to justice and the public good. The apportionment of taxes on the various descriptions of property is an act which seems to require the most exact impartiality; yet there is, perhaps, no legislative act in which greater opportunity and temptation are given to a predominant party to trample on the rules of justice. Every shilling with which they overburden the inferior number is a shilling saved to their own pockets.

It is vain to say that enlightened statesmen will be able to adjust these clashing interests and render them all subservient to the public good. Enlightened statesmen will not always be at the helm. Nor, in many cases, can such an adjustment be made at all without taking into view indirect and remote considerations, which will rarely prevail over the immediate interest which one party may find in disregarding the rights of another or the good of the whole.

The inference to which we are brought is that the *causes* of faction cannot be removed and that relief is only to be sought in the means of controlling its *effects.*

If a faction consists of less than a majority, relief is supplied by the republican principle, which enables the majority to defeat its sinister views by regular vote. It may clog the administration, it may convulse the society; but it will be unable to execute and mask its violence under the forms of the Constitution. When a majority is included in a faction, the form of popular government, on the other hand, enables it to sacrifice to its ruling passion or interest both the public good and the rights of other citizens. To secure the public good and private rights against the danger of such a faction, and at the same time to preserve the spirit and the form of popular government, is then the great object to which our inquiries are directed. Let me add that it is the great desideratum by which this form of government can be rescued from the opprobrium under which it has so long labored and be recommended to the esteem and adoption of mankind.

By what means is this object attainable? Evidently by one of two only. Either the existence of the same passion or interest in a majority at the same time must be prevented, or the majority, having such coexistent passion or interest, must be rendered, by their number and local situation, unable to concert and carry into effect schemes of oppression. If the impulse and the opportunity be suffered to coincide, we well know that neither moral nor religious motives can be relied on as an adequate control. They are not found to be such on the injustice and violence of individuals, and lose their efficacy in proportion to the number combined together, that is, in proportion as their efficacy becomes needful.

From this view of the subject it may be concluded that a pure democracy, by which I mean a society consisting of a small number of citizens, who assemble and administer the government in person, can admit of no cure for the mischiefs of faction. A common passion or interest will, in almost every case, be felt by a majority of the whole; a communication and concert result from the form of government itself; and there is nothing to check the inducements to sacrifice the weaker party or an obnoxious individual. Hence it is that such democracies have ever been spectacles of turbulence and contention; have ever been found incompatible with personal security or the rights of property; and have in general been as short in their lives as they have been violent in their deaths. Theoretic politicians, who have patronized this species of government, have erroneously supposed that by reducing mankind to a perfect equality in their political rights, they would at the same time be perfectly equalized and assimilated in their possessions, their opinions, and their passions.

A republic, by which I mean a government in which the scheme of representation takes place, opens a different prospect and promises the cure for which we are seeking. Let us examine the points on which it varies from pure democracy, and we shall comprehend both the nature of the cure and the efficacy which it must derive from the Union.

The two great points of difference between a democracy and a republic are: first, the delegation of the government, in the latter, to a small number of citizens elected by the rest; secondly, the greater number of citizens and greater sphere of country over which the latter may be extended.

The effect of the first difference is, on the one hand, to refine and enlarge the public views by passing them through the medium of a chosen body of citizens, whose wisdom may best discern the true interest of their country and whose patriotism and love of justice will be least likely to sacrifice it to temporary or partial considerations. Under such a regulation it may well happen that the public voice, pronounced by the representatives of the people, will be more consonant to the public good than if pronounced by the people themselves, convened for the purpose. On the other hand, the effect may be inverted. Men of factious tempers, of local prejudices, or of sinister designs, may, by intrigue, by corruption, or by other means, first obtain the suffrage, and then betray the interests of the people. The question resulting is, whether small or extensive republics are most favorable to the election of proper guardians of the public weal; and it is clearly decided in favor of the latter by two obvious considerations.

In the first place it is to be remarked that however small the republic may be the representatives must be raised to a certain number in order to guard against the cabals of a few; and that however large it may be they must be limited to a certain number in order to guard against the confusion of a multitude. Hence, the number of representatives in the two cases not being in proportion to that of the two constituents, and being proportionally greatest in the small republic, it follows that if the proportion of fit characters be not less in the large than in the small republic, the former will present a greater option, and consequently a greater probability of a fit choice.

In the next place, as each representative will be chosen by a greater number of citizens in the large than in the small republic, it will be more difficult for unworthy candidates to practise with success the vicious arts by which elections are too often carried; and the suffrages of the people being more free, will be more likely to center on men who possess the most attractive merit and the most diffusive and established characters. . . .

COUNTERPOINT
The Continental Army

What kinds of men made up the Continental Army that George Washington led to victory over the British forces in the American Revolution? By analyzing Army muster rolls and the New Jersey state tax lists for the late 1770s, Mark Edward Lender has been able to gather data for the following two tables.

Table 2.1 concerns the distribution of farmland in New Jersey. In it soldiers and officers are compared with the general citizenry in terms of land ownership. In those times, affluence was judged mainly according to the land one owned, so the table reveals much about the soldiers' wealth as compared with the officers', as well as something about New Jersey enlistment patterns. The figures show that New Jersey soldiers were poorer than the general population, and that officers hailed from the upper reaches of the social hierarchy. What other generalizations can you draw from the table? Does it say something about the average size of New Jersey farms? What does it suggest about the type of person who tended to enlist in the Continental Army?

Table 2.2 divides officers and enlisted men according to their wealth —whether they belonged to the lower third, middle third, or upper third of the state population. The data show that there were eight times as many officers in the upper third as there were soldiers. Can you find the figures that reveal this fact in the table? What does this disparity suggest about the nature of social relations between officers and soldiers in the Continental Army? How might they have differed from social relations in the broader society?

Taken together, the tables indicate that the "pluralist" society of James Madison existed well before 1787. They also suggest that the Continentals were not the "citizen soldiers" that Thomas Paine's rhetoric made them out to be. Middle-class yeomen tended, in fact, to fight (when they fought) as short-term militiamen rather than as Continentals. The tables thus show that the Army was precisely the combination of aristocrats and plebians, "distinct from the rest of the citizens," that patriots like Thomas Jefferson dreaded. Little wonder that he feared the Army as being "dangerous to liberty" and incorporated the militia's right to bear arms in the Bill of Rights.

TABLE 2.1 New Jersey Landowners Compared: The General State Population, Continental Army Soldiers, and Officers (late 1770s)

Acres	All New Jersey	Soldiers	Officers
Landless	37.0%	56.7%	2.3%
1-24	12.8	12.5	6.8
25-99	20.5	21.8	20.4
100-199	18.7	7.6	38.6
200-299	6.7	1.4	18.2
300-399	2.1	0.0	4.5
400-	2.2	0.0	9.1

Source: From *The Military in America: From the Colonial Era to the Present* by Peter Karsten, Ed. Reprinted with permission of Macmillan Publishing Company. Copyright © 1980 by The Free Press, a Division of Macmillan Publishing Company.

TABLE 2.2 New Jersey Continental Army Soldiers and Officers Compared According to Wealth of the General State Population (late 1770s)

Percentage of Enlisted Men from:

Lower Third	Middle Third	Upper Third
61%	29%	10%

Percentage of Officers from:

Lower Third	Middle Third	Upper Third
0	16	84

Source: From *The Military in America: From the Colonial Era to the Present* by Peter Karsten, Ed. Reprinted with permission of Macmillan Publishing Company. Copyright © 1980 by The Free Press, a Division of Macmillan Publishing Company.

The inauguration of Washington as first president of the United States in New York City on April 30, 1789. (Library of Congress)

CHAPTER THREE

Nationalists and Partisans

14. The Industrial Vision
Alexander Hamilton,
ON MANUFACTURES (1791)

Under the new Constitution, Congress had the power to tax, borrow, and regulate trade and money. But the president was also important; he could recommend to Congress "such measures" as he thought "necessary and expedient." While George Washington was president, he established many precedents of economic policy and behavior. Probably the most important recommendations made during his presidency came from Secretary of the Treasury Alexander Hamilton. Hamilton's four reports to Congress on economic and financial policies were crucial in shaping the development of the new nation. In them Hamilton sought to make the Constitution's promise of a "more perfect Union" a reality by recommending governmental policies that fostered private enterprise and economic growth.

Hamilton's first three reports had to do with funding the national debt and creating a national bank. Hamilton wanted the federal government to take over the old Revolutionary debt as well as the debts incurred by the states during the Revolution, convert them into bonds, and pay for the interest on the bonds by levying excise taxes on distilled spirits and by imposing customs duties on such imports as tea, coffee, and wine. Congress adopted his funding proposals; it also accepted his plan for a large national bank that could make loans to businesses and issue currency backed by federal bonds. Hamilton's fourth report, "On Manufactures," urged a system of import taxes ("protective tariffs"), better roads and harbors ("internal improvements"), and subsidies ("bounties") in order to spur manufacturing.

Hamilton's four reports, with their emphasis on national rather than state power, on industry rather than agriculture, and on public spending to promote private enterprise, had a tremendous political impact. First, they triggered the birth of the earliest formal party system: Hamiltonian Federalists urging passage of the program and Democratic Republicans, followers of Secretary of State Thomas Jefferson, trying to modify or block it. Second, the reports helped establish the questions of governmental power and the nature of the economy as basic issues of political debate over the next half-century, as urgent for South Carolina in 1828 (Document 19) and Andrew Jackson in 1832 (Document 20) as for the politicians of the 1790s. Finally, Hamilton's reports became a veritable fountainhead for Americans concerned with the enhancement of capitalism and national power. Hamiltonian conservatives did not want an uninvolved government; they wanted to forge a partnership between government and business in which federal policies would actively promote business enterprise.

Congress did not immediately adopt Hamilton's recommendations for manufacturing. Protective tariffs, internal improvements, and bounties came much later and were adopted in a piecemeal fashion. Still, "On Manufactures" is important in its prevision of the future. Hamilton was perceptive in foreseeing that America's destiny was an industrial one. Long after he had passed from the scene, industrialism did overtake and surpass agriculture (with the encouragement of the states as well as of the federal government) as the driving force of the American economy. The observations Hamilton made in 1791 enable us to see the beginnings of the trend toward industrialization and help explain its seemingly inexorable inner logic.

Hamilton himself was concerned more with the political implications of his reports than their economic effects. His major aim was to strengthen the Union. This strong nationalism probably came from Hamilton's lack of state loyalties. He was born in 1755 in the West Indies (Hamilton claimed 1757). Orphaned at the age of thirteen, he was sent by relatives to the colony of New York in 1772. After preliminary study in New Jersey, he entered King's College (now Columbia University). When war with Britain broke out, he joined the army; in 1777 George Washington made him his aide-de-camp and personal secretary. After the Revolution he studied law, married well, rose rapidly in New York society, and became a dominant force in the Washington administration and the Federalist party. Overbearing and ambitious as well as bright and energetic, he proceeded to alienate important party leaders such as John Adams, and his career declined steadily after Washington left office. In 1804, Vice President Aaron Burr, a long-time political adversary who had just been defeated in the election for governor of New York, demanded a duel of honor with Hamilton because of some alleged derogatory remarks. On July 11, Burr shot Hamilton at their meeting in a field near Weehawken, New Jersey. He died the following day.

Questions to consider. Hamilton's report on manufactures reveals as well as recommends: it provides interesting glimpses into American society in 1791. For example, Hamilton argued for manufacturing on the ground that it would attract immigrants and employ women and children. What does this prediction tell us about the availability and condition of labor in early America and about the attitudes of American leaders toward the work force? Note, too, that Hamilton argued not just for the specialization of labor but even more for the easier application of machinery that would result from labor specialization. What two models did he suggest for combining machinery and labor, and what does his simultaneous use of these two very different models indicate about the state of American industry at the time he was writing? Again, Hamilton thought that the spirit of capitalist enterprise must be fostered by government. How did Hamilton's spirit of enterprise differ from that of Benjamin Franklin's "Poor Richard" a half-century earlier (Document 10)? Why, if this spirit was so prevalent, did Hamilton feel the need for special measures to promote it? How compatible was Hamilton's economic nationalism with Madison's political federalism (Document 13)?

ON MANUFACTURES (1791)

It is now proper to proceed a step further, and to enumerate the principal circumstances, from which it may be inferred that manufacturing establishments not only occasion a position augmentation of the produce and revenue of the society, but that they contribute essentially to rendering them greater than they could possible be without such establishments. These circumstances are:

1. The division of labor.
2. An extension of the use of machinery.
3. Additional employment to classes of the community not ordinarily engaged in the business.
4. The promoting of emigration from foreign countries.
5. The furnishing greater scope for the diversity of talents and dispositions, which discriminate men from each other.
6. The affording a more ample and various field for enterprize.
7. The creating, in some instances, a new, and securing, in all, a more certain and steady demand for the surplus produce of the soil.

Each of these circumstances has a considerable influence upon the total mass of industrious effort in a community; together, they add to it a degree of energy and effect which is not easily conceived. Some comments upon each of them, in the order in which they have been stated, may serve to explain their importance.

1. AS TO THE DIVISION OF LABOR

It has justly been observed, that there is scarcely any thing of greater moment in the economy of a nation than the proper division of labor. The separation of occupations causes each to be carried to a much greater perfection than it could possibly acquire if they were blended. This arises principally from three circumstances:

1st. The greater skill and dexterity naturally resulting from a constant and undivided application to a single object. It is evident that these properties must increase in proportion to the separation and simplification of objects, and the steadiness of the attention devoted to each; and must be less in proportion to the complication of objects, and the number among which the attention is distracted.

2nd. The economy of time, by avoiding the loss of it, incident to a frequent transition from operation to another of a different nature. This depends on various circumstances; the transition itself, the orderly disposition of the implements, machines, and materials employed in the operation to be relinquished, the preparatory steps to the commencement of a new one, the interruption of the impulse which the mind of the workman acquires from

From Henry Cabot Lodge, ed., *The Works of Alexander Hamilton* (12 v., G. P. Putnam's Sons, New York, 1904), IV: 70-198.

being engaged in a particular operation, the distractions, hesitations, and reluctances which attend the passage from one kind of business to another.

3rd. An extension of the use of machinery. A man occupied on a single object will have it more in his power, and will be more naturally led to exert his imagination, in devising methods to facilitate and abridge labor, than if he were perplexed by a variety of independent and dissimilar operations. Besides this, the fabrication of machines, in numerous instances, becoming itself a distinct trade, the artist who follows it has all the advantages which have been enumerated, for improvement in his particular art; and, in both ways, the invention and application of machinery are extended.

And from these causes united, the mere separation of the occupation of the cultivator from that of the artificer has the effect of augmenting the productive powers of labor, and with them, the total mass of the produce or revenue of a country. In this single view of the subject, therefore, the utility of artificers or manufacturers, towards promoting an increase of productive industry, is apparent.

2. AS TO AN EXTENSION OF THE USE OF MACHINERY, A POINT WHICH, THOUGH PARTLY ANTICIPATED, REQUIRES TO BE PLACED IN ONE OR TWO ADDITIONAL LIGHTS

The employment of machinery forms an item of great importance in the general mass of national industry. It is an artificial force brought in aid of the natural force of man; and, to all the purposes of labor, is an increase of hands, an accession of strength, unencumbered too by the expense of maintaining the laborer. May it not, therefore, be fairly inferred, that those occupations which give greatest scope to the use of this auxiliary, contribute most to the general stock of industrious effort, and, in consequence, to the general product of industry?

It shall be taken for granted, and the truth of the position referred to observation, that manufacturing pursuits are susceptible, in a greater degree, of the application of machinery, than those of agriculture. If so, all the difference is lost to a community which, instead of manufacturing for itself, procures the fabrics requisite to its supply from other countries. The substitution of foreign for domestic manufactures is a transfer to foreign nations of the advantages accruing from the employment of machinery, in the modes in which it is capable of being employed with most utility and to the greatest extent.

The cotton mill, invented in England, within the last twenty years, is a signal illustration of the general proposition which has been just advanced. In consequence of it, all the different processes for spinning cotton are performed by means of machines, which are put in motion by water, and attended chiefly by women and children—and by a smaller number of persons, in the whole, than are requisite in the ordinary mode of spinning. And it is an advantage of great moment, that the operations of this mill continue with convenience during the night as well as through the day. The prodigious effect of such a machine is easily conceived. To this invention is to be attributed, essentially, the immense progress, which has been so suddenly made in Great Britain, in the various fabrics of cotton.

3. AS TO THE ADDITIONAL EMPLOYMENT OF CLASSES OF THE COMMUNITY NOT ORIGINALLY ENGAGED IN THE PARTICULAR BUSINESS

This is not among the least valuable of the means by which manufacturing institutions contribute to augment the general stock of industry and production. In places where those institutions prevail, besides the persons regularly engaged in them, they afford occasional and extra employment to industrious individuals and families, who are willing to devote the leisure resulting from the intermissions of their ordinary pursuits to collateral labours, as a resource for multiplying their acquisitions or their enjoyments. The husbandman himself experiences a new source of profit and support from the increased industry of his wife and daughters, invited and stimulated by the demands of the neighboring manufactories.

Besides this advantage of occasional employment to classes having different occupations, there is another, of a nature allied to it, and of a similar tendency. This is the employment of persons who would otherwise be idle, and in many cases a burthen on the community, either from the bias of temper, habit, infirmity of body, or some other cause, indisposing or disqualifying them for the toils of the country. It is worthy of particular remark that, in general, women and children are rendered more useful, and the latter more early useful by manufacturing establishments, than they would otherwise be. Of the number of persons employed in the cotton manufactories of Great Britain, it is computed that four sevenths nearly are women and children, of whom the greatest proportion are children, and many of them of a very tender age.

And thus it appears to be one of the attributes of manufactures, and one of no small consequence, to give occasion to the exertion of a greater quantity of industry, even by the same number of persons, where they happen to prevail, than would exist if there were no such establishments.

4. AS TO THE PROMOTING OF EMIGRATION FROM FOREIGN COUNTRIES

Men reluctantly quit one course of occupation and livelihood for another, unless invited to it by very apparent and proximate advantages. Many who would go from one country to another, if they had a prospect of continuing with more benefit the callings to which they have been educated, will often not be tempted to change their situation by the hope of doing better in some other way. Manufacturers who, listening to the powerful invitations of a better price for their fabrics, or their labor, of greater cheapness of provisions and raw materials, of an exemption from the chief part of the taxes, burthens and restraints, which they endure in the Old World, of greater personal independence and consequence, under the operation of a more equal government, and of what is far more precious than mere religious toleration, a perfect equality of religious privileges, would probably flock from Europe to the United States to pursue their own trades or professions, if they were once made sensible of the advantages they would enjoy, and were inspired with an assurance of encouragement and employment, will with difficulty, be induced to transplant themselves, with a view to becoming cultivators of Land.

If it be true, then, that it is in the interest of the United States to open every possible avenue to imigration from abroad, it affords a weighty argument for the encouragement of manufactures; which, for the reasons just assigned, will have the strongest tendency to multiply the inducements to it.

Here is perceived an important resource, not only for extending the population, and with it the useful and productive labor of the country, but likewise for the prosecution of manufactures, without deducting from the number of hands which might otherwise be drawn to tillage, and even for the indemnification of agriculture for such as might happen to be diverted from it. Many, whom manufacturing views would induce to emigrate, would, afterwards, yield to the temptations which the particular situation of this country holds out to agricultural pursuits. And while agriculture would, in other respects, derive many signal and unmingled advantages from the growth of manufactures, it is a problem whether it would gain or lose, as to the article of the number of persons employed in carrying it on.

5. AS TO THE FURNISHING GREATER SCOPE FOR THE DIVERSITY OF TALENTS AND DISPOSITIONS, WHICH DISCRIMINATE MEN FROM EACH OTHER

This is a much more powerful means of augmenting the fund of national industry, than may at first sight appear. It is a just observation, that minds of the strongest and most active powers for their proper objects, fall below mediocrity, and labor without effect, if confined to uncongenial pursuits. And it is thence to be inferred, that the results of human exertion may be immensely increased by diversifying its objects. When all the different kinds of industry obtain in a community, each individual can find his proper element, and can call into activity the whole vigor of his nature. And the community is benefited by the services of its respective members, in the manner in which each can serve it with most effect.

If there be any thing in a remark often to be met with, namely, that there is, in the genius of the people of this country, a peculiar aptitude for mechanic improvements, it would operate as a forcible reason for giving opportunities to the exercise of that species of talent, by the propagation of manufactures.

6. AS TO THE AFFORDING A MORE AMPLE AND VARIOUS FIELD FOR ENTERPRISE

This also is of greater consequence in the general scale of national exertion than might, perhaps, on a superficial view be supposed, and has effects not altogether dissimilar from those of the circumstance last noticed. To cherish and stimulate the activity of the human mind, by multiplying the objects of enterprise, is not among the least considerable of the expedients by which the wealth of a nation may be promoted. Even things in themselves not positively advantageous sometimes become so, by their tendency to provoke exertion. Every new scene which is opened to the busy nature of man to rouse and exert itself, is the addition of a new energy to the general stock of effort.

The spirit of enterprise, useful and prolific as it is, must necessarily be contracted or expanded, in proportion to the simplicity or variety of the occupations and productions which are to be found in a society. It must be less in a nation of mere cultivators, than in a nation of cultivators and merchants; less in a nation of cultivators and merchants, than in a nation of cultivators, artificers and merchants.

7. AS TO THE CREATING, IN SOME INSTANCES, A NEW, AND SECURING IN ALL, A MORE CERTAIN AND STEADY DEMAND FOR THE SURPLUS PRODUCE OF THE SOIL

This is among the most important of the circumstances which have been indicated. It is a principal means by which the establishment of manufactures contributes to an augmentation of the produce or revenue of a country, and has an immediate and direct relation to the prosperity of agriculture.

It is evident that the exertions of the husbandman will be steady or fluctuating, vigorous or feeble, in proportion to the steadiness or fluctuation, adequateness or inadequateness, of the markets on which he must depend for the vent of the surplus which may be produced by his labor; and that such surplus, in the ordinary course of things, will be greater or less in the same proportion.

For the purpose of this vent, a domestic market is greatly to be preferred to a foreign one; because it is, in the nature of things, far more to be relied upon.

15. Beyond Entanglement

George Washington,

FAREWELL ADDRESS (1796)

Long before his second term was over, George Washington had decided not to seek a third term. Having served his country, in war and peace, for many years, he was becoming weary of public life and was eager to retire to the peace and quiet of his Mount Vernon estate. He was also anxious for the young nation to prove to the world that it could change rulers peacefully. With the help of James Madison and Alexander Hamilton he prepared a public letter to the American people announcing his intentions; on September 19, 1796, a Philadelphia newspaper published it as his "Farewell Address" to the nation. It was a moving appeal for unity, patriotism, and devotion to the common good. It was also a warning against the major evils that Washington thought might wreck the American experiment in self-government.

Washington saw several threats to the new nation's well-being. One was party strife. He was afraid that the acrimonious controversy between Federalists and Republicans over Hamilton's economic policies might tear the nation apart, and he warned against "the baneful effects of the spirit of party." He was also bothered by the way Americans developed "inveterate antipathies against particular nations and passionate attachments for others" without regard for the national interest. When Britain and France went to war in 1793, he issued a proclamation of neutrality, and when British interference with America's neutral rights at sea threatened to produce war, he sponsored the unpopular Jay's treaty in 1795 to keep the peace with Britain. Washington's neutrality policy pleased few people. The Federalists were pro-British and anti-French; they looked on France after the Revolution of 1789 as a threat to property, authority, and order everywhere. Most Republicans, for their part, were anti-British and pro-French; they regarded America's former Revolutionary ally, now a republic, as a comrade-in-arms in the fight against privilege and oppression throughout the world. Washington himself deplored "an habitual hatred or an habitual fondness," as he put it, by Americans toward other nations; he thought they crippled foreign policy. He wanted the United States to remain aloof from the wars of Britain and France, if possible, because he thought peace was an absolute necessity for the young developing nation. The United States, he insisted, should keep out of wars not involving its basic national interests and be prepared to fight only in self-defense. He was concerned about the militarism that comes with wars, just as another general-president, Dwight D. Eisenhower, was, over one hundred fifty years later (Vol. 2, Document 35). In one part of the Farewell Address, not included here, Washington urged Americans to avoid "the necessity of

those overgrown military establishments, which, under any form of government, are inauspicious to liberty, and which are to be regarded as
particularly hostile to republican liberty."

George Washington was born in 1732 on the family tobacco plantation in Westmoreland County, Virginia. Little is known of his childhood;
after his father died in 1753 he lived with various relatives, finally coming
into the care of his elder half-brother Lawrence, owner of the Mount
Vernon estate. At age fifteen he became a surveyor, an occupation he kept
until age twenty, when he inherited Mount Vernon upon the death of
Lawrence. After this time he obtained various political and militia appointments. He married a wealthy widow, Martha Custis, in 1759 and over the
next fifteen years he lived as a gentleman farmer, managing Mount Vernon
and growing tobacco with slave labor. He also entered the Virginia House
of Burgesses. His years as commander in chief of the Continental Army
from 1775-1783 were followed by service in the Constitutional Convention
in 1787 and election to the presidency in 1789. Though he was a Virginia
planter like Jefferson, he showed himself increasingly sympathetic as
president to the ideas of Secretary of the Treasury Hamilton rather than to
those of Secretary of State Jefferson. Rejecting pleas to accept a third term,
he retired to Mount Vernon in 1797 and died there two years later.

Questions to consider. In reading the excerpt from Washington's
Farewell Address, note the specific grounds on which Washington opposed
alliances with the nations of the Old World. Did he believe these were
permanent considerations or only temporary reflections of the current
international turmoil? What types of contact with foreign countries did he
view with favor? What did he mean by saying that "habitual hatred" and
"habitual fondness" in foreign affairs makes people "in some degree a
slave"? Compare Washington's anxieties about the impact of international
politics on domestic political passions with what the supposed radical,
Thomas Jefferson, had to say about these matters in his inaugural address
in 1801 (Document 16). Were Washington's fears justified? How does his
conception of America's place in the world compare with that of modern
political leaders?

FAREWELL ADDRESS (1796)

Observe good faith and justice toward all nations. Cultivate peace and
harmony with all. Religion and morality enjoin this conduct. And can it be
that good policy does not equally enjoin it? It will be worthy of a free,
enlightened, and, at no distant period, a great nation to give to mankind the
magnanimous and too novel example of a people always guided by an exalted
justice and benevolence. Who can doubt that in the course of time and things

From Jared Sparks, ed., *The Writings of George Washington* (12 v., Little, Brown and Co., Boston,
1855), XII: 214-235.

the fruits of such a plan would richly repay any temporary advantages which might be lost by a steady adherence to it? Can it be that Providence has not connected the permanent felicity of a nation with its virtue? The experiment, at least, is recommended by every sentiment which ennobles human nature. Alas! is it rendered impossible by its vices?

In the execution of such a plan nothing is more essential than that permanent, inveterate antipathies against particular nations and passionate attachments for others should be excluded, and that in place of them, just and amicable feelings toward all should be cultivated. The nation which indulges toward another an habitual hatred or an habitual fondness is in some degree a slave. It is a slave to its animosity or to its affection, either of which is sufficient to lead it astray from its duty and its interest. Antipathy in one nation against another disposes each more readily to offer insult and injury, to lay hold of slight causes of umbrage, and to be haughty and intractable when accidental or trifling occasions of dispute occur. . . .

So, likewise, a passionate attachment of one nation for another produces a variety of evils. Sympathy for the favorite nation, facilitating the illusion of an imaginary common interest in cases where no real common interest exists, and infusing into one of the enmities of the other, betrays the former into a participation in the quarrels and wars of the latter without adequate inducement or justification. It leads also to concessions to the favorite nation of privileges denied to others, which is apt doubly to injure the nation making the concessions by unnecessarily parting with what ought to have been retained, and by exciting jealousy, ill will, and a disposition to retaliate in the parties from whom equal privilieges are withheld; and it gives to ambitious, corrupted, or deluded citizens (who devote themselves to the favorite nation) facility to betray or sacrifice the interests of their own country without odium, sometimes even with popularity, gilding with the appearances of a virtuous sense of obligation, a commendable deference for public opinion, or a laudable zeal for public good, the base or foolish compliances of ambition, corruption, or infatuation. . . .

Against the insidious wiles of foreign influence (I conjure you to believe me, fellow-citizens) the jealousy of a free people ought to be constantly awake, since history and experience prove that foreign influence is one of the most baneful foes of republican government. But that jealousy, to be useful, must be impartial, else it becomes the instrument of the very influenced to be avoided, instead of a defense against it. Excessive partiality for one foreign nation and excessive dislike of another cause those whom they actuate to see danger only on one side, and serve to veil and even second the arts of influence on the other. Real patriots who may resist the intrigues of the favorite are liable to become suspected and odious, while its tools and dupes usurp the applause and confidence of the people to surrender their interests.

The great rule of conduct for us in regard to foreign nations is, in extending our commercial relations to have with them as little political connection as possible. So far as we have already formed engagements, let them be fulfilled with perfect good faith. Here let us stop.

Europe has a set of primary interests which to us have none or a very remote relation. Hence she must be engaged in frequent controversies, the causes of which are essentially foreign to our concerns. Hence, therefore, it must be unwise in us to implicate ourselves by artificial ties in the ordinary vicissitudes of her politics or the ordinary combinations and collisions of her friendships or enmities.

Our detached and distant situation invites and enables us to pursue a different course. If we remain one people, under an efficient government, the period is not far off when we may defy material injury from external annoyance; when we may take such an attitude as will cause the neutrality, we may at any time resolve upon, to be scrupulously respected; when belligerent nations, under the impossibility of making acquisitions upon us, will not lightly hazard the giving us provocation; when we may choose peace or war, as our interest, guided by justice, shall counsel.

Why forego the advantages of so peculiar a situation? Why quit our own to stand upon foreign ground? Why, by interweaving our destiny with that of any part of Europe, entangle our peace and prosperity in the toils of European ambition, rivalship, interest, humor, or caprice?

It is our true policy to steer clear of permanent alliances with any portion of the foreign world, so far, I mean, as we are now at liberty to do it; for let me not be understood as capable of patronizing infidelity to existing engagements. I hold the maxim no less applicable to public than to private affairs that honesty is always the best policy. I repeat, therefore, let those engagements be observed in their genuine sense. But in my opinion it is unnecessary and would be unwise to extend them.

Taking care always to keep ourselves by suitable establishments on a respectable defensive posture, we may safely trust to temporary alliances for extraordinary emergencies.

Harmony, liberal intercourse with all nations are recommended by policy, humanity, and interest. But even our commercial policy should hold an equal and impartial hand, neither seeking nor granting exclusive favors or preferences; consulting the natural course of things; diffusing and diversifying by gentle means the streams of commerce, but forcing nothing; establishing with powers so disposed, in order to give trade a stable course, to define the rights of our merchants, and to enable the Government to support them, conventional rules of intercourse, the best that present circumstances and mutual opinion will permit, but temporary and liable to be from time to time abandoned or varied as experience and circumstances shall dictate; constantly keeping in view that it is folly in one nation to look for disinterested favors from another; that it must pay with a portion of its independence for whatever it may accept under that character; that by such acceptance it may place itself in the condition of having given equivalents for nominal favors, and yet of being reproached with ingratitude for not giving more. There can be no greater error than to expect or calculate upon real favors from nation to nation. It is an illusion which experience must cure, which a just pride ought to discard.

16. A Call for Unity
Thomas Jefferson,
FIRST INAUGURAL ADDRESS (1801)

The election of 1800 was a stormy one. During the campaign Demo-cratic-Republican Thomas Jefferson was called a dangerous radical and Federalist John Adams a high-toned royalist. The House of Representatives, voting by states in February 1801, finally picked Jefferson as president on the thirty-sixth ballot. Jefferson called his election "the revolution of 1800." Reacting against what he regarded as monarchical tendencies in the Federalists, he insisted on "republican simplicity" in his administration. He stopped using the fancy carriage of state and rode horseback through the streets of Washington like any other citizen. He refused to wear "court dress" when receiving foreign diplomats, and his casual demeanor shocked some of the diplomatic corps. The British minister was so outraged by the informality of dinners at the Executive Mansion that he began refusing invitations to dine with the president.

Jefferson's first inaugural address, given on March 4, 1801, was a beautifully phrased exposition of his republican philosophy. The American republic, he declared, was founded on the sacred principle of majority rule; but the majority, he added, must respect the rights of the minority. He went on to make an appeal for the restoration of good feeling between the Federalists and the Republicans after the bitter campaign of 1800. The two parties differed on many points, he acknowledged, but they agreed on their devotion to the basic principles of the American system of govern-ment: equal justice for all; peace and friendship with all nations; support of the state governments in their rights; the right of election by the people; the supremacy of the civil over military authority; freedom of religion, freedom of the press, and freedom of person, under the protection of habeas corpus; and trial by juries impartially selected. "Sometimes," said Jefferson, "it is said that man can not be trusted with government of himself. Can he, then, be trusted with the government of others? Or have we found angels in the form of kings to govern him? Let history answer this question." History, Jefferson thought, showed the failure of undemocratic governments. He placed his faith in the future in governments resting on the consent of the people.

Thomas Jefferson was born in 1743 on his father's Virginia tobacco plantation. After graduating from William and Mary College in 1762, he studied law and entered politics, joining the Virginia House of Burgesses in 1769. In 1775 he became a delegate to the Continental Congress and was chosen to draft the Declaration of Independence. He served as governor of Virginia from 1779 to 1781 and as U.S. minister to France from 1785 to 1789. Insistent, in his correspondence with James Madison, on the necessity of adding a Bill of Rights to the Constitution, he became increasingly disturbed by the policies of Hamilton and Washington and saw his election as president as partial vindication of his own views on the importance of land, liberty, and localism in the new republic. His reputation as a scholar and architect flourished after his retirement from office in 1809, although his personal finances did not. He died, deeply revered as the Sage of Monticello but still an indebted slaveholder, at his Monticello estate on July 4, 1826, fifty years to the day after the adoption of his Declaration of Independence. On the same day John Adams died in Quincy, Massachusetts. Jefferson and Adams had been friends at the time of the American Revolution, became political enemies during the early years of the American republic, and then became reconciled later in life and entered into a lively correspondence which has delighted generations of Americans. Just before he died Adams exclaimed: "Thomas Jefferson survives!"

Questions to consider. In reading Jefferson's address several questions come at once to mind. In what ways did Jefferson perceive the United States as different from the countries of Europe? What did he mean by saying that "every difference of opinion is not a difference of principle"? After the bitter political strife of the 1790s, how could Jefferson argue that "we are all Republicans, we are all Federalists"? What role did the accidents of geography—physical separation from Europe and what Jefferson called "a chosen country, with room enough for our descendants"—play in his optimistic expectations? Did any of the themes appearing in Jefferson's inaugural address clash with those put forth by Federalists like Hamilton in 1791 (Document 14), Washington in 1796 (Document 15), and John Marshall in 1803 (Document 17)? Is it possible to summarize Jefferson's "essential principles of our Government" even more than he was able or willing to do? In view of these principles, how could a Massachusetts Federalist like John Adams believe that Jefferson's election as president would produce "the loathsome steam of human victims offered in sacrifice"?

FIRST INAUGURAL ADDRESS (1801)

Called upon to undertake the duties of the first executive office of our country, I avail myself of the presence of that portion of my fellow-citizens which is here assembled to express my grateful thanks for the favor with which they have been pleased to look toward me, to declare a sincere consciousness that the task is above my talents, and that I approach it with those anxious and awful presentiments which the greatness of the charge and the weakness of my powers so justly inspire. A rising nation, spread over a wide and fruitful land, traversing all the seas with the rich productions of their industry, engaged in

From James D. Richardson, ed., *A Compilation of the Messages and Papers of the Presidents* (Government Printing Office, Washington, D.C., 1897-1907), I: 322-326.

commerce with nations who feel power and forget right, advancing rapidly to destinies beyond the reach of mortal eyes—when I contemplate these transcendent objects, and see the honor, the happiness, and the hopes of this beloved country committed to the issue and the auspices of this day, I shrink from the contemplation, and humble myself before the magnitude of the undertaking. Utterly, indeed, should I despair did not the presence of many whom I here see remind me that in the other high authorities provided by our Constitution I shall find resources of wisdom, of virtue, and of zeal on which to rely under all difficulties. To you, then, gentlemen, who are charged with the sovereign functions of legislation, and to those associated with you, I look with encouragement for that guidance and support which may enable us to steer with safety the vessel in which we are all embarked amidst the conflicting elements of a troubled world.

During the contest of opinion through which we have passed the animation of discussions and of exertions has sometimes worn an aspect which might impose on strangers unused to think freely and to speak and to write what they think; but this being now decided by the voice of the nation, announced according to the rules of the Constitution, all will, of course, arrange themselves under the will of the law, and unite in common efforts for the common good. All, too, will bear in mind this sacred principle, that though the will of the majority is in all cases to prevail, that will to be rightful must be reasonable; that the minority possess their equal rights, which equal law must protect, and to violate would be oppression. Let us, then, fellow-citizens, unite with one heart and one mind. Let us restore to social intercourse that harmony and affection without which liberty and even life itself are but dreary things. And let us reflect that, having banished from our land that religious intolerance under which mankind so long bled and suffered, we have yet gained little if we countenance a political intolerance as despotic, as wicked, and capable of as bitter and bloody persecutions. During the throes and convulsions of the ancient world, during the agonizing spasms of infuriated man, seeking through blood and slaughter his long-lost liberty, it was not wonderful that the agitation of the billows should reach even this distant and peaceful shore; that this should be more felt and feared by some and less by others, and should divide opinions as to measures of safety. But every difference of opinion is not a difference of principle. We have called by different names brethren of the same principle. We are all Republicans, we are all Federalists. If there be any among us who would wish to dissolve this Union or to change its republican form, let them stand undisturbed as monuments of the safety with which error of opinion may be tolerated where reason is left free to combat it. I know, indeed, that some honest men fear that a republican government can not be strong, that this Government is not strong enough; but would the honest patriot, in the full tide of successful experiment, abandon a government which has so far kept us free and firm on the theoretic and visionary fear that this Government, the world's best hope, may by possibility want energy to preserve itself? I trust not. I believe this, on the contrary, the strongest Government on earth. I believe it the only one where every man, at the call of the law, would fly to the standard of the law, and would meet invasions of the public order as his own personal concern. Sometimes it is said that man can not be

Thomas Jefferson seated at his desk. Jefferson, third president of the United States and the first to be inaugurated in Washington, was one of the most gifted men in America. There was almost nothing in human affairs that did not attract his eager attention, and he acquired an expert knowledge in an amazing variety of fields. He spoke or read seven languages and was familiar with both ancient and modern literature. He wrote an essay on English poetry, a book on rules for debate in the Senate, and a long article on standards of weights and measures. He collected paintings, played the violin, and took a serious interest in both science and religion. He was also a distinguished architect and designed his home at Monticello in Virginia. (Library of Congress)

trusted with government of himself. Can he, then, be trusted with the government of others? Or have we found angels in the forms of kings to govern him? Let history answer this question.

Let us, then, with courage and confidence pursue our own Federal and Republican principles, our attachment to union and representative government. Kindly separated by nature and a wide ocean from the exterminating havoc of one quarter of the globe; too high-minded to endure the degradations of the others; possessing a chosen country, with room enough for our descendants to the thousandth and thousandth generation; entertaining a due sense of our own faculties, to the acquisitions of our own industry, to honor and confidence from our fellow-citizens, resulting not from birth, but from our actions and their sense of them; enlightened by a benign religion, professed, indeed, and practiced in various forms, yet all of them inculcating honesty, truth, temperance, gratitude, and the love of man; acknowledging and adoring an overruling Providence, which by all its dispensations proves that it delights in the happiness of man here and his greater happiness hereafter—with all these blessings, what more is necessary to make us a happy and prosperous people? Still one thing more, fellow-citizens—a wise and frugal Government, which shall restrain men from injuring one another, shall leave them otherwise free to regulate their own pursuits of industry and improvement, and shall not take from the mouth of labor the bread it has earned. This is the sum of good government, and this is necessary to close the circle of our felicities.

About to enter, fellow-citizens, on the exercise of duties which comprehend everything dear and valuable to you, it is proper you should understand what I deem the essential principles of our Government, and consequently those which ought to shape its Administration. I will compress them within the narrowest compass they will bear, stating the general principle, but not all its limitations. Equal and exact justice to all men, of whatever state or persuasion, religious or political; peace, commerce, and honest friendship with all nations, entangling alliances with none; the support of the State governments in all their rights, as the most competent administrations for our domestic concerns and the surest bulwarks against antirepublican tendencies; the preservation of the General Government in its whole constitutional vigor, as the sheet anchor of our peace at home and safety abroad; a jealous care of the right of election by the people—a mild and safe corrective of abuses which are lopped by the sword of revolution where peaceable remedies are unprovided; absolute acquiescence in the decisions of the majority, the vital principle of republics, from which is no appeal but to force, the vital principle and immediate parent of despotism; a well-disciplined militia, our best reliance in peace and for the first moments of war, till regulars may relieve them; the supremacy of the civil over the military authority; economy in the public expense, that labor may be lightly burthened; the honest payment of our debts and sacred preservation of the public faith; encouragement of agriculture, and of commerce as its handmaid; the diffusion of information and arraignment of all abuses at the bar of the public reason; freedom of religion; freedom of the press, and freedom of person under the protection of the habeas corpus, and trial by juries impartially selected. These principles form the bright constellation which has gone before us and guided our steps through an age of revolution and reformation.

The wisdom of our sages and blood of our heroes have been devoted to their attainment. They should be the creed of our political faith, the text of civic instruction, the touchstone by which to try the services of those we trust; and should we wander from them in moments of error or of alarm, let us hasten to retrace our steps and to regain the road which alone leads to peace, liberty, and safety.

I repair, then, fellow-citizens, to the post you have assigned me. With experience enough in subordinate offices to have seen the difficulties of this the greatest of all, I have learnt to expect that it will rarely fall to the lot of imperfect man to retire from this station with the reputation and the favor which bring him into it. Without pretensions to that high confidence you reposed in our first and greatest revolutionary character, whose preeminent services had entitled him to the first place in his country's love and destined for him the fairest page in the volume of faithful history, I ask so much confidence only as may give firmness and effect to the legal administration of your affairs. I shall often go wrong through defect of judgment. When right, I shall often be thought wrong by those whose positions will not command a view of the whole ground. I ask your indulgence for my own errors, which will never be intentional, and your support against the errors of others, who may condemn what they would not if seen in all its parts. The approbation implied by your suffrage is a great consolation to me for the past, and my future solicitude will be to retain the good opinion of those who have bestowed it in advance, to conciliate that of others by doing them all the good in my power, and to be instrumental to the happiness and freedom of all.

Relying, then, on the patronage of your good will, I advance with obedience to the work, ready to retire from it whenever you become sensible how much better choice it is in your power to make. And may that infinite Power which rules the destinies of the universe lead our councils to what is best, and give them a favorable issue for your peace and prosperity.

17. The Constitution Protected
MARBURY v. MADISON (1803)

Marbury v. *Madison* was the first case in which the Supreme Court exercised the right of "judicial review" over laws passed by Congress. In February 1803, Chief Justice John Marshall, a staunch Federalist, speaking for the majority of justices on the Supreme Court, announced his opinion in the case. William Marbury had been appointed justice of the peace for the District of Columbia by John Adams in the last hours of his adminis-tration. But because Marbury was a Federalist, James Madison, Jefferson's secretary of state, withheld the commission from him. Marbury appealed to the Supreme Court for a writ of mandamus, that is, a court order compelling Madison to deliver the commission.

Marshall did not believe that Madison was justified in denying Marbury his commission as justice of the peace. But in his opinion he declared that the Supreme Court could not force Madison to deliver the commission. The Constitution, he said, in defining the original jurisdiction of the Supreme Court, did not include the issue of writs to executive officers. Nonetheless, section 13 of the Judiciary Act of 1789 did give the Supreme Court the power to issue such writs, and it was under this law that Marbury had applied to the Court. Marshall, however, declared that section 13 of the Judiciary Act was unconstitutional and that therefore the Court could not take jurisdiction. He then went on to assert the right of the Supreme Court to pass on the constitutionality of laws passed by Congress. "It is a proposition too plain to be contested," he declared, "that the constitution controls any legislative act repugnant to it" and that "a legislative act contrary to the constitution is not law. . . ." He added: "It is emphatically the province and duty of the judicial department to say what the law is." And he concluded that "a law repugnant to the constitution is void, and that courts, as well as other departments, are bound by that instrument." By claiming for the Court the duty of deciding whether acts of Congress were constitutional, Marshall upheld the prestige of the judiciary, even though he was unable to do anything for Marbury. But it was not until the *Dred Scott* case (Document 28), more than half a century later, that the Supreme Court invalidated a Congressional act for the second time.

Born in 1755 to well-to-do Virginians, John Marshall received little formal schooling. He studied law, however, and eventually became active in state politics. His service in the army during the American Revolution helped develop his nationalistic outlook. A distant cousin of Thomas Jefferson but a devoted Federalist nonetheless, Marshall served on a commission to France in 1797 and was elected to Congress in 1799. In 1801 President John Adams named him to the U.S. Supreme Court, where he served as chief justice for the next thirty-four years. Among his notable decisions besides *Marbury* v. *Madison* were *McCulloch* v. *Maryland* (1819), which protected federal agencies such as the Bank of the United States from state taxes; *Dartmouth College* v. *Woodward* (1819), which upheld the sanctity of contracts; and *Gibbons* v. *Ogden* (1824), which established federal authority over interstate and foreign commerce. In these and other cases Marshall sought to protect the rights of property, increase the power of the federal government, and raise the prestige of the federal judiciary. Personally convivial, gossipy, courtly with women, and in general, reveling in the social life of the slaveholding gentry, Marshall in public remained a figure of controversy throughout his career. He died in Philadelphia in 1835.

Questions to consider. Why, according to Chief Justice Marshall, should the Constitution and its principles be considered permanent? How important was it to Marshall's argument that the U.S. Constitution was written? What alternative did he have in mind, and why did he feel compelled to assert the special character of a written document? Why did he single out the legislative branch as opposed to the executive (or judiciary) as the chief danger to the permanence of the Constitution and its principles? On what grounds, according to Marshall, did the judiciary become the final arbiter of constitutional quarrels with the right to annul legislation? How persuasive will present-day readers find Marshall's examples of the centrality of the courts and the Constitution in the American system? Why, finally, was Marshall's decision seen as a political victory for the Federalist party?

MARBURY v. MADISON (1803)

. . . The question whether an act repugnant to the constitution can become the law of the land is a question deeply interesting to the United States; but, happily not of an intricacy proportioned to its interest. It seems only necessary to recognize certain principles supposed to have been long and well established, to decide it.

That the people have an original right to establish for their future government such principles as, in their opinion, shall most conduce to their own happiness, is the basis on which the whole American fabric has been erected. The exercise of this original right is a very great exertion, nor can it nor ought it to be frequently repeated. The principles therefore so established are deemed fundamental. And as the authority from which they proceed is supreme and can seldom act, they are designed to be permanent.

This original and supreme will organizes the government, and assigns to different departments their respective powers. It may either stop here or establish certain limits not to be transcended by those departments.

The government of the United States is of the latter description. The powers of the legislature are defined and limited; and that those limits may not be mistaken or forgotten, the constitution is written. To what purpose are

From 1 Craven 137 (1803).

powers limited, and to what purpose is that limitation committed to writing, if these limits may, at any time, be passed by those intended to be restrained? The distinction between a government with limited and unlimited powers is abolished if those limits do not confine the persons on whom they are imposed and if acts prohibited and acts allowed are of equal obligation. It is a proposition too plain to be contested, that the constitution controls any legislative act repugnant to it, or, that the legislature may alter the constitution by an ordinary act.

Between these alternatives there is no middle ground. The constitution is either a superior paramount law, unchangeable by ordinary means, or it is on a level with ordinary legislative acts, and, like other acts, is alterable when the legislature shall please to alter it.

If the former part of the alternative be true, then a legislative act contrary to the constitution is not law; if the latter part be true, then written constitutions are absurd attempts, on the part of the people, to limit a power in its own nature illimitable.

Certainly all those who have framed written constitutions contemplate them as forming the fundamental and paramount law of the nation, and consequently the theory of every such government must be that an act of the legislature repugnant to the Constitution is void.

This theory is essentially attached to a written constitution, and is consequently to be considered, by this court, as one of the fundamental principles of our society. It is not, therefore, to be lost sight of in the further consideration of this subject.

If an act of the legislature repugnant to the constitution is void, does it, notwithstanding its invalidity, bind the courts and oblige them to give it effect? Or, in other words, though it be not law, does it constitute a rule as operative as if it was a law? This would be to overthrow in fact what was established in theory, and would seem, at first view, an absurdity too gross to be insisted on. It shall, however, receive a more attentive consideration.

It is emphatically the province and duty of the judicial department to say what the law is. Those who apply the rule to particular cases must of necessity expound and interpret that rule. If two laws conflict with each other, the courts must decide on the operation of each.

So if a law be in opposition to the constitution; if both the law and the constitution apply to a particular case, so that the court must either decide that case conformably to the law, disregarding the constitution, or conformably to the constitution, disregarding the law, the court must determine which of these conflicting rules governs the case. This is of the very essence of judicial duty.

If, then, the courts are to regard the constitution, and the constitution is superior to any ordinary act of the legislature, the constitution, and not such ordinary act, must govern the case to which they both apply.

Those, then, who controvert the principle that the constitution is to be considered in court as a paramount law, are reduced to the necessity of maintaining that courts must close their eyes on the constitution and see only the law.

This doctrine would subvert the very foundation of all written constitutions. It would declare that an act which, according to the principles and theory of our government, is entirely void, is yet, in practice, completely obligatory. It would declare that if the legislature shall do what is expressly forbidden, such act, notwithstanding the express prohibition, is in reality effectual. It would be giving to the legislature a practical and real omnipotence with the same breath which professes to restrict their powers within narrow limits. It is prescribing limits and declaring that those limits may be passed at pleasure.

That it thus reduces to nothing what we have deemed the greatest improvement on political institutions, a written constitution, would of itself be sufficient, in America, where written constitutions have been viewed with so much reverence, for rejecting the construction. But the peculiar expressions of the constitution of the United States furnish additional arguments in favor of its rejection.

The judicial power of the United States is extended to all cases arising under the constitution.

Could it be the intention of those who gave this power to say that in using it the constitution should not be looked into? That a case arising under the constitution should be decided without examining the instrument under which it arises?

This is too extravagant to be maintained.

In some cases, then, the constitution must be looked into by the judges. And if they can open it at all, what part of it are they forbidden to read or to obey?

There are many other parts of the constitution which serve to illustrate this subject.

It is declared that "no tax or duty shall be laid on articles exported from any state." Suppose a duty on the export of cotton, of tobacco, or of flour, and a suit instituted to recover it, ought judgment to be rendered in such a case? Ought the judges to close their eyes on the constitution, and only see the law?

The constitution declares "that no bill of attainder of *ex post facto* law shall be passed." If, however, such a bill should be passed, and a person should be prosecuted under it, must the court condemn to death those victims whom the constitution endeavors to preserve?

"No person," says the constitution, "shall be convicted of treason unless on the testimony of two witnesses to the same overt act, or on confession in open court."

Here the language of the constitution is addressed especially to the courts. It prescribes, directly for them, a rule of evidence not to be departed from. If the legislature should change that rule, and declare one witness, or a confession out of court, sufficient for conviction, must the constitutional principle yield to the legislative act?

From these, and many other selections which might be made, it is apparent that the framers of the constitution contemplated that instrument as a rule for the government of *courts*, as well as of the legislature. Why otherwise does it direct the judges to take an oath to support it? This oath certainly applies in an especial manner to their conduct in their official character. How immoral to impose it on them if they were to be used as the instruments, and the knowing instruments, for violating what they swear to support!

The oath of office, too, imposed by the legislature, is completely demonstrative of the legislative opinion on this subject. It is in these words: "I do solemnly swear that I will administer justice without respect to persons, and do equal right to the poor and to the rich; and that I will faithfully and impartially discharge all the duties incumbent on me as —————, according to the best of my abilities and understanding, agreeably to *the constitution* and laws of the United States." Why does a judge swear to discharge his duties agreeably to the constitution of the United States, if that constitution forms no rule for his government—if it is closed upon him, and cannot be inspected by him?

If such be the real state of things, this is worse than solemn mockery. To prescribe, or to take this oath, becomes equally a crime.

It is also not entirely unworthy of observation, that in declaring what shall be the *supreme* law of the land, the constitution itself is first mentioned, and not the laws of the United States generally, but those only which shall be made in *pursuance* of the constitution, have that rank.

Thus, the particular phraseology of the constitution of the United States confirms and strengthens the principle, supposed to be essential to all written constitutions, that a law repugnant to the constitution is void, and that courts, as well as other departments, are bound by that instrument.

18. A Hemispheric Interest
THE MONROE DOCTRINE (1823)

In the early part of the nineteenth century, Spain's colonies in Latin America revolted, declared their independence, and received diplomatic recognition from the United States. In 1823, however, a group of European powers known as the Holy Alliance talked of sending an expedition to the New World to restore Spain's control over her former colonies. President James Monroe was alarmed at the prospect. So was George Canning, the British foreign minister, who was afraid that British trade with the new American nations might be disrupted by European intervention. Canning asked the United States to join Britain in a declaration warning the European nations against attempts to retake Spain's former colonies by force.

Monroe liked Canning's proposal, but Secretary of State John Quincy Adams argued forcefully for a unilateral statement by the United States. Not only was Adams concerned about intervention in South America, he was also disturbed by Russian expansion (from Alaska, which Russia owned, southward) on the Pacific Coast. He wanted the United States to make it clear to the European powers that all parts of the New World were closed to further colonization, and he wanted to send direct warnings to all the nations involved.

Adams managed to win Monroe to his views. The president agreed to drop the idea of a joint declaration with England in favor of an independent statement. He also adopted Adams's view that the statement should apply the noncolonization principle to the New World as a whole. But he insisted on making the declaration in a public document rather than in notes sent directly to the nations involved.

The Monroe Doctrine, as the declaration came to be called, appeared in Monroe's annual message to Congress on December 2, 1823. The declaration consisted of two sections. The first was a warning to Russia in the Pacific Northwest and contained the following noncolonization principle: "The American continents, by the free and independent condition which they have assumed and maintain, are henceforth not to be considered as subjects for future colonization by any European power." The second section was directed against the powers that might intervene in South America. It declared that the United States would not interfere with "existing colonies or dependencies of any European power" in the New World, but that any attempt to reconquer the independent republics of Latin America would be considered "the manifestation of an unfriendly disposition toward the United States."

Monroe's message pleased most Americans but irritated Europeans; they knew the young nation was not strong enough to back up its words. The British, whose navy was primarily responsible for keeping Europeans from meddling in America, were particularly irked. They realized Monroe's principles could be used against them as well as against other nations. But Monroe's statement was soon forgotten. The expression *Monroe Doctrine* did not become common until the 1850s. And it was not until the late nineteenth century that the Monroe Doctrine itself came to be regarded as one of the cornerstones of American foreign policy.

Monroe was born in Virginia in 1758. After two years of study at the College of William and Mary, he left to take part in the Revolution and was wounded at the battle of Trenton. After leaving the service, he studied law with Jefferson, served in Congress from 1783 to 1786, and was elected to the new U.S. Senate in 1790. An ally from the start of his friend and sponsor, Thomas Jefferson, he went to France in 1803 to help Robert R. Livingston negotiate the Louisiana Purchase. From 1799 to 1800 and in 1811 he was governor of Virginia. He held a cabinet post during the War of 1812 and easily went on to win election to the presidency in 1816 and again in 1820. The last of the "Virginia dynasty" to occupy the White House and also the last president to wear the wig and small clothes (knee breeches) of eighteenth-century gentlemen, Monroe presided over the nation during a period of reduced sectional and party rivalry known as the Era of Good Feelings, which his moderate outlook and instinct for harmonizing different political interests did much to produce. He retired to Virginia in 1825, where he succeeded Jefferson as regent of the University of Virginia and, also like Jefferson, sank into genteel poverty. He died while visiting New York City on July 4, 1831, the third president (after John Adams and Jefferson) to die on the anniversary of American independence.

Questions to consider. Note the extent to which Monroe's message derives from the notion of American separateness and exceptionalism that George Washington had emphasized in 1796 (Document 15). Note, too, how Thomas Jefferson's roomy chosen country had become with Monroe a good deal roomier just twenty-two years later. As for the security issue that concerned Monroe, how important was it that the European powers were not merely strong but also had political systems different from that of the United States? Was it an alien system or an alien force, or some combination of the two, that disturbed Monroe? How important, finally, were the wishes of "our southern brethren," meaning the Latin Americans, for U.S. policymakers? Why did Monroe refer to them? Does the reference make the American system more or less justifiable? More or less defensible? More or less open-ended and subject to the vagaries of domestic politics and international upheavals?

THE MONROE DOCTRINE (1823)

At the proposal of the Russian Imperial Government, made through the minister of the Emperor residing here, a full power and instructions have been transmitted to the minister of the United States at St. Petersburg to arrange by amicable negotiation the respective rights and interests of the two nations on the northwest coast of this continent. A similar proposal has been made by His Imperial Majesty to the Government of Great Britain, which has likewise been acceded to. The Government of the United States has been desirous by this friendly proceeding of manifesting the great value which they have invariably attached to the friendship of the Emperor and their solicitude to cultivate the best understanding with his Government. In the discussion to which this interest has given rise and in the arrangements by which they may terminate the occasion has been judged proper for asserting, as a principle in which the rights and interests of the United States are involved, that the American continents, by the free and independent condition which they have assumed and maintain, are henceforth not to be considered as subjects for future colonization by any European power.

It was stated at the commencement of the last session that a great effort was then making in Spain and Portugal to improve the condition of the people of those countries, and that it appeared to be conducted with extraordinary moderation. It need scarcely be remarked that the result has been so far very different from what was then anticipated. Of events in that quarter of the globe, with which we have so much intercourse and from which we derive our origin, we have always been anxious and interested spectators. The citizens of the United States cherish sentiments the most friendly in favor of the liberty and happiness of their fellow-men on that side of the Atlantic. In the wars of the European powers in matters relating to themselves we have never taken any part, nor does it comport with our policy so to do. It is only when our rights are invaded or seriously menaced that we resent injuries or make preparations for our defense. With the movements in this hemisphere we are of necessity more immediately connected, and by causes which must be obvious to all enlightened and impartial observers. The political system of the allied powers is essentially different in this respect from that of America. This difference proceeds from that which exists in their respective Governments; and to the defense of our own, which has been achieved by the loss of so much blood and treasure, and matured by the wisdom of their most enlightened citizens, and under which we have enjoyed unexampled felicity, this whole nation is devoted. We owe it, therefore, to candor and to the amicable relations existing between the United States and those powers to declare that we should consider any attempt on their part to extend their system to any portion of this hemisphere as dangerous to our peace and safety. With the existing colonies or dependencies of any European power we have not interfered and shall not interfere. But with the Governments who have declared their independence and maintained it, and whose independence we have, on great consideration

From James D. Richardson, ed., *A Compilation of the Messages and Papers of the Presidents* (Government Printing Office, Washington, D.C., 1897-1907), I: 322-326.

James Monroe. Elected president in 1816 and re-elected in 1820, James Monroe, with his knee breeches, silk stockings, cockade, and sword, was the "last of the cocked hats." His career dated back to the period of the American Revolution, in which he had served as a soldier. After the war he served on several diplomatic missions for the new nation and was James Madison's secretary of state just before becoming president. The United States entered an "Era of Good Feelings" during Monroe's presidency and, with the demise of the Federalist party, party strife on the national level came to an end. For a time, the United States was a one-party state. (Library of Congress)

and on just principles, acknowledged, we could not view any interposition for the purpose of oppressing them, or controlling in any other manner their destiny, by any European power in any other light than as the manifestation of an unfriendly disposition toward the United States. In the war between those new Governments and Spain we declared our neutrality at the time of their recognition, and to this we have adhered, and shall continue to adhere, provided no change shall occur which, in the judgment of the competent authorities of this Government, shall make a corresponding change on the part of the United States indispensable to their security.

The late events in Spain and Portugal shew that Europe is still unsettled. Of this important fact no stronger proof can be adduced than that the allied powers should have thought it proper, on any principle satisfactory to themselves, to have interposed by force in the internal concerns of Spain. To what extent such interposition may be carried, on the same principle, is a question in which all independent powers whose governments differ from theirs are interested, even those most remote, and surely none more so than the United States. Our policy in regard to Europe, which was adopted at an early stage of the wars which have so long agitated that quarter of the globe, nevertheless remains the same, which is, not to interfere in the internal concerns of any of its powers; to consider the government *de facto* as the legitimate government for us; to cultivate friendly relations with it, and to preserve those relations by a frank, firm, and manly policy, meeting in all instances the just claims of every power, submitting to injuries from none. But in regard to these continents circumstances are eminently and conspicuously different. It is impossible that the allied powers should extend their political system to any portion of either continent without endangering our peace and happiness; nor can anyone believe that our southern brethren, if left to themselves, would adopt it of their own accord. It is equally impossible, therefore, that we should behold such interposition in any form with indifference. If we look to the comparative strength and resources of Spain and those new Governments, and their distance from each other, it must be obvious that she can never subdue them. It is still the true policy of the United States to leave the parties to themselves, in the hope that other powers will pursue the same course. . . .

19. The Sectional Specter

John C. Calhoun,

SOUTH CAROLINA EXPOSITION AND PROTEST (1828)

The first great sectional struggle in the United States (after the Missouri crisis over slavery) was over the tariff. Northern industrialists favored high tariffs to protect their products from foreign competition. But the South was an agricultural region, and southerners complained that protective tariffs raised the price of manufactured goods and prevented them from importing low-priced goods from abroad. On May 20, 1828, Congress passed a tariff bill with rates so high that South Carolina's John C. Calhoun (vice president at the time) called it a "Tariff of Abominations." He presented a lengthy statement of the southern position on tariffs in which he developed his theory of nullification.

Calhoun believed in the "compact theory" of the Union. He maintained that the Constitution was a contract into which the states had entered of their own free will. The states retained their sovereignty and the federal government was merely their agent for general purposes. If the federal government exceeded its authority and encroached on the powers of the states, the states had a right to resist. Calhoun thought the constitutionality of acts of Congress should be decided by state conventions called for that purpose. If such a convention declared an act of Congress in violation of the Constitution, that act became null and void within the borders of that state. Calhoun insisted that the Constitution did not give Congress the right to levy protective tariffs and that the states had a right to nullify tariff legislation.

On December 19, 1828, the South Carolina legislature published Calhoun's statement (without mentioning his name) as "South Carolina Exposition and Protest," together with resolutions, reproduced below, condemning the tariff. For the time being, South Carolina contented itself with making this protest, hoping that the tariff would be revised after Andrew Jackson became president. But in July 1832, when a new tariff bill was passed by Congress and signed by Jackson, South Carolinians decided to put Calhoun's theory into practice. On November 4, 1832, a special state convention met in Columbia, adopted an ordinance declaring the tariffs of 1828 and 1832 unconstitutional, and announced that no tariff duties would be collected in the state after February 1, 1833. Jackson at once denounced South Carolina's action and asked Congress to give him authority to use the army and navy, if necessary, to compel South Carolina to obey the law. South Carolina continued defiant. When Congress passed a compromise bill lowering the tariff rate, the "nullies" (as they were called) repealed the nullification ordinance. But they did not disavow the nullification theory.

Calhoun was born in South Carolina in 1782 to an upcountry farmer. After graduating from Yale, he practiced law briefly and then married a wealthy Charleston woman and began a political climb that led to Congress, a post in James Monroe's cabinet, and the vice presidency under both John Quincy Adams and Andrew Jackson. He began as a vigorous nationalist, favoring the protective tariff, but moved to states' rights and an antitariff position when it became clear that South Carolina had more to gain from free trade. During the nullification crisis he resigned from the vice presidency in December 1832 for a seat in the Senate, where he became one of the "great triumvirate" (along with Henry Clay and Daniel Webster), an implacable foe of Jackson, and a staunch supporter of South Carolina, the South, and slavery. He died in Washington, D.C., in early 1850.

Questions to consider. Both economic and political issues are raised by Calhoun in "South Carolina Exposition and Protest." As to the former, why was a protective tariff considered so threatening to the Carolinians? Were they fearful of higher prices for imported goods or of reduced markets for their own product, cotton? Why did the "encouragement of domestic industry," originally urged by Alexander Hamilton in 1791 (Document 14), cause such a fierce blowup in 1828 but not before? Was Calhoun trying to speak for all of American agriculture or only for a certain kind? Why did South Carolina receive so little support from other states, including the other "cotton states"? Was it the threat to agriculture or to something else that most disturbed Calhoun? Which of the eight articles of the "Protest" furnishes the best clue to the situation in South Carolina? As to the political issue, why did Calhoun fear what he called "simple consolidated government" as a threat to freedom? To what extent could he draw support for this idea from the writings of James Madison in 1787 (Document 13) and Thomas Jefferson in 1801 (Document 16)? What would John Marshall (Document 17) have made of the theory of nullification? Could the theory have helped in a practical way to resolve constitutional disputes?

SOUTH CAROLINA EXPOSITION AND PROTEST (1828)

The Senate and House of Representatives of South Carolina, now met, and sitting in General Assembly, through the Hon. William Smith and the Hon. Robert Y. Hayne, the representatives in the Senate of the United States, do, in the name and on behalf of the good people of the said commonwealth, solemnly PROTEST against the system of protecting duties, lately adopted by the federal government, for the following reasons:—

From Jonathan Elliot, ed., *The Debates in the Several State Conventions on the Adoption of the Federal Constitution, &c* (5 v., J. B. Lippincott, Philadelphia, 1836), IV: 580–582.

John C. Calhoun. Calhoun, who served as congressman, vice president under Andrew Jackson, and then senator from South Carolina, started out as a strong nationalist and then became one of the most vigorous states-righters in the nation. He insisted that sovereignty (supreme power) resided in "the people of the several states" rather than in the people making up the nation as a whole, and that the people of the states had the right to nullify any federal laws they thought threatened their state's welfare. Calhoun developed his doctrine of nullification as a reaction against protective-tariff measures designed to encourage Northern industries but which he thought hurt South Carolina and other Southern states with little or no manufacturing. He was also a states-righter because he wanted to safeguard the institution of slavery from interference by antislavery crusaders in the North. (Library of Congress)

1st. *Because* the good people of this commonwealth believe that the powers of Congress were delegated to it in trust for the accomplishment of certain specified objects which limit and control them, and that every exercise of them for any other purposes, is a violation of the Constitution as unwarrantable as the undisguised assumption of substantive, independent powers not granted or expressly withheld.

2d. *Because* the power to lay duties on imports is, and in its very nature can be, only a means of effecting objects specified by the Constitution; since no free government, and least of all a government of enumerated powers, can of right impose any tax, any more than a penalty, which is not at once justified by public necessity, and clearly within the scope and purview of the social compact; and since the right of confining appropriations of the public money to such legitimate and constitutional objects is as essential to the liberty of the people as their unquestionable privilege to be taxed only by their own consent.

3d. *Because* they believe that the tariff law passed by Congress at its last session, and all other acts of which the principal object is the protection of manufactures, or any other branch of domestic industry, if they be considered as the exercise of a power in Congress to tax the people at its own good will and pleasure, and to apply the money raised to objects not specified in the Constitution, is a violation of these fundamental principles, a breach of a well-defined trust, and a perversion of the high powers vested in the federal government for federal purposes only.

4th. *Because* such acts, considered in the light of a regulation of commerce, are equally liable to objection; since, although the power to regulate commerce may, like all other powers, be exercised so as to protect domestic manufactures, yet it is clearly distinguishable from a power to do so *eo nomine*, both in the nature of the thing and in the common acception of the terms; and because the confounding of them would lead to the most extravagant results, since the encouragement of domestic industry implies an absolute control over all the interests, resources, and pursuits of a people, and is inconsistent with the idea of any other than a simple, consolidated government.

5th. *Because*, from the contemporaneous exposition of the Constitution in the numbers of the *Federalist*, (which is cited only because the Supreme Court has recognized its authority), it is clear that the power to regulate commerce was considered by the Convention as only incidentally connected with the encouragement of agriculture and manufactures; and because the power of laying imposts and duties on imports was not understood to justify in any case, a prohibition of foreign commodities, except as a means of extending commerce, by coercing foreign nations to a fair reciprocity in their intercourse with us, or for some *bona fide* commercial purpose.

6th. *Because*, whilst the power to protect manufactures is nowhere expressly granted to Congress, nor can be considered as necessary and proper to carry into effect any specified power, it seems to be expressly reserved to the states, by the 10th section of the 1st article of the Constitution.

7th. *Because* even admitting Congress to have a constitutional right to protect manufactures by the imposition of duties, or by regulations of commerce, designed principally for that purpose, yet a tariff of which the operation is grossly unequal and oppressive, is such an abuse of power as is incompatible with the principles of a free government and the great ends of civil society, justice, and equality of rights and protection.

8th. *Finally*, because South Carolina, from her climate, situation, and peculiar institutions, is, and must ever continue to be, wholly dependent upon agriculture and commerce, not only for her prosperity, but for her very existence as a state; because the valuable products of her soil—the blessings by which Divine Providence seems to have designed to compensate for the great disadvantages under which she suffers in other respects—are among the very few that can be cultivated with any profit by slave labor; and if, by the loss of her foreign commerce, these products should be confined to an inadequate market, the fate of this fertile state would be poverty and utter desolation; her citizens, in despair, would emigrate to more fortunate regions, and the whole frame and constitution of her civil policy be impaired and deranged, if not dissolved entirely.

Deeply impressed with these considerations, the representatives of the good people of this commonwealth, anxiously desiring to live in peace with their fellow-citizens, and to do all that in them lies to preserve and perpetuate the union of the states, and liberties of which it is the surest pledge, but feeling it to be their bounden duty to expose and resist all encroachments upon the true spirit of the Constitution, lest an apparent acquiescence in the system of protecting duties should be drawn into precedent—do, in the name of the commonwealth of South Carolina, claim to enter upon the Journal of the Senate their *protest* against it as unconstitutional, oppressive, and unjust.

20. Assaulting Monopoly
Andrew Jackson,
BANK VETO MESSAGE (1832)

The Bank of the United States (BUS), chartered by Congress in 1816 for twenty years, was a powerful institution. It performed several important functions: it served as a depository for government funds, it marketed government securities, it made loans to businesses, and, by maintaining specie payments (gold and silver) on its bank notes, it provided the country with a sound currency. With headquarters in Philadelphia and twenty-nine branches in other cities, the BUS contained private funds as well as government money and controlled one-fifth of the bank notes and one-third of the bank deposits and specie of the country. Advocates of "cheap money"—state bankers, land speculators, and some small business-owners—were hostile to the bank because it restricted the amount of paper money in circulation—they hoped to benefit from an abundance of paper currency. But those who favored "hard money" also disliked the bank. Eastern working people were suspicious of wages paid in paper money and southern planters and western farmers also tended to look on any money but gold and silver as dishonest. Andrew Jackson, who had an unpleasant experience with banks as a young man, was a hard-money man and distrustful of all banks.

In the spring of 1832, friends of the BUS in Congress, particularly Henry Clay, urged Nicholas Biddle, the bank's president, to seek a renewal of the bank's charter. The charter did not actually expire until 1836, but Clay was sure that Congress would approve a new charter at once. He was right; after investigating the bank's operations, Congress passed a recharter bill by large majorities. But on July 10, 1832, President Jackson vetoed the bill. In his veto message, he denounced the bank bill as an unconstitutional violation of states' rights as well as an endorsement of a dangerous monopoly whose profits came from "the earnings of the American people" and went to the benefit of foreign stockholders and "a few hundred of our own citizens, chiefly of the richest class."

When Jackson ran for re-election in 1832 the BUS was the main campaign issue. Henry Clay, the candidate of the National Republicans, was a strong supporter of the bank, and so were most eastern merchants and businessmen. They insisted that the bank performed an essential function in managing the country's finances. But working people in the East and farmers in the West tended to support Jackson. They felt that Nicholas Biddle followed policies that favored the rich and powerful at the expense of the plain people. Biddle himself continually boasted about the great powers at his disposal and made no secret of his contempt for popular government. During the 1832 campaign he worked hard to defeat

Jackson by lending large sums of money to Jackson's opponents. Biddle's behavior convinced the Jacksonians that the BUS represented a dangerous "concentration of power in the hands of a few men irresponsible to the people."

After his triumphant re-election Jackson decided to move against the bank at once without waiting for its charter to expire. He directed Secretary of the Treasury Roger B. Taney to place government funds in state banks rather than in the BUS, where they were usually deposited. By the end of 1833, some twenty-three state banks, called "pet banks" by Jackson's enemies, were handling funds of the federal government. Jackson's with-holding of federal funds effectively killed Biddle's bank. Although it remained in operation until its charter expired in 1836, the BUS was no longer a powerful force. In 1836 it was reorganized as a state bank in Pennsylvania. The decline of the BUS was accompanied by increasing disarray in the nation's economy. In 1837 came a financial panic, followed by the country's worst depression up to that time.

Andrew Jackson was born in 1767 on the Carolina frontier; his parents were poor Scotch-Irish immigrants. But Jackson climbed rapidly to wealth and status through land speculation and law practice. Before he was thirty, in 1795, he established the Hermitage, a splendid plantation near Nashville, Tennessee, and headed for Congress the next year. As major-general of his state's militia, Jackson won a victory over the British at the battle of New Orleans in 1815 that catapulted him to national prominence and led to a Senate seat in 1823 and the presidency in 1828. Known as Old Hickory and famous as a champion of the West and the common man, Jackson quarreled with Calhoun over nullification as well as with Biddle over the BUS. These conflicts added to his popularity and enabled him to build a strong Democratic party based on patronage and personality as well as on appeals to regional and class interests. Having survived the first attempt to assassinate a president when an unemployed housepainter attacked him in 1835, Jackson retired at the end of his second term to the Hermitage, where he died in 1845.

Questions to consider. Jackson, as you will see, opposed the BUS as a monopoly. Why did he attack monopolies so strongly? Were there other monopolies in the country at that time besides the bank? Did banks in general trouble Jackson, or only this particular bank? How did his casti-gation of foreign control strengthen Jackson's position with the people? Note, too, the president's concern for the right of states to tax the bank and of state-chartered banks to prosper. Is it surprising that a vigorous chief executive and strong opponent of nullification should here be a champion of states' rights? In assuming this stance, was Jackson acting in the tradition of Thomas Jefferson (Document 16) or of John C. Calhoun (Document 19)? Consider, finally, Jackson's appeal to the low and poor against the high and rich. Did this appeal to class differences, as opposed to occupational or sectional ones, signal a new turn in American politics? If so, why do you suppose it occurred in 1832 rather than, say, in 1816 or 1824? Who were Jackson's poor anyway?

BANK VETO MESSAGE (1832)

The bill "to modify and continue" the act entitled "An act to incorporate the subscribers to the Bank of the United States" was presented to me on the 4th July instant. Having . . . come to the conclusion that it ought not to become a law, I herewith return it to the Senate, in which it originated, with my objections.

A bank of the United States is in many respects convenient for the Government and useful to the people. Entertaining this opinion, and deeply impressed with the belief that some of the powers and privileges possessed by the existing bank are unauthorized by the Constitution, subversive of the rights of the States, and dangerous to the liberties of the people, I felt it my duty at an early period of my Administration to call the attention of Congress to the practicability of organizing an institution combining all its advantages and obviating these objections. I sincerely regret that in the act before me I can perceive none of these modifications of the bank charter which are necessary, in my opinion, to make it compatible with justice, with sound policy, or with the Constitution of our country.

The present corporate body . . . enjoys an exclusive privilege of banking under the authority of the General Government, a monopoly of its favor and support, and, as a necessary consequence, almost a monopoly of the foreign and domestic exchange. The powers, privileges, and favors bestowed upon it in the original charter, by increasing the value of the stock far above its par value, operated as a gratuity of many millions to the stockholders . . .

The act before me proposes another gratuity to the holders of the same stock. . . . On all hands it is conceded that its passage will increase at least 20 or 30 per cent more the market price of the stock, subject to the payment of the annuity of $200,000 per year secured by the act, thus adding in a moment one-fourth to its par value. It is not our own citizens only who are to receive the bounty of our Government. More than eight millions of the stock of this bank are held by foreigners. By this act the American Republic proposes virtually to make them a present of some millions of dollars. For these gratuities to foreigners and to some of our own opulent citizens the act secures no equivalent whatever. . . .

Every monopoly and all exclusive privileges are granted at the expense of the public, which ought to receive a fair equivalent. The many millions which this act proposes to bestow on the stockholders of the existing bank must come directly or indirectly out of the earnings of the American people. It is due to them, therefore, if their Government sell monopolies and exclusive privileges, that they should at least exact for them as much as they are worth in open market. The value of the monopoly in this case may be correctly ascertained. The twenty-eight millions of stock would probably be at an advance of 50 per cent, and command in market at least $42,000,000, subject to the payment of the present bonus. The present value of the monopoly, therefore, is $17,000,000,

From James D. Richardson, ed., *A Compilation of the Messages and Papers of the Presidents* (Government Printing Office, Washington, D.C., 1897-1907), II: 217-218.

and this the act proposes to sell for three millions, payable in fifteen annual installments of $200,000 each.

It is not conceivable how the present stockholders can have any claim to the special favor of the Government. The present corporation has enjoyed its monopoly during the period stipulated in the original contract. If we must have such a corporation, why should not the Government sell out the whole stock and thus secure to the people the full market value of the privileges granted? Why should not Congress create and sell twenty-eight millions of stock, incorporating the purchasers with all the powers and privileges secured in this act and putting the premium upon the sales into the Treasury?

The modifications of the existing charter proposed by this act are not such, in my view, as make it consistent with the rights of the States or the liberties of the people. The qualification of the right of the bank to hold real estate, the limitation of its power to establish branches, and the power reserved to Congress to forbid the circulation of small notes are restrictions comparatively of little value or importance. All the objectionable principles of the existing corporation, and most of its odious features, are retained without alleviation. . . .

Is there no danger to our liberty and independence in a bank that in its nature has so little to bind it to our country? The president of the bank has told us that most of the State banks exist by its forbearance. Should its influence become concentrated, as it may under the operation of such an act as this, in the hands of a self-elected directory whose interests are identified with those of the foreign stockholders, will there not be cause to tremble for the purity of our elections in peace and for the independence of our country in war? Their power would be great whenever they might choose to exert it; but if this monopoly were regularly renewed every fifteen or twenty years on terms proposed by themselves, they might seldom in peace put forth their strength to influence elections or control the affairs of the nation. But if any private citizen or public functionary should interpose to curtail its powers or prevent a renewal of its privileges, it can not be doubted that he would be made to feel its influence. . . .

If we must have a bank with private stockholders, every consideration of sound policy and every impulse of American feeling admonishes that it should be *purely American*. Its stockholders should be composed exclusively of our own citizens, who at least ought to be friendly to our Government and willing to support it in times of difficulty and danger. . . . To a bank exclusively of American stockholders, possessing the powers and privileges granted by this act, subscriptions for $200,000,000 could be readily obtained. . . .

The principle is conceded that the States can not rightfully tax the operations of the General Government. They can not tax the money of the Government deposited in the State banks, nor the agency of those banks in remitting it; but will any man maintain that their mere selection to perform this public service for the General Government would exempt the State banks and their ordinary business from State taxation? Had the United States, instead of establishing a bank at Philadelphia, employed a private banker to keep and transmit their funds, would it have deprived Pennsylvania of the right to tax his bank and his usual banking operations? . . .

General Jackson, president-elect, on his way to Washington.
Andrew Jackson was one of the most popular presidents
ever to occupy the White House. On his way to Washington
for his inauguration on March 4, 1829, he was greeted by
crowds of enthusiastic people everywhere. Backwoodsmen,
hunters, farmers, woodcutters, teamsters, and steamboat
captains poured into Washington to see their hero take the
oath of office. After his inaugural address men, women,
and children rushed past the police and up the steps to
shake hands with him. Jackson finally managed to get
away, mounted his horse, and started for the White House
followed by a wildly cheering throng. When the crowd
reached the White House, people poured into the reception
rooms, through windows as well as doors, and the building
became so jammed that one could hardly move. The attempt to serve refreshments almost led to a riot. Waiters
emerging from the kitchen with loaded trays were pushed
to the floor by the crowd, china and glassware were
smashed, and gallons of punch spilled on the carpets.
(Library of Congress)

It can not be *necessary* to the character of the bank as a fiscal agent of the Government that its private business should be exempted from that taxation to which all the State banks are liable, nor can I conceive it *"proper"* that the substantive and most essential powers reserved by the State shall be thus attacked and annihilated as a means of executing the powers delegated to the General Government. It may be safely assumed that none of those sages who had an agency in forming or adopting our Constitution ever imagined that any portion of the taxing power of the States not prohibited to them nor delegated to Congress was to be swept away and annihilated as a means of executing certain powers delegated to Congress.

If our power over means is so absolute that the Supreme Court will not call in question the constitutionality of an act of Congress the subject of which "is not prohibited, and is really calculated to effect any of the objects intrusted to the Government," although, as in the case before me, it takes away powers expressly granted to Congress and rights scrupulously reserved to the States, it becomes us to proceed in our legislation with the utmost caution. Though not directly, our own powers and the rights of the States may be indirectly legislated away in the use of means to execute substantive powers. We may not enact that Congress shall not have the power of exclusive legislation over the District of Columbia, but we may pledge the faith of the United States that as a means of executing other powers it shall not be exercised for twenty years or forever. We may not pass an act prohibiting the States to tax the banking business carried on within their limits, but we may, as a means of executing our powers over other objects, place that business in the hands of our agents and then declare it exempt from State taxation in their hands. Thus may our own powers and the rights of the States, which we can not directly curtail or invade, be frittered away and extinguished in the use of means employed by us to execute other powers. That a bank of the United States, competent to all the duties which may be required by the Government, might be so organized as not to infringe on our own delegated powers or the reserved rights of the States I do not entertain a doubt. . . .

The bank is professedly established as an agent of the executive branch of the Government, and its constitutionality is maintained on that ground. Neither upon the propriety of present action nor upon the provisions of this act was the Executive consulted. It has had no opportunity to say that it neither needs nor wants an agent clothed with such powers and favored by such exemptions. There is nothing in its legitimate functions which makes it necessary or proper. Whatever interest or influence, whether public or private, has given birth to this act, it can not be found either in the wishes or necessities of the executive department, by which present action is deemed premature, and the powers conferred upon its agent not only unnecessary, but dangerous to the Government and country. . . .

There are no necessary evils in government. Its evils exist only in its abuse. If it would confine itself to equal protection, and, as Heaven does its rains, shower its favors alike on the high and the low, the rich and the poor, it would be an unqualified blessing. In the act before me there seems to be a wide and unnecessary departure from these just principles. . . .

Experience should teach us wisdom. Most of the difficulties our Government now encounters and most of the dangers which impend over our Union have sprung from an abandonment of the legitimate objects of Government by our national legislation, and the adoption of such principles as are embodied in this act. Many of our rich men have not been content with equal protection and equal benefits, but have besought us to make them richer by act of Congress. By attempting to gratify their desires we have in the results of our legislation arrayed section against section, interest against interest, and man against man, in a fearful commotion which threatens to shake the foundations of our Union. It is time to pause in our career to review our principles, and if possible revive that devoted patriotism and spirit of compromise which distinguished the sages of the Revolution and the fathers of our Union.

21. To the Farthest Shores
Thomas Hart Benton,
THE DESTINY OF THE RACE (1846)

When James K. Polk ran for president in 1844, the Democrats campaigned for the reannexation of Texas and the reoccupation of Oregon. Texas, they insisted, had been acquired by the Louisiana Purchase of 1803 and had been unwisely returned to Spain in a later treaty. The Oregon country, too, they maintained, had become part of the United States by virtue of American settlements there in the early nineteenth century; they felt that British claims there were unjustified. Polk agreed heartily with the Democratic platform on both of these issues. In May 1844 he declared, "Let Texas be reannexed and the authority and laws of the United States be established and maintained within her limits, as also in the Oregon Territory, and let the fixed policy of our government be, not to permit Great Britain or any other foreign power to plant a colony or hold dominion over any portion of the people or territory of either."

Polk compromised with Britain on Oregon, signing a treaty in 1846 fixing the boundary there at the 49th parallel. But his administration went to war with Mexico from 1846 to 1848 over Texas and ended by acquiring California and the Southwest for the United States. Polk's territorial conquests produced a lively debate over the meaning of expansionism for the United States. Some people, especially in New England, thought the Mexican War had been inspired by Southern planters (like Polk himself) greedy for new lands into which to extend slavery. Others saw both Oregon and the Southwest as tokens in a Northern drive for more farmland and for harbors on the West Coast for the China trade. Another group, perhaps the largest, saw expansion in terms of "manifest destiny," the right of a teeming, vigorous American nation to fill up a continent either empty or held by "inferior" peoples and thus destined almost by nature itself to be absorbed.

One of the most articulate representatives of the manifest destiny school was Senator Thomas Hart Benton of Missouri, a long-time supporter of Jackson, Polk, and the Democratic party. Benton was a tireless promoter of midwestern agricultural and commercial interests that looked favorably on the acquisition of new lands and ports. But he also took the "higher" ground of national destiny. Benton, born in North Carolina in 1782, briefly attended the University of North Carolina before moving to Tennessee, where he practiced law and served in the militia under Andrew Jackson. In 1815 he moved to St. Louis, Missouri, on the raw frontier. Here Benton prospered as a lawyer, newspaper editor, and land speculator. In 1820 he was elected to the Senate, where he remained, a champion of the Midwest and of Jackson and the Democratic party, until 1850. In that year his growing opposition to slavery cost him his Senate seat. The same stand also cost him the Missouri governor's race in 1856, the year in which he published his masterpiece of political autobiography, *Thirty Years' View*. A loyal Democrat to the end, Benton refused to bolt his party even after the Republicans nominated his son-in-law, John C. Frémont, for president in 1856. He died in Washington, D.C., in 1858.

Questions to consider. Several questions are raised in a reading of "The Destiny of the Race." First, by placing expansionism within a context of age-old population movements, did Benton make it seem inevitable and irresistible and therefore not really open to political criticism? Second, by explaining expansionism in terms of white superiority, did he encourage Americans to think according to racial categories about all issues, including slavery and political rights for dark-skinned people in the United States? Finally, did he encourage Americans to pursue their destiny still further? Did his trans-Pacific vision involve conquest and colonization as well as trade? In what sense would Americans and Asians be common foes of the "great Powers of Europe"? How, precisely, would the "van of the Caucasian race" wake up the "torpid body of old Asia"? Does this somewhat surprising prediction in any way modify Benton's racism?

THE DESTINY OF THE RACE (1846)

Since the dispersion of man upon earth, I know of no human event, past or present, which promises a greater, a more beneficent change upon earth than the arrival of the van of the Caucasian race (the Celtic-Anglo-Saxon division) upon the border of the sea which washes the shore of eastern Asia. The Mongolian, or Yellow race, is there, four hundred million in number, spreading almost to Europe; a race once the foremost of the human family in the arts of civilization, but torpid and stationary for thousands of years. It is a race far above the Ethiopian, or Black—above the Malay, or Brown (if we must admit five races)—and above the American Indian, or Red; it is a race far above all these, but still, far below the White; and, like all the rest, must receive an impression from the superior race whenever they come in contact. It would seem that the White race alone received the divine command, to subdue and replenish the earth! for it is the only race that has obeyed it—the only one that hunts out new and distant lands, and even a New World, to subdue and replenish. Starting from western Asia, taking Europe for their field, and the Sun for their guide, and leaving the Mongolians behind, they arrived, after many ages, on the shores of the Atlantic, which they lit up with the lights of science and religion, and adorned with the useful and the elegant arts. Three and a half centuries ago, this race, in obedience to the great command, arrived in the New World, and found new lands to subdue and replenish. For a long time, it was confined to the border of the new field (I now mean the Celtic-

From the *Congressional Globe*, May 28, 1846.

Battle of Buena Vista. In February 1847, American forces led by General Zachary Taylor met Mexican forces commanded by General Antonio López de Santa Anna in battle three miles north of the hacienda of Buena Vista. On the first day the Americans lost ground, but on the second day they beat Santa Anna's forces badly. Buena Vista ended the war in northern Mexico, and later that year General Winfield Scott completed the conquest of Mexico by occupying the capital, Mexico City. (Library of Congress)

Anglo-Saxon division); and even fourscore years ago the philosophic Burke was considered a rash man because he said the English colonists would top the Alleghanies, and descend into the valley of the Mississippi, and occupy without parchment if the Crown refused to make grants of land.

What was considered a rash declaration eighty years ago, is old history, in our young country, at this day. Thirty years ago I said the same thing of the Rocky Mountains and the Columbia: it was ridiculed then: it is becoming history to-day. The venerable Mr. Macon [North Carolina senator] has often told me that he remembered a line low down in North Carolina, fixed by a royal governor as a boundary between the whites and the Indians: where is the boundary now? The van of the Caucasian race now top the Rocky Mountains, and spread down to the shores of the Pacific. In a few years a great population will grow up there, luminous with the accumulated lights of European and American civilization. Their presence in such a position cannot be without its influence upon eastern Asia. The sun of civilization must shine across the sea: socially and commercially, the van of the Caucasians, and the rear of the Mongolians, must intermix. They must talk together, and trade together, and marry together. Commerce is a great civilizer—social intercourse as great— and marriage greater. The White and Yellow races can marry together, as well as eat and trade together. Moral and intellectual superiority will do the rest: the White race will take the ascendant, elevating what is susceptible of improvement—wearing out what is not. The Red race has disappeared from the Atlantic coast: the tribes that resisted civilization, met extinction. This is a cause of lamentation with many. For my part, I cannot murmur at what seems to be the effect of divine law. I cannot repine that this Capitol has replaced the wigwam—this Christian people, replaced the savages—white matrons, the red squaws—and that such men as Washington, Franklin, and Jefferson, have taken the place of Powhattan, Opechonecanough, and other red men, howsoever respectable they may have been as savages.

Civilization, or extinction, has been the fate of all people who have found themselves in the track of the advancing Whites, and civilization, always the preference of the Whites, has been pressed as an object, while extinction has followed as a consequence of its resistance. The Black and the Red races have often felt their ameliorating influence. The Yellow race, next to themselves in the scale of mental and moral excellence, and in the beauty of form, once their superiors in the useful and elegant arts, and in learning, and still respectable though stationary; this race cannot fail to receive a new impulse from the approach of the Whites, improved so much since so many ages ago they left the western borders of Asia. The apparition of the van of the Caucasian race, rising upon them in the east after having left them on the west, and after having completed the circumnavigation of the globe, must wake up and reanimate the torpid body of the old Asia. Our position and policy will commend us to their hospitable reception: political considerations will aid the action of social and commercial influences. Pressed upon by the great Powers of Europe—the same that press upon us—they must in our approach see the advent of friends, not of foes—of benefactors, not of invaders. The moral and intellectual superiority of the White race will do the rest: and thus the youngest people, and the newest land, will become the reviver and the regenerator of the oldest.

COUNTERPOINT
Work and Wealth in Philadelphia, 1820–1860

Did the advent of Jacksonian Democracy inaugurate an era of the common man characterized by high upward social mobility? Stuart Blumin has explored this and other questions by examining the distribution of wealth and the occupational structure of Philadelphia between 1820 and 1860. He derived the following tables from information drawn from city directories, assessors' lists, and manuscript census returns. It is possible, from studying the tables, to get a sense of Philadelphia's economy and society in the four decades preceding the Civil War.

Table 3.1 provides evidence about the number and variety of occupations in Philadelphia in 1860, about their relative earning power, and therefore about class distinctions in the city. The figures reveal wide disparities of wealth. They also show that merchants were the wealthiest group in society, which is not altogether surprising since Philadelphia was a leading port city. It is still noteworthy, however, that manufacturers possessed only one-third the wealth of merchants. What does this suggest about the scale of production in ante-bellum Philadelphia? Much else can be learned about the city from a careful examination of the figures. What, for example, does the relative prosperity of bricklayers, carpenters, and stonecutters suggest about the city's architecture? Why do you think low-paid, female domestic servants acquired greater wealth than males in some occupations? Can you think of further ways in which the data shed light on the nature of this society?

Table 3.2 shows what proportion of the labor force belonged to broad occupational categories in 1820 and 1860. It thus fills in the picture of Philadelphia as of 1820 and enables us to see how the city's economy and society changed over a forty-year period. Which occupational groups expanded during these years? Which contracted? What explanation can you give for these changes? Does the table provide any evidence to support the contention that this was a period of high upward social mobility? What overall trend do the figures suggest?

We can see by examining these tables that the Democrats were less than successful in bridging the chasm between the low and poor and the high and rich. We can also see that, despite Alexander Hamilton's vision of a manufacturing nation, some major cities in 1860 were still largely places of trade and small-scale production. Yet it should be noted that in 1860 Philadelphia was not the whole world. Can you think of any mid-century cities in which manufacturing, rather than commerce, dominated the economy? Compared with Philadelphia, what differences might you find were you to examine occupational structure and wealth distribution in these locales?

TABLE 3.1   Rank Order of Occupations According to Mean Wealth, 1860

Rank	Occupation	Mean Wealth
1	Merchant	$50,357
2	Attorney	34,948
3	M.D.	23,879
4	Watchmaker	20,972
5	Broker	16,961
6	Manufacturer	16,910
7	Druggist	12,281
8	Agent	10,369
9	Saddler	9,980
10	Tanner and currier	8,950
11	Brickmaker	8,433
12	Cabinetmaker	7,272
13	Grocer	5,767
14	Bricklayer	4,308
15	Storekeeper	4,062
16	Carpenter	3,755
17	Teacher	3,746
18	Machinist	3,627
19	Tobacconist	3,512
20	Printer	3,510
21	Baker	3,507
22	Victualler (butcher)	3,414
23	Coachmaker	3,371
24	Plasterer	3,243
25	Hatter	3,175
26	Cooper	3,020
27	Shipwright	2,935
28	Confectioner	2,662
29	Stonecutter	2,425
30.5	Innkeeper	2,324
30.5	Gardener	2,324
32	Tailor	2,317
33	Bookbinder	2,300
34	Shoemaker	2,114
35	Blacksmith	2,089
36	Painter	1,788
37	Carter	1,727
38	Tinsmith	1,625
39	Clerk	1,410
40	Stonemason	1,150
41	Salesman	546
42	Watchman	457

TABLE 3.1 *(cont.)*

Rank	Occupation	Mean Wealth
43	Conductor	454
44	Domestic servant	328
45	Carpet weaver	186
46	Laborer	180
47	Coachman	170
48	Mariner	113
49	Weaver	106
50	Ironworker	88
51	Boatman	50

Source: From Stuart Blumin, "Mobility and Change in Ante-Bellum Philadelphia," in Stephen Thernstrom and Richard Sennett, eds., *Nineteenth-Century Cities* (Yale University Press, New Haven, Conn., 1969). Copyright © 1969 by Yale University.

TABLE 3.2   Occupational Structure of the Adult Male Work Force, 1820 and 1860

	1820	1860
Merchants and professionals	21.5%	24.2%
Manufacturers	1.0	2.3
Total nonmanual proprietors	22.5	26.5
Clerical workers	4.6	2.9
Total nonmanual	27.1	29.4
Master craftsmen	34.3	na
Journeymen craftsmen	21.9	na
Total craftsmen	56.2	47.0
Day laborers	5.8	13.9
Other unskilled and service workers	10.9	9.7
Total unskilled workers	16.7	23.6
Total manual	72.9	70.6
Total	100.0	100.0

Source: From Stuart Blumin, "Mobility and Change in Ante-Bellum Philadelphia," in Stephen Thernstrom and Richard Sennett, eds., *Nineteenth-Century Cities* (Yale University Press, New Haven, Conn., 1969). Copyright © 1969 by Yale University.

An 1851 temperance banner promotes the domestic rewards of abstention from alcohol. (Library of Congress)

CHAPTER FOUR

The Age of Reform

22. A Call to Arms
David Walker,
APPEAL TO THE COLOURED CITIZENS OF THE WORLD (1829)

With the publication in Boston of the first issue of William Lloyd Garrison's *Liberator* in January 1831, the antislavery movement turned toward militancy. But Garrison's call for immediate emancipation was preceded by David Walker's *Appeal to the Coloured Citizens of the World,* published in September 1829. In one place in his impassioned pamphlet, not appearing in the excerpt below, Walker called American blacks the "most wretched, degraded and abject sort of beings that ever lived since the world began," blasted American whites for their condescension, insensitivity, and cruelty, and demanded that they end slavery and begin treating blacks as human beings with all the rights of other citizens. "Treat us like men," he cried, "and we will be friends."

In composing his *Appeal* Walker knew whereof he wrote. A free black born in North Carolina in 1785, he managed to get an education. He traveled widely in the South observing slavery before he settled in Boston in 1827 and opened a shop that sold old clothes. When *Freedom's Journal,* the first American black newspaper, began publication in New York in 1827, Walker began contributing articles to it; he also lectured against slavery to small groups in Boston. He wrote his *Appeal* at high speed, printed it at his own expense, and saw to it that copies made their way into the South. The reaction to the *Appeal* was not surprising. Prominent Southerners demanded its suppression; even Bostonians called it "wicked and inflammatory." Garrison himself praised its "impassioned and determined spirit," but regretted its publication; later he changed his mind and reprinted most of it in the *Liberator.* Though there were threats on his life, Walker prepared new editions of his *Appeal.* But on June 28, 1830, he was found dead near the doorway of his shop, possibly the victim of poisoning.

Questions to consider. Walker's *Appeal* shocked even those whites opposed to slavery. Why do you suppose this was so? To whom was he addressing his plea: to slaves, free blacks, or whites? Do you think he was exaggerating the misery of blacks in the United States? Is there any resemblance between his method of presenting the facts and that of Dorothea Dix (Document 24)? How radical does his *Appeal* sound today? What kind of action did he call upon American blacks to take? What part did religion play in his view of things?

APPEAL TO THE COLOURED CITIZENS
OF THE WORLD (1829)

I know that the blacks, take them half enlightened and ignorant, are more humane and merciful than the most enlightened and refined European that can be found in all the earth. Let no one say that I assert this because I am prejudiced on the side of my colour, and against the whites or Europeans. For what I write, I do it candidly, for my God and the good of both parties: Natural observations have taught me these things; there is a solemn awe in the hearts of the blacks, as it respects *murdering* men; whereas the whites (though they are great cowards) where they have the advantage, or think that there are any prospects of getting it, they murder all before them, in order to subject men to wretchedness and degradation under them. This is the natural result of pride and avarice. . . . Should the lives of such creatures be spared? Are God and Mammon in league? What has the Lord to do with a gang of desperate wretches, who go *sneaking about the country like robbers*—light upon his people wherever they can get a chance, binding them with chains and handcuffs, beat and murder them as they would *rattle-snakes*? Are they not the Lord's enemies? Ought they not to be destroyed? Any person who will save such wretches from destruction, is fighting against the Lord, and will receive his just recompense. . . . The whites have had us under them for more than three centuries, murdering, and treating us like brutes; and, as Mr. Jefferson wisely said, they have never *found us out*—they do not know, indeed, that there is an unconquerable disposition in the breasts of the blacks, which, when it is fully awakened and put in motion, will be subdued, only with the destruction of the animal existence. Get the blacks started, and if you do not have a gang of tigers and lions to deal with, I am a deceiver of the blacks and of the whites.

Now, I ask you, had you not rather be killed than to be a slave to a tyrant, who takes the life of your mother, wife, and dear little children? Look upon your mother, wife and children, and answer God Almighty; and believe this, that it is no more harm for you to kill a man, who is trying to kill you, than it is for you to take a drink of water when thirsty; in fact, the man who will stand still and let another murder him, is worse than an infidel, and, if he has common sense, ought not to be pitied. . . . Oh! coloured people of these United States, I ask you, in the name of that God who made us, have we, in consequence of oppression, nearly lost the spirit of man, and, in no very trifling degree, adopted that of brutes? Do you answer, no? I ask you, then, what set of men can you point me to, in all the world, who are so abjectly employed by their oppressors, as we are by our *natural enemies*? How can, Oh! how can those enemies but say that we and our children are not of the HUMAN FAMILY, but were made by our Creator to be an inheritance to them and theirs for ever? How can the slaveholders but say that they can bribe the best coloured person in the country, to sell his brethren for a trifling sum of

From David Walker, *Walker's Appeal, in Four Articles; Together with a Preamble to Coloured Citizens of the World* (D. Walker, Boston, 1830), 11-87.

CASH!

All persons that have SLAVES to dispose of, will do well by giving me a call, as I will give the

HIGHEST PRICE FOR

Men, Women, &
CHILDREN.

Any person that wishes to sell, will call at Hill's tavern, or at Shannon Hill for me, and any information they want will be promptly attended to.

Thomas Griggs.

Charlestown, May 7, 1835.

PRINTED AT THE FREE PRESS OFFICE, CHARLESTOWN.

Broadside, Charleston, 1835. The African slave trade ended in 1808, but the domestic trade flourished thereafter. Breeding slaves for the market became a lucrative business in the South in the four decades before the Civil War. Cried one European after observing an auction in the nation's capital: "You call this the land of liberty, and every day that passes things are done in it at which the despotisms of Europe would be horror-struck and disgusted!" (Library of Congress) money, and take that atrocity to confirm them in their avaricious opinion, that we were made to be slaves to them and their children? . . .

I aver, that when I look over these United States of America, and the world, and see the ignorant deceptions and consequent wretchedness of my brethren, I am brought ofttimes solemnly to a stand, and in the midst of my reflections I exclaim to my God, "Lord didst thou make us to be slaves to our brethren, the whites?" But when I reflect that God is just, and that millions of my wretched brethren would meet death with glory — yea, more, would plunge into the very mouths of cannons and be torn into particles as minute as the atoms which compose the elements of the earth, in preference to a mean submission to the lash of tyrants, I am with streaming eyes, compelled to shrink back into nothingness before my Maker, and exclaim again, thy will be done, O Lord God Almighty.

Men of colour, who are also of sense, for you particularly is my APPEAL designed. Our more ignorant brethren are not able to penetrate its value. I call upon you therefore to cast your eyes upon the wretchedness of your brethren, and to do your utmost to enlighten them — *go to work and enlighten your brethren!* — Let the Lord see you doing what you can to rescue them and yourselves from degradation. Do any of you say that you and your family are free and happy, and what have you to do with the wretched slaves and other people? So can I say, for I enjoy as much freedom as any of you, if I am not quite as well off as the best of you. Look into our freedom and happiness, and see of what kind they are composed!! They are of the very lowest kind — they are the very *dregs*! — they are the most servile and abject kind, that ever a people was in possession of! If any of you wish to know how FREE you are, let one of you start and go through the southern and western States of this country, and unless you travel as a slave to a white man (a servant is a *slave* to the man whom he serves) or have your free papers (which if you are not careful they will get from you) if they do not take you up and put you in jail, and if you cannot give good evidence of your freedom, sell you into eternal slavery, I am not a living man: or any man of colour, immaterial who he is, or where he came from, if he is *the fourth from the negro race!!* (as we are called) the white Christian of America will serve him the same they will sink him into wretchedness and degradation for ever while he lives. And yet some of you have the hardihood to say that you are free and happy! May God have mercy on your freedom and happiness!! I met a coloured man in the street a short time since, with a string of boots on his shoulders; we fell into conversation, and in course of which, I said to him, what a miserable set of people we are! He asked, why? — Said I, we are so subjected under the whites, that we cannot obtain the comforts of life, but by cleaning their boots and shoes, old clothes, waiting on them, shaving them &c. Said he, (with the boots on his shoulders) "I am completely happy!!! I never want to live any better or happier than when I get a plenty of boots and shoes to clean!!!!" Oh! how can those who are actuated by avarice only, but think, that our Creator made us to be an inheritance to them for ever, when they see that our greatest glory is centered in such mean and low objects? Understand me, brethren, I do not mean to speak against the occupations by which we acquire enough and sometimes scarcely that, to render ourselves and families comfortable through life. I am subjected to the same inconvenience, as you all. — My objections are, to our *glorying* and being *happy* in such low employments; for if we are men, we ought to be thankful to the Lord for the past, and for the future. Be looking forward with thankful hearts to higher attainments than *wielding the razor* and *cleaning boots and shoes*. The man whose aspirations are not *above*, and even *below* these, is indeed, ignorant and wretched enough. I advanced it therefore to you, not as a *problematical*, but as an unshaken and for ever immovable *fact*, that your full glory and happiness, as well as all other coloured people under Heaven, shall never be fully consummated, but with the *entire emancipation of your enslaved brethren all over the world*. You may therefore, go to work and do what you can to rescue, or join in with tyrants to oppress them and yourselves, until the Lord shall come upon you all like a thief in the night. For I believe it is the will of the Lord that our greatest happiness shall consist in working for the salvation of our whole body. When this is accomplished a burst of glory will shine upon you, which will indeed astonish you and the world. Do any of you say this never will be done? I assure you that God will accomplish it—if nothing else will answer, he will hurl tyrants and devils into *atoms* and make way for his people. But O my brethren! I say unto you again, you must go to work and prepare the way of the Lord.

23. The Trail of Tears
APPEAL OF THE CHEROKEE NATION (1830)

American attitudes toward the Indian nations varied widely in the first part of the nineteenth century. Some people urged a policy of assimilation; others proposed the voluntary removal of the Indians to lands in the West. But land-hungry Americans in the South and West wanted to push the Indians off their ancestral lands by force, and a few people even favored extermination. When Andrew Jackson, an old Indian fighter, became president in March 1829, he adopted a policy of forcing the Indian tribes to move to the trans-Mississippi West. The Removal Act of 1830, passed by Congress with his encouragement, ordered the Indians to trade their tribal lands in the United States for new homes in federal territory west of the Mississippi River.

Indians everywhere objected to the removal policy, but there was little they could do about it. In Illinois and Florida the Indians put up forceful resistance, but after several years of bloody warfare they were finally subdued. In Georgia, the Cherokees, an Indian nation in the northwestern part of the state, tried to protect their rights peacefully. Refuting the average white's contention that Indians were "savages," the Cherokees had become skilled in agriculture, built fine homes and roads, accepted Christian missionaries, adopted a constitution, and published books in an alphabet invented by Sequoya, a talented hunter who had become a silversmith and a scholar. The Cherokees had treaty commitments from the U.S. government, but neither President Jackson nor the state of Georgia was willing to respect them. In July 1830, when Georgia decided to take over their lands, the Cherokees made a moving appeal to the American people to respect their "national and individual rights" and permit them "to remain on the land of our fathers."

The Cherokees' appeal was in vain. Although some northeastern humanitarians sympathized with the Cherokees, and the Supreme Court in two decisions written by Chief Justice John Marshall ruled in the Cherokees' favor, the state of Georgia asserted its sovereignty over their territory, and Jackson sent an army of 7,000 to drive the Indians westward at bayonet point. Over 4,000 of the 15,000 Cherokees who went west along the Trail of Tears in 1838 perished en route. By the time Jackson left office he could boast that his removal policy was rapidly nearing completion. The "shotgun removal," as it was called, shocked Ralph Waldo Emerson, one of America's greatest writers. "Such a dereliction of all faith and virtue," he cried, "such a denial of justice, and such deafness to screams for mercy were never heard of in time of peace and in the dealing of a nation with its own allies and wards, since the earth was made."

Questions to consider. In the first part of their appeal the Cherokees reviewed the history of their relations with American presidents, beginning with George Washington, called attention to the "solemn treaties" guaranteeing their rights, as well as the oral and written promises made to them by high U.S. officials, discussed their own efforts to "become civilized," and expressed gratification for the petitions on their behalf pouring into Congress from every part of the United States. In the final section of the appeal, which appears below, note the style in which the Cherokees state their case. Is it coolly argued or does it contain deep-seated feelings? How united were the Cherokees? What rights did they cite? What were their major objections to moving to a new location?

APPEAL OF THE CHEROKEE NATION (1830)

We are aware that some persons suppose it will be for our advantage to remove beyond the Mississippi. We think otherwise. Our people universally think otherwise. Thinking that it would be fatal to their interests, they have almost to a man sent their memorial to Congress, deprecating the necessity of a removal. This question was distinctly before their minds when they signed their memorial. Not an adult person can be found, who has not an opinion on the subject; and if the people were to understand distinctly, that they could be protected against the laws of the neighboring States, there is probably not an adult person in the nation, who would think it best to remove; though possibly a few might emigrate individually. There are doubtless many who would flee to an unknown country, however beset with dangers, privations and sufferings, rather than be sentenced to spend six years in a Georgia prison for advising one of their neighbors not to betray his country. And there are others who could not think of living as outlaws in their native land, exposed to numberless vexations, and excluded from being parties or witnesses in a court of justice. It is incredible that Georgia should ever have enacted the oppressive laws to which reference is here made, unless she had supposed that something extremely terrific in its character was necessary, in order to make the Cherokees willing to remove. We are not willing to remove; and if we could be brought to this extremity, it would be, not by argument; not because our judgment was satisfied; not because our condition will be improved—but only because we cannot endure to be deprived of our national and individual rights, and subjected to a process of intolerable oppression.

We wish to remain on the land of our fathers. We have a perfect and original right to claim this, without interruption or molestation. The treaties with us, and laws of the United States made in pursuance of treaties, guaranty our residence, and our privileges, and secure us against intruders. Our only request is, that these treaties may be fulfilled, and these laws executed.

From E. C. Tracy, *Memoir of the Life of Jeremiah Evarts* (Boston, 1845), 149-158.

But if we are compelled to leave our country, we see nothing but ruin before us. The country west of the Arkansas territory is unknown to us. From what we can learn of it, we have no prepossessions in its favor. All the inviting parts of it, as we believe, are preoccupied by various Indian nations, to which it has been assigned. They would regard us as intruders, and look upon us with an evil eye. The far greater part of that region is, beyond all controversy, badly supplied with wood and water; and no Indian tribe can live as agriculturists without these articles. All our neighbors, in case of our removal, though crowded into our near vicinity, would speak a language totally different from ours, and practice different customs. The original possessors of that region are now wandering savages, lurking for prey in the neighborhood. They have always been at war, and would be easily tempted to turn their arms against peaceful emigrants. Were the country to which we are urged much better than it is represented to be, and were it free from the objections which we have made to it, still it is not the land of our birth, nor of our affections. It contains neither the scenes of our childhood, nor the graves of our fathers.

24. Balm for the Afflicted
Dorothea L. Dix,
MEMORIAL ON ASYLUMS (1843)

The period from the 1830s until the Civil War was a period of reform movements, especially in the Northeast. "In the history of the world," exclaimed Ralph Waldo Emerson, "the doctrine of Reform had never such a scope as at the present hour." Most of the reformers were deeply religious; they took seriously Christianity's emphasis on the spiritual equality of all human beings and Jesus' special concern for the lowly and humble. They were also inspired by the Declaration of Independence, with its insistence on inalienable rights, and were eager to make its social and political ideals a reality. Many reformers believed that human nature was perfectible, and that with better social arrangements men and women would be able to live fuller and freer lives than they ever had before.

During the Age of Reform the antislavery movement became important; so did the temperance movement (the movement against alcohol consumption) and the struggles for enlarging women's rights, expanding public education, improving the lot of working people, and reforming prisons. Dorothea L. Dix, a Boston schoolteacher, took an interest in all these reforms, but she was especially interested in the treatment of the mentally ill. One Sunday, in March 1841, she went to the House of Correction in East Cambridge to hold a Sunday school class for the women inmates there. She was horrified by the filth, neglect, and misery she discovered among the insane who were kept in the jail.

Dix's experience in East Cambridge turned her into an earnest reformer. She persuaded local authorities to improve conditions in the jail. She also began touring Massachusetts, visiting jails, almshouses, and houses of correction in order to gather information about the treatment of the mentally ill throughout the state. Having gathered a shocking collection of facts about the situation, she drew up a tract entitled *Memorial to the Legislature of Massachusetts,* which called for drastic reforms, and had it presented to the Massachusetts legislature in January 1843. The memorial raised a storm; Dix was called a sensationalist, a troublemaker, and a liar. But leading humanitarians supported her, and in the end the lawmakers appropriated money for enlarging and improving the state hospital for the insane in Worcester.

Dorothea L. Dix, born in Hampden, Maine, in 1802, and brought up by her grandmother in Boston, had never intended to be a reformer. Shy and sickly as a young woman, she taught in a girls' school, wrote children's stories and books on religious subjects, and led a retired life. But she was a friend and disciple of the great Unitarian preacher William Ellery Channing, who believed human nature could be bettered, and she also knew reformers like Samuel Gridley Howe, who ran a school for the blind and agitated for prison reform. There was something natural, then, about her turn to activism after her Sunday morning in East Cambridge in 1841. After the Massachusetts legislature responded affirmatively to her 1843 petition, she was in the field of reform for good. She continued her crusade for better asylums until the end of her life. She went from one state to another, following the procedure she had used in Massachusetts: gathering facts, drawing up petitions, winning public opinion over to the need for reform, and persuading states to do something about it. "I have travelled over more than ten thousand miles in the last three years," she wrote in 1845. "Have visited eighteen state penitentiaries, three hundred county jails and houses of correction, more than five hundred almshouses and other institutions, besides hospitals and houses of refuge." Altogether she was responsible for the founding or enlarging of thirty-two mental hospitals in the United States and abroad. Her success owed much, no doubt, to the public's desire to control social deviants. But her own motivations were profoundly humanitarian. By the time she died in 1887 in a New Jersey hospital founded by her efforts she was regarded as one of the most distinguished women in the nation.

Questions to consider. Notice the method that Dix employed in her *Memorial* to rouse the interest of the Massachusetts legislators and persuade them to take action—that is, reporting in horrendous detail the conditions she had uncovered. Do you think the technique is convincing? Are there any similarities between Dix's method and those of investigative reporters today? For what reasons were the mentally ill badly treated? Why did Dix think the mentally ill should be separated from criminals? To what motives in the legislators did she appeal in her call for action? What did she reveal about her own motivations and outlook?

MEMORIAL ON ASYLUMS (1843)

Gentlemen, —I respectfully ask to present this Memorial, believing that the cause, which actuates to and sanctions so unusual a movement, presents no equivocal claim to public consideration and sympathy. . . .

About two years since leisure afforded opportunity and duty prompted me to visit several prisons and almshouses in the vicinity of this metropolis, I found, near Boston, in the jails and asylums for the poor, a numerous class brought into unsuitable connection with criminals and the general mass of paupers. I refer to idiots and insane persons, dwelling in circumstances not only adverse to their own physical and moral improvement, but productive of extreme disadvantages to all other persons brought into association with them.

From D. L. Dix, *Memorial to the Legislature of Massachusetts* (Munroe and Francis, Boston, 1843), 3-32.

I applied myself diligently to trace the causes of these evils, and sought to supply remedies. As one obstacle was surmounted, fresh difficulties appeared. Every new investigation has given depth to the conviction that it is only by decided, prompt, and vigorous legislation the evils to which I refer, and which I shall proceed more fully to illustrate, can be remedied. I shall be obliged to speak with great plainness, and to reveal many things revolting to the taste, and from which my woman's nature shrinks with peculiar sensitiveness. But truth is the highest consideration. *I tell what I have seen* — painful and shocking as the details often are — that from them you may feel more deeply the imperative obligation which lies upon you to prevent the possibility of a repetition or continuance of such outrages upon humanity. . . .

I come to present the strong claims of suffering humanity. I come to place before the Legislature of Massachusetts the condition of the miserable, the desolate, the outcast. I come as the advocate of helpless, forgotten, insane, and idiotic men and women; of beings sunk to a condition from which the most unconcerned would start with real horror; of beings wretched in our prisons, and more wretched in our almshouses. . . .

I must confine myself to few examples, but am ready to furnish other and more complete details, if required.

If my pictures are displeasing, coarse, and severe, my subjects, it must be recollected, offer no tranquil, refined, or composing features. The condition of human beings, reduced to the extremest states of degradation and misery cannot be exhibited in softened language, or adorn a polished page.

I proceed, gentlemen, briefly to call your attention to the *present state* of insane persons confined within this Commonwealth, *in cages, closets, cellars, stalls, pens! Chained, naked, beaten with rods,* and *lashed* into obedience. . . .

It is the Commonwealth, not its integral parts, that is accountable for most of the abuses which have lately and do still exist. I repeat it, it is defective legislation which perpetuates and multiplies these abuses. In illustration of my subject, I offer the following extracts from my Note-book and Journal: —

Springfield. In the jail, one lunatic woman, furiously mad, a State pauper, improperly situated, both in regard to the prisoners, the keepers, and herself. It is a case of extreme self-forgetfulness and oblivion to all the decencies of life, to describe which would be to repeat only the grossest scenes. She is much worse since leaving Worcester. In the almshouse of the same town is a woman apparently only needing judicious care, and some well-chosen employment, to make it unnecessary to confine her in solitude, in a dreary unfurnished room. Her appeals for employment and companionship are most touching, but the mistress replied "she had no time to attend to her." . . .

Lincoln. A woman in a cage. *Medford.* One idiotic subject chained, and one in a close stall for seventeen years. *Pepperell.* One often doubly chained, hand and foot; another violent; several peaceable now. *Brookfield.* One man caged, comfortable. *Granville.* One often closely confined; now losing the use of his limbs from want of exercise. *Charlemont.* One man caged. *Savoy.* One man caged. *Lenox.* Two in the jail, against whose unfit condition there the jailer protests.

Dedham. The insane disadvantageously placed in the jail. In the almshouse, two females in stalls, situated in the main building; lie in wooden bunks

Dorothea Dix. For fifty years Dorothea Dix devoted her energies to improving the attitudes of people toward the mentally ill and to providing better treatment for them. She was horrified by conditions in the East Cambridge (Massachusetts) House of Correction, which she visited in 1841, and became convinced it was necessary to establish asylums, supervised by intelligent and compassionate people and supported by taxation, to cope with the problem. Dix never appeared in public to push her cause. Her greatest disappointment came in 1854 when Franklin Pierce vetoed a bill passed by Congress that would have provided ample funds for the care of the insane. (National Archives)

filled with straw; always shut up. One of these subjects is supposed curable. The overseers of the poor have declined giving her a trial at the hospital, as I was informed, on account of expense.

Besides the above, I have seen many who, part of the year, are chained or caged. The use of cages all but universal. Hardly a town but can refer to some not distant period of using them; chains are less common; negligences frequent; wilful abuse less frequent than sufferings proceeding from ignorance, or want of consideration. I encountered during the last three months many poor creatures wandering reckless and unprotected through the country. . . . But I cannot particularize. In traversing the State, I have found hundreds of insane persons in every variety of circumstance and condition, many whose situation could not and need not be improved; a less number, but that very large, whose lives are the saddest pictures of human suffering and degradation.

I give a few illustrations; but description fades before reality.

Danvers. November. Visited the almshouse. A large building, much out of repair. Understand a new one is in contemplation. Here are from fifty-six to sixty inmates, one idiotic, three insane; one of the latter in close confinement at all times.

Long before reaching the house, wild shouts, snatches of rude songs, imprecations and obscene language, fell upon the ear, proceeding from the occupant of a low building, rather remote from the principal building to which my course was directed. Found the mistress, and was conducted to the place which was called "the home" of the *forlorn* maniac, a young woman, exhibiting a condition of neglect and misery blotting out the faintest idea of comfort, and outraging every sentiment of decency. She had been, I learnt, "a respectable person, industrious and worthy. Disappointments and trials shook her mind, and, finally, laid prostrate reason and self-control. She became a maniac for life. She had been at Worcester Hospital for a considerable time, and had been returned as incurable." The mistress told me she understood that, "while there, she was comfortable and decent." Alas, what a change was here exhibited! She had passed from one degree of violence to another, in swift progress. There she stood, clinging to or beating upon the bars of her caged appartment, the contracted size of which afforded space only for increasing accumulations of filth, a *foul* spectacle. There she stood with naked arms and dishevelled hair, the unwashed frame invested with fragments of unclean garments, the air so extremely offensive, though ventilation was afforded on all sides save one, that it was not possible to remain beyond a few moments without retreating for recovery to the outward air. Irritation of body, produced by utter filth and exposure, incited her to the horrid process of tearing off her skin by inches. Her face, neck, and person were thus disfigured to hideousness. To my exclamation of horror, the mistress replied: "Oh, we can't help it. Half the skin is off sometimes. We can do nothing with her; and it makes no difference what she eats, for she consumes her own filth as readily as the food which is brought her."

Men of Massachusetts, I beg, I implore, I demand pity and protection for these of my suffering, outraged sex. Fathers, husbands, brothers, I would supplicate you for this boon; but what do I say? I dishonor you, divest you at once of Christianity and humanity, does this appeal imply distrust. If it comes burdened with a doubt of your righteousness in this legislation, then blot it out; while I declare confidence in your honor, not less than your humanity. Here you will put away the cold, calculating spirit of selfishness and self-seeking; lay off the armor of local strife and political opposition; here and now, for once, forgetful of the earthly and perishable, come up to these halls and consecrate them with one heart and one mind to works of righteousness and just judgment.

Become the benefactors of your race, the just guardians of the solemn rights you hold in trust. Raise up the fallen, succor the desolate, restore the outcast, defend the helpless, and for your eternal and great reward receive the benediction. "Well done, good and faithful servants, become rulers over many things!" . . .

Injustice is also done to the *convicts*; it is certainly very wrong that they should be doomed day after day and night to listen to the ravings of madmen and madwomen. This is a kind of punishment that is not recognized by our statutes, and is what the criminal ought not to be called upon to undergo. The confinement of the criminal and of the insane in the same building is subversive of that good order and discipline which should be observed in every well-regulated prison. I do most sincerely hope that more permanent provision will be made for the pauper insane by the State, either to restore Worcester Insane Asylum to what it was originally designed to be or else make some just appropriation for the benefit of this very unfortunate class of our "fellow-beings."

Gentlemen, I commit to you this sacred cause. Your action upon this subject will affect the present and future condition of hundreds and of thousands. In this legislation, as in all things, may you exercise that "wisdom which is the breath of the power of God."

25. The Utopians
THE CONSTITUTION OF THE
BROOK FARM ASSOCIATION (1841)

The Brook Farm Association was established in 1841 in a rural area nine miles from Boston. One of many utopian communities that sprang up in the United States in the first part of the nineteenth century, Brook Farm was an experiment in cooperative living. Of the two hundred cooperative colonies that flowered from New England to Utah during this period, Brook Farm was probably the most famous because of its proximity to a large city and because many well-known literary people were associated with it. The Farmers, dedicated to "plain living and high thinking," engaged in agriculture, lived communally, operated an excellent school, and held dances, games, picnics, plays, lectures, and discussions. It was, said one visitor, "rich in cheerful buzz." Praised by Ralph Waldo Emerson for their experimentalism, but disparaged by Henry David Thoreau for their conformity, the Brook Farmers, like other utopians, emphasized the equality of the sexes and the rights and dignity of labor. In 1844, the association adopted Fourierism, a socialist doctrine originating in France, introduced more organization into their community, and published the *Harbinger,* a Fourierist journal with a nationwide circulation. In 1847 a fire destroyed the main building at Brook Farm; the association, which was heavily in debt, disbanded soon after.

The constitution of the Brook Farm Association was written chiefly by George Ripley, who was born in Greenfield, Massachusetts, in 1802. He studied at the Harvard Divinity School and served as a Unitarian minister in Boston for more than a decade. He also edited the *Christian Register,* was a member of the informal Transcendental Club, to which Emerson also belonged, and became increasingly preoccupied with literary matters. In 1841 he left the Unitarian church, helped edit the *Dial,* an organ of transcendentalist writers, and, with the help of his wife, launched the Brook Farm Institute of Agriculture and Education, commonly called "Mr. Ripley's community," in East Roxbury. With the collapse of Brook Farm he moved to Long Island and became literary critic for Horace Greeley's *New York Tribune.* For thirty-one years Ripley reviewed books for the *Tribune,* including Nathaniel Hawthorne's *Scarlet Letter* and Charles Darwin's *Origin of Species,* and was also editor of the literary department of *Harper's New Monthly Magazine.* He died in 1880.

Questions to consider. Ripley was a close friend of such transcendentalists as Emerson and Thoreau and infused his association with the transcendentalist belief in the spirituality of physical nature and the superiority of intuitive insight to logical reasoning. What objectives were announced in the Brook Farm constitution's preamble? What do these objectives reveal about American society in 1841? What does the constitution say about religion? How much freedom was there to be in the new community? Would you characterize Brook Farm as capitalistic, socialistic, or communistic? How democratic was the community?

THE CONSTITUTION OF THE BROOK FARM ASSOCIATION (1841)

In order more effectually to promote the great purposes of human culture; to establish the external relations of life on a basis of wisdom and purity; to apply the principles of justice and love to our social organization in accordance with the laws of Divine Providence; to substitute a system of brotherly cooperation for one of selfish competition; to secure to our children and those who may be entrusted to our care, the benefits of the highest physical, intellectual and moral education, which in the progress of knowledge the resources at our command will permit; to institute an attractive, efficient, and productive system of industry; to prevent the exercise of worldly anxiety, by the competent supply of our necessary wants; to diminish the desire of excessive accumulation, by making the acquisition of individual property subservient to upright and disinterested uses; to guarantee to each other forever the means of physical support, and of spiritual progress; and thus to impart a greater freedom, simplicity, truthfulness, refinement, and moral dignity, to our mode of life; —we the undersigned do unite in a voluntary Association, and adopt and ordain the following articles of agreement, to wit:

ARTICLE I

Sec. 1 The name of this Association shall be "THE BROOK-FARM ASSOCIATION FOR INDUSTRY AND EDUCATION." All persons who shall hold one or more shares in its stock, or whose labor and skill shall be considered an equivalent for capital, may be admitted by the vote of two-thirds of the Association, as members thereof.

Sec. 2 No member of the Association shall ever be subjected to any religious test; nor shall any authority be assumed over individual freedom of opinion by the Association, nor by any one member over another; nor shall any one be held accountable to the Association, except for such overt acts, omissions of duty, as violate the principles of justice, purity, and love, on which it is founded; and in such cases the relation of any member may be suspended, or discontinued, at the pleasure of the Association.

From O. B. Frothingham, *Transcendentalism in New England* (G. P. Putnam's Sons, New York, 1876), 159-164.

ARTICLE II

Sec. 1   The members of this Association shall own and manage such real and personal estate in joint stock proprietorship, divided into shares of one hundred dollars, each, as may from time to time be agreed on. . . .

Sec. 4   The shareholders on their part, for themselves, their heirs and assigns, do renounce all claim on any profits accruing to the Association for the use of their capital invested in the stock of the Association, except five percent interest on the amount of stock held by them, payable in the manner described in the preceding section.

ARTICLE III

Sec. 1   The Association shall provide such employment for all its members as shall be adapted to their capacities, habits, and tastes; and each member shall select and perform such operations of labor, whether corporal or mental, as shall be deemed best suited to his own endowments, and the benefit of the Association.

Sec. 2   The Association guarantees to all its members, their children, and family dependents, house-rent, fuel, food, and clothing, and the other necessaries of life, without charge, not exceeding a certain fixed amount to be decided annually by the Association; no charge shall ever be made for support during inability to labor from sickness or old age, or for medical or nursing attendance, except in case of shareholders, who shall be charged therefor . . . but no charge shall be made to any members for education or the use of library and public rooms. . . .

ARTICLE V

Sec. 1   The government of the Association shall be vested in a board of Directors, divided into four departments as follows: 1st, General Direction; 2d, Direction of Education; 3d, Direction of Industry; 4th, Direction of Finance; consisting of three persons each. . . .

Sec. 5   The departments of Education and Finance shall be under the control each of its own Direction, which shall select, and in concurrence with the General Direction, shall appoint such teachers, officers, and agents, as shall be necessary to the complete and systematic organization of the department. No Directors or other officers shall be deemed to possess any rank superior to the other members of the Association, nor shall they receive any extra remuneration for their official services.

Sec. 6   The department of Industry shall be arranged in groups and series, as far as practicable, and shall consist of three primary series; to wit, Agricultural, Mechanical, and Domestic Industry. The chief of each series shall be elected every two months by the members thereof. . . .

26. Women's Rights
THE SENECA FALLS DECLARATION OF 1848

In March 1776, when the Continental Congress in Philadelphia was beginning to contemplate independence from Britain, Abigail Adams wrote her husband, John, from Braintree, Massachusetts: "I long to hear that you have declared an independency. And, by the way," she added, "in the new code of laws which I suppose it will be necessary for you to make, I desire you would remember the ladies and be more generous and favorable to them than your ancestors. Do not put unlimited power into the hands of the husbands. Remember, all men would be tyrants if they could. If particular care and attention is not paid to the ladies, we are determined to foment a rebellion, and will not hold ourselves bound by any laws in which we have no voice or representation. That your sex are naturally tyrannical is a truth so thoroughly established as to admit of no dispute. . . ." Adams wrote back good-humoredly. "We are obliged to go fairly and softly," he told his wife, "and, in practice, you know we are the subjects. We have only the name of masters, and rather than give this up, which would completely subject us to the despotism of the petticoat, I hope General Washington and all our brave heroes would fight. . . ."*

Adams wasn't being accurate. American men had more than "the name of masters." The status of women in Adams's day and for many years afterward was distinctly inferior. Sir William Blackstone, the great eighteenth-century British legal authority, set the standard for the American view. "The husband and wife are one," he proclaimed, "and that one is the husband." Women were regarded as the wards of their husbands, were barred from professions like the law, medicine, and the ministry, and had few opportunities for higher education. According to a little verse composed in 1844:

> The father gives his kind command
> The mother joins, approves,
> And children all attentive stand,
> Then each, obedient, moves.

Abigail Adams wasn't the only woman to chafe at the situation. In 1832 Lydia Maria Child published a two-volume *History of the Condition of Woman in All Ages*, deploring woman's subservience, and in 1843 Margaret Fuller published a long essay, later expanded and published as *Woman in the Nineteenth Century*, in which she declared: "What woman needs is not as a woman to act or rule, but as a nature to grow, as an intellect to discern, as a soul to live freely and unimpeded, to unfold such powers as

---

* Charles Francis Adams, ed., *Familiar Letters of John Adams and His Wife During the Revolution* (New York, 1876), 149-150, 155.

were given her when we left our common home." In the first part of the nineteenth century women in increasing numbers began asking for equality before the law and asserting their right to be educated, enter the professions, and participate in public affairs along with men. Some women became active in reform, participating in the temperance movement, the fight against slavery, and the crusade for world peace. But even as reformers they were required to take a subordinate position. When a woman tried to speak at a temperance convention in New York she was shouted down. One man yelled, "Shame on the woman, shame on the woman!" And when several women attended the World Anti-Slavery Convention in London in 1840, men refused to seat them as delegates and made them sit in a curtained enclosure out of the public view. Two delegates—Lucretia Mott and Elizabeth Cady Stanton—began talking of holding a convention to battle for their own rights.

In July 1848 the first organized meeting for women's rights ever held met in Seneca Falls, New York, attended by two hundred delegates, including thirty-two men. Stanton drew up the Declaration of Sentiments, using the Declaration of Independence as a model. She also drafted a series of resolutions that were adopted by the convention. Only one of her demands ran into trouble: the right to vote. Woman suffrage still seemed so outlandish that it took the eloquence of Frederick Douglass, a black abolitionist and journalist, to persuade the delegates to adopt it by a small majority. Many people were shocked by the Seneca Falls convention. They denounced the "Reign of Petticoats" and warned against the "Insurrection among Women." But many distinguished Americans—including Ralph Waldo Emerson, John Greenleaf Whittier, and William Lloyd Garrison—supported the movement.

Elizabeth Cady Stanton, who drafted the Seneca Falls Declaration, was born in Johnstown, New York, in 1815. She attended Emma Willard's seminary in Troy, and while studying law with her father, became aware of the injustices suffered by women from American legal practices. When she married the abolitionist lawyer Henry B. Stanton in 1840, she insisted that the word *obey* be omitted from the ceremony. At an antislavery convention that she attended with her husband that same year, she got to know Lucretia Mott, and the two of them began working together for women's rights. Following the Seneca Falls Conference, Stanton joined Mott (and later Susan B. Anthony) in sponsoring conventions, writing articles, delivering lectures, and appearing before legislative bodies on behalf of the cause. Despite Stanton's grace and charm, she was considered a dangerous radical for espousing woman suffrage and easier divorce laws for women. During the Civil War she helped organize the Women's Loyal National League and urged emancipation. After the war she resumed her work for woman suffrage, became president of the National Woman Suffrage Association, lectured on family life, wrote for *Revolution*, a women's rights weekly, and contributed to the three-volume *History of Woman Suffrage*, published in the 1880s. One of the most distinguished feminist leaders in the country, she died in New York City in 1902.

Questions to consider. Many years passed before the women's rights movement in America began achieving some of its objectives. But the Seneca Falls convention marks the formal beginning of the organized movement to advance women's position, so it merits careful study. Do you think there were any advantages in using the Declaration of Independence (Document 11) as a model for the Declaration of Sentiments? How do the grievances listed by Stanton compare with those cited by Jefferson? Where does the emphasis of the Seneca Falls Declaration lie: in legal, in economic, or in political rights? Were any rights overlooked by Stanton? The demand for suffrage raised the biggest storm; some of those who signed the declaration withdrew their names when the suffrage resolution met with ridicule. Why do you suppose this happened? How radical do the Seneca Falls demands seem today? Which demands have been met by legislation since 1848?

THE SENECA FALLS DECLARATION OF 1848

When, in the course of human events, it becomes necessary for one portion of the family of man to assume among the people of the earth a position different from that which they have hitherto occupied, but one to which the laws of nature and of nature's God entitle them, a decent respect to the opinions of mankind requires that they should declare the causes that impel them to such a course.

We hold these truths to be self-evident: that all men and women are created equal; that they are endowed by their Creator with certain inalienable rights; that among these are life, liberty, and the pursuit of happiness; that to secure these rights governments are instituted, deriving their just powers from the consent of the governed. Whenever any form of government becomes destructive of these ends, it is the right of those who suffer from it to refuse allegiance to it, and to insist upon the institution of a new government, laying its foundations on such principles, and organizing its powers in such form, as to them shall seem most likely to effect their safety and happiness. Prudence, indeed, will dictate that governments long established should not be changed for light and transient causes; and accordingly all experience hath shown that mankind are more disposed to suffer, while evils are sufferable, than to right themselves by abolishing the forms to which they were accustomed. But when a long train of abuses and usurpations, pursuing invariably the same object evinces a design to reduce them under absolute despotism, it is their duty to throw off such government, and to provide new guards for their future security. Such has been the patient sufferance of the women under this

From Susan B. Anthony, Elizabeth Cady Stanton, and Matilda Joslyn Gage, eds., *History of Woman Suffrage* (3 v., Susan B. Anthony, Elizabeth Cady Stanton, and Matilda Joslyn Gage, Rochester, N.Y., 1889), I: 75-80.

Lydia Maria Child

Susan B. Anthony

Lucretia Mott

Elizabeth Cady Stanton

Representative women. These four women were all ardent reformers. Lydia Maria Child (1802–1880) was active in the antislavery movement, published many articles and pamphlets depicting the moral and economic evils of slavery, and with her husband edited the *National Anti-Slavery Standard* in New York. Susan B. Anthony (1820–1906), an independent-minded Quaker, started out as a temperance reformer but soon became an energetic women's-rights crusader with a special interest in woman suffrage. Lucretia Coffin Mott (1793–1880), also a Quaker, started out as an antislavery worker and then, like Elizabeth Cady Stanton (1815–1902), turned to women's rights when the two women were refused recognition as delegates to the world anti-slavery convention in London in 1840. Mott and Stanton were prime movers behind the first women's-rights convention, held in Seneca Falls, New York, in July 1848. (Library of Congress) government, and such is now the necessity which constrains them to demand the equal station to which they are entitled.

The history of mankind is a history of repeated injuries and usurpations on the part of man toward woman, having in direct object the establishment of an absolute tyranny over her. To prove this, let facts be submitted to a candid world.

He has never permitted her to exercise her inalienable right to the elective franchise.

He has compelled her to submit to laws, in the formation of which she had no voice.

He has withheld from her rights which are given to the most ignorant and degraded men—both natives and foreigners.

Having deprived her of this first right of a citizen, the elective franchise, thereby leaving her without representation in the halls of legislation, he has opposed her on all sides.

He has made her, if married, in the eye of the law, civilly dead.

He has taken from her all right in property, even to the wages she earns.

He has made her, morally, an irresponsible being, as she can commit many crimes with impunity, provided they be done in the presence of her husband. In the covenant of marriage, she is compelled to promise obedience to her husband, he becoming, to all intents and purposes, her master—the law giving him power to deprive her of her liberty, and to administer chastisement.

He has so framed the laws of divorce, as to what shall be the proper causes, and in case of separation, to whom the guardianship of the children shall be given, as to be wholly regardless of the happiness of women—the law, in all cases, going upon a false supposition of the supremacy of man, and giving all power into his hands.

After depriving her of all rights as a married woman, if single, and the owner of property, he has taxed her to support a government which recognizes her only when her property can be made profitable to it.

He has monopolized nearly all the profitable employments, and from those she is permitted to follow, she receives but a scanty remuneration. He closes against her all the avenues to wealth and distinction which he considers most honorable to himself. As a teacher of theology, medicine, or law, she is not known.

He has denied her the facilities for obtaining a thorough education, all colleges being closed against her.

He allows her in Church, as well as State, but a subordinate position, claiming Apostolic authority for her exclusion from the ministry, and, with some exceptions, from any public participation in the affairs of the Church.

He has created a false public sentiment by giving to the world a different code of morals for men and women, by which moral delinquencies which exclude women from society, are not only tolerated, but deemed of little account in man.

He has usurped the prerogative of Jehovah himself, claiming it as his right to assign for her a sphere of action, when that belongs to her conscience and to her God.

He has endeavored, in every way that he could, to destroy her confidence in her own powers, to lessen her self-respect, and to make her willing to lead a dependent and abject life.

Now, in view of this entire disfranchisement of one-half the people of this country, their social and religious degradation—in view of the unjust laws above mentioned, and because women do not feel themselves aggrieved, oppressed, and fraudulently deprived of their most sacred rights, we insist that they have immediate admission to all the rights and privileges which belong to them as citizens of the United States.

In entering upon the great work before us, we anticipate no small amount of misconception, misrepresentation, and ridicule; but we shall use every instrumentality within our power to effect our object. We shall employ agents, circulate tracts, petition the State and National legislatures, and endeavor to enlist the pulpit and the press in our behalf. We hope this Convention will be followed by a series of Conventions embracing every part of the country.

RESOLUTIONS

WHEREAS, The great precept of nature is conceded to be, that "man shall pursue his own true and substantial happiness." Blackstone in his Commentaries remarks, that this law of Nature being coequal with mankind, and dictated by God himself, is of course superior in obligation to any other. It is binding over all the globe, in all countries and at all times; no human laws are of any validity if contrary to this, and such of them as are valid, derive all their force, and all their validity, and all their authority, mediately and immediately, from this original; therefore,

Resolved, That such laws as conflict, in any way, with the true and substantial happiness of woman, are contrary to the great precept of nature and of no validity, for this is "superior in obligation to any other."

Resolved, That all laws which prevent woman from occupying such a station in society as her conscience shall dictate, or which place her in a position inferior to that of man, are contrary to the great precept of nature, and therefore of no force or authority.

Resolved, That woman is man's equal—was intended to be so by the Creator, and the highest good of the race demands that she should be recognized as such.

Resolved, That the women of this country ought to be enlightened in regard to the laws under which they live, that they may no longer publish their degradation by declaring themselves satisfied with their present position, nor their ignorance, by asserting that they have all the rights they want.

Resolved, That inasmuch as man, while claiming for himself intellectual superiority, does accord to woman moral superiority, it is pre-eminently his duty to encourage her to speak and teach, as she has an opportunity, in all religious assemblies.

Resolved, That the same amount of virtue, delicacy, and refinement of behavior that is required of woman in the social state, should also be required of man, and the same transgressions should be visited with equal severity on both man and woman.

Resolved, That the objection of indelicacy and impropriety, which is so often brought against woman when she addresses a public audience, comes with a very ill-grace from those who encourage, by their attendance, her appearance on the stage, in the concert, or in feats of the circus.

Resolved, That woman has too long rested satisfied in the circumscribed limits which corrupt customs and a perverted application of the Scriptures have marked out for her, and that it is time she should move in the enlarged sphere which her great Creator has assigned her.

Resolved, That it is the duty of the women of this country to secure to themselves their sacred right to the elective franchise.

Resolved, That the equality of human rights results necessarily from the fact of the identity of the race in capabilities and responsibilities.

Resolved, therefore, That, being invested by the Creator with the same capabilities, and the same consciousness of responsibility for their exercise, it is demonstrably the right and duty of woman, equally with man, to promote every righteous cause by every righteous means; and especially in regard to the great subjects of morals and religion, it is self-evidently her right to participate with her brother in teaching them, both in private and in public, by writing and by speaking, by any instrumentalities proper to be used, and in any assemblies proper to be held; and this being a self-evident truth growing out of the divinely implanted principles of human nature, any custom or authority adverse to it, whether modern or wearing the hoary sanction of antiquity, is to be regarded as a self-evident falsehood, and at war with mankind.

27. Demon Rum
T. S. Arthur,
TEN NIGHTS IN A BAR-ROOM (1854)

In the early part of the nineteenth century the United States was a hard-drinking nation. European visitors were struck by the amount of alcohol consumed in the young republic. One English observer declared that Americans consumed more "spirits of all kinds" in proportion to population than any other people in the world.

Distilled spirits were easy to come by in the new nation. Farmers disposed of their surplus fruit and grain by processing them into spirits, which were easily stored and shipped to market. A bushel of corn worth $0.25 yielded two and a half gallons of whiskey worth $1.25 or more. Corn whiskey and apple cider, the most popular beverages, were considered nutritious and healthful; they were far cheaper than coffee or tea, which had to be imported, and preferable to water, which was often impure and shunned as drink fit for pigs. Alcohol was commonly drunk at meals; it made up for the monotonous diet of many Americans. During a good part of the year, people depended on dry, salty foods—parched corn, smoked ham, salt pork—that didn't spoil rapidly. Many Americans ate corn three times a day in the form of johnnycake, corn bread, corn mush, or Indian pudding. They also consumed great quantities of salt pork fried in lard. Whiskey made greasy food taste better; it was also supposed to cure a variety of ailments, including headaches, nausea, and indigestion.

In 1812, Mason Locke ("Parson") Weems, an Episcopalian clergyman and popular writer, published a little temperance tract. Its ebullient title was *The Drunkard's Looking Glass, Reflecting a Faithful Likeness of the Drunkard in Sundry Very Interesting Attitudes, with Lively Representations of the Many Strange Capers which he cuts at different Stages of his Disease; as first, when he has only "a drop in his eye"; second, when he is "half-shaved"; third, when he is getting "a little on the staggers or so"; and fourth and fifth, and so on, till he is "quite capsized"; "Snug under the table with the dogs", and "sticks to the floor without holding on."* Weems was bothered by American drinking habits. He estimated that there were a hundred thousand habitual drunkards in a population of six million. He was not alone in his concern. Clergymen in other denominations, and laymen as well, became increasingly alarmed by the spread of alcoholism in young America. Basil Hall, a British traveler, reported that "a deeper curse never afflicted any nation. The evil is manifested in almost every walk of life, contaminating all it touches."

In 1826, concerned citizens, led by a Congregational clergyman, organized the American Society for the Promotion of Temperance in Boston and dedicated themselves to encouraging abstinence from spiritous liquors. The organization grew rapidly. By 1835 it had attracted more than a million members, established five thousand local branches, and was distributing thousands of tracts and pamphlets picturing the evils of alcohol. The Temperance Society sought pledges of abstinence; it also sponsored "Cold Water Armies" for children. For a time it was the largest of all the reform movements agitating the nation. Hundreds of temperance stories, songs, poems, and plays poured from the press, and a revivalistic fervor permeated the earnest meetings of the temperance advocates.

Eventually the temperance movement split over purposes and procedures. Conservatives favored moderation in drinking and the rejection of distilled spirits but not of wine and beer. Radicals insisted on total abstinence; they also switched from moral suasion to promotion of laws prohibiting the manufacture and sale of intoxicating beverages. In 1846 Maine passed the first prohibition law; in the 1850s several other states did the same. The prohibitionists looked upon liquor as the root of all evil. They insisted that it destroyed the home, encouraged crime and violence, and transformed hard-working, law-abiding citizens into besotted loafers who threatened to make a mockery of the American experiment in self-government.

In 1854 Timothy Shay Arthur published a novel, *Ten Nights in a Bar-Room and What I Saw There,* dramatizing all these points. In Arthur's novel everything goes wrong in Cedarville when the Sickle and Sheaf tavern is opened: diligent workers become shiftless slobs, civility gives way to coarseness, and violence and degradation wreck the lives of several of the town's most promising young men. But there is one bright note. Joe Morgan, the leading drunk in town when the novel opens, decides to reform. When his little girl, Mary (who comes regularly to the tavern to take him home), is mortally wounded in a tavern brawl, Joe takes the pledge.

T. S. Arthur was born in New York City in 1809. Although he did poorly in school, he became a competent magazine editor and prolific writer of children's stories, self-help manuals, and sentimental novels dealing with marital problems. But his most successful books dealt with temperance. He regarded saloons as "nurseries of vice and crime" and waged his fight against them until long after the Civil War. *Ten Nights in a Bar-Room* sold several hundred thousand copies and was made into a play that rivaled a play based on Harriet Beecher Stowe's *Uncle Tom's Cabin* in popularity. Arthur was editor of the *Home Magazine,* which dealt with family problems, when he died in 1885.

Questions to consider. The final chapter of *Ten Nights in a Bar-Room,* reprinted below, has an upbeat ending. Hargrove, an opponent of taverns from the outset, tells the villagers the sad story of Simon Slade, a once-industrious mill operator who turned to tavern keeping and was eventually killed by his own son. Hargrove, speaking for Arthur, also recommends immediate action. Why does he think that prohibition is the only safeguard against the abuse of alcohol? How does he handle the clash between prohibition laws and the rights of individuals? What does he say about property rights? What does Arthur's chapter reveal about American culture in the 1850s?

TEN NIGHTS IN A BAR-ROOM (1854)

On the day that succeeded the evening of this fearful tragedy, placards were to be seen all over the village, announcing a mass meeting at the "Sickle and Sheaf" that night.

By early twilight, the people commenced assembling. The bar, which had been closed all day, was now thrown open, and lighted; and in this room, where so much of evil had been originated, encouraged, and consummated, a crowd of earnest-looking men were soon gathered. Among them I saw the fine person of Mr. Hargrove. Joe Morgan — or rather Mr. Morgan — was also of the number. The latter I would scarcely have recognized, had not some one near me called him by name. He was well dressed, stood erect, and, though there were many deep lines on his thoughtful countenance, all traces of his former habits were gone. While I was observing him, he arose, and addressing a few words to the assemblage, nominated Mr. Hargrove as chairman of the meeting. To this a unanimous assent was given.

On taking the chair, Mr. Hargrove made a brief address, something to this effect.

"Ten years ago," said he, his voice evincing a light unsteadiness as he began, but growing firmer as he proceeded, "there was not a happier spot in Bolton country than Cedarville. Now, the marks of ruin are everywhere. Ten years ago, there was a kind-hearted, industrious miller in Cedarville, liked by every one, and as harmless as a little child. Now, his bloated, disfigured body lies in that room. His death was violent, and by the hand of his own son!"

Mr. Hargrove's words fell slowly, distinctly, and marked by the most forcible emphasis. There was scarcely one present who did not feel a low shudder run along his nerves, as the last words were spoken in a husky whisper.

"Ten years ago," he proceeded, "the miller had a happy wife, and two innocent, glad-hearted children. Now, his wife, bereft of reason, is in a mad-house, and his son the occupant of a felon's cell, charged with the awful crime of patricide!"

Briefly he paused, while his audience stood gazing upon him with half-suspended respiration.

"Ten years ago," he went on, "Judge Hammond was accounted the richest man in Cedarville. Yesterday he was carried, a friendless pauper, to the Almshouse; and to-day he is the unmourned occupant of a pauper's grave! Ten years ago, his wife was the proud, hopeful, loving mother of a most promising son. I need not describe what Willy Hammond was. All here knew him well.

From Timothy Shay Arthur, *Ten Nights in a Bar-Room* (J. W. Bradley, Philadelphia, 1860), 68-81.

BLACK VALLEY RAILROAD!

GREAT CENTRAL, BROAD GAUGE, FAST ROUTE,

From Sippington, through Tippleton and Topersville,

VIA

BEGGARSTOWN, DEMONLAND AND BLACK VALLEY,

TO

DESTRUCTION!

ACCIDENTS BY COLLISIONS ENTIRELY AVOIDED AS NO UP TRAINS ARE RUN OVER THE ROAD.

TICKETS SOLD AT ALL LIQUOR SHOPS.

Anti-alcohol poster of the Massachusetts Temperance Alliance, Boston. Until the antislavery campaign began to gather force in the 1830s, the crusade for temperance was the most popular of all the reform movements before the Civil War. There were numerous temperance organizations at the local and national level and countless temperance meetings marked by dramatic confessions by reformed alcoholics and enthusiastic pledge-signings. There were also many corny jokes. A man sees his little girl dipping her doll's dress in a cup, according to a typical temperance tale, and asks what she's doing. "I'm coloring my doll's dress red, Pa," she explains. "With what?" he asks. "With beer, Pa." "You can't color red with beer." "Yes, I can," insists the girl. "Ma said it was beer that colored your nose so red." (Library of Congress)

Ah! what shattered the fine intellect of that noble-minded woman? Why did her heart break? Where is she? Where is Willy Hammond?"

A low, half repressed groan answered the speaker.

"Ten years ago, you! sir," pointing to a sad-looking old man, and calling him by name, "had two sons—generous, promising, manly-hearted boys. What are they now? You need not answer the question. Too well is their history and your sorrow known. Ten years ago, I had a son—amiable, kind, loving, but weak. Heaven knows how I sought to guard and protect him! But he fell also. The arrows of destruction darkened the very air of our once secure and happy village. And who was safe? Not mine, nor yours!

"Shall I go on? Shall I call up and pass in review before you, one after another, all the wretched victims who have fallen in Cedarville during the last ten years? Time does not permit. It would take hours for the enumeration! No: I will not throw additional darkness into the picture. Heaven knows it is black enough already! But what is the root of this great evil? Where lies the fearful secret? Who understands the disease? A direful pestilence is in the air—it walketh in darkness, and wasteth at noonday. It is slaying the firstborn in our houses, and the cry of anguish is swelling on every gale. Is there no remedy?"

"Yes! yes! There is a remedy!" was the spontaneous answer from many voices.

"Be it our task, then, to find and apply it this night," answered the chairman as he took his seat.

"And there is but one remedy," said Morgan, as Mr. Hargrove sat down. "The accursed traffic must cease among us. You must cut off the fountain, if you would dry up the stream. If you would save the young, the weak, and the innocent—on you God has laid the solemn duty of their protection—you must cover them from the tempter. Evil is strong, wily, fierce, and active in the pursuit of its ends. The young, the weak, and the innocent can no more resist its assaults, than the lamb can resist the wolf. They are helpless, if you abandon them to the powers of evil. Men and brethren! as one who has himself been wellnigh lost—as one who, daily, feels and trembles at the dangers that beset his path—I do conjure you to stay the fiery stream that is bearing every thing good and beautiful among you to destruction. Fathers! for the sake of your young children, be up now and doing. Think of Willy Hammond, Frank Slade, and a dozen more whose names I could repeat, and hesitate no longer! Let us resolve, this night, that from henceforth, the traffic shall cease in Cedarville. Is there not a large majority of citizens in favour of such a measure? And whose rights or interest can be affected by such a restriction? Who, in fact, has any right to sow disease and death in our community? The liberty, under sufferance, to do so, wrongs the individual who uses it, as well as those who become his victims. Do you want proof of this. Look at Simon Slade, the happy, kind-hearted miller; and at Simon Slade, the tavern-keeper. Was he benefited by the liberty to work harm to his neighbour? No! no! In heaven's name, then, let the traffic cease! To this end, I offer these resolutions: —

"Be it resolved by the inhabitants of Cedarville, That from this day henceforth, no more intoxicating drink shall be sold within the limits of the corporation.

"Resolved, further, That all the liquors in the 'Sickle and Sheath' be forthwith destroyed, and that a fund be raised to pay the creditors of Simon Slade therefor, should they demand compensation.

"Resolved, That in closing up all other places where liquor is sold, regard shall be had to the right of property which the law secures to every man.

"Resolved, That with the consent of the legal authorities, all the liquor for sale in Cedarville be destroyed; provided the owners thereof be paid its full value out of a fund specially raised for that purpose."

But for the calm, yet resolute opposition of one or two men, these resolutions would have passed by acclamation. A little sober argument showed the excited company that no good end is ever secured by the adoption of wrong means.

There were, in Cedarville, regularly constituted authorities, which alone had the power to determine public measures; or to say what business might or might not be pursued by individuals. And through these authorities they must act in an orderly way.

There was some little chafing at this view of the case. But good sense and reason prevailed. Somewhat modified, the resolution passed, and the more ultra-inclined contented themselves with carrying out the second resolution, to destroy forthwith all liquor to be found on the premises; which was immediately done. After which the people dispersed to their home, each with a lighter heart, and better hopes for the future of their village.

On the next day, as I entered the stage that was to bear me from Cedarville, I saw a man strike his sharp axe into the worn, faded, and leaning post that had, for so many years, borne aloft the 'Sickle and Sheaf'; and just as the driver gave word to his horses, the false emblem which had invited so many to enter the way of destruction, fell crashing to the earth.

28. Race, Slavery, and the Constitution
DRED SCOTT v. SANFORD (1857)

The spread of slavery during the early nineteenth century divided the nation and so fanned the flames of sectionalism that the United States was able to remain united only by careful political compromise between North and South. The Missouri Compromise of 1820 admitted Maine, a free state, and Missouri, a slave state, to the Union about the same time, thus preserving the balance between the two sections; it also barred slavery from all territories north of a line (36°30'N) drawn westward from Missouri's southern border. The Compromise of 1850 admitted California as a free state but organized New Mexico and Utah on the principle of popular sovereignty, with slavery left to the inhabitants' decision.

In 1854 Congress violated the Missouri Compromise line. By the Kansas-Nebraska Act of that year, sponsored by Illinois Senator Stephen A. Douglas, who wanted settlers to decide whether or not to have slavery, territory north of 36°30'N was opened to slavery on a "local option" basis. The result was a bloody conflict in Kansas between free-soil settlers opposed to slavery there and those favoring slavery. In 1857, moreover, Chief Justice Roger B. Taney's opinion in the *Dred Scott* case placed the Supreme Court squarely behind the institution of slavery. (A Missouri slave, Dred Scott, had sued his master for freedom, basing his case on the fact that they had lived for a time in free territory.) Speaking for the majority of the justices, Taney announced that blacks could not be American citizens and that Congress could not prohibit slavery even in territories under its direct jurisdiction. The *Dred Scott* decision made all previous compromises over slavery unconstitutional. It also exacerbated sectional tensions. Proslavery Southerners were anxious to extend slavery into new areas; antislavery Northerners were just as determined to do all they could to prevent the further expansion of human bondage despite the Court's ruling. Even Northerners who were not abolitionists opposed Taney's decision. They did not like the idea of Southerners bringing their slaves into the federal territories.

Roger Taney was born in 1777 in Maryland, where he practiced law for a time and then entered politics. An early supporter of Andrew Jackson, he became attorney general in 1831 and helped draft Jackson's message to Congress in 1832 vetoing the recharter bill for the Bank of the United States (Document 20). In 1836 Jackson made Taney chief justice of the Supreme Court. Taney's major opinion before *Dred Scott* was an antimonopoly decision in the *Charles River Bridge* case in 1837. After the *Dred Scott* decision, Taney's prestige declined rapidly, and it all but disappeared after the Republican victory in 1860. He died in Washington four years later.

Scott himself became free because when his master died, the widow married an abolitionist who arranged for Scott's freedom. Scott became a hotel porter in St. Louis and died there of tuberculosis a year after the Supreme Court decision.

Questions to consider. The *Dred Scott* decision purports to cite historical facts as well as advance opinions about those facts. How accurate is Taney's statement that American blacks had never possessed any of the rights and privileges the U.S. Constitution confers on citizens? Why did he make a careful distinction between the rights of citizenship that a state may confer and the rights conferred by the federal Constitution? Do you think Taney's position on the right of states "to confer on whomever it pleased the character of citizen" had implications that he did not intend? Note that Taney insisted that Dred Scott, not being a citizen, was "not entitled to sue in the courts." If he believed this, why did he agree to rule on the case at all? Was he correct in saying that when the nation was founded "no one thought of disputing" the idea that "the negro might justly and lawfully be reduced to slavery"? Do you think his reference to the constitutional provision permitting the slave trade until 1808 strengthened his argument? Note that in order to find the Missouri Compromise unconstitutional, Taney maintained that the clause in the Constitution giving Congress power to regular the federal territories applied only to territories belonging to the United States at the time the Constitution was adopted. Do you think he made a convincing case for this assertion? Would Taney's insistence that Congress cannot prohibit slavery in the federal territories logically apply to whites as well as blacks? Was he correct in asserting that the 1787 document made no distinction between property in goods and property in slaves? William Lloyd Garrison called the Constitution a "slaveholder's document," and Taney obviously agreed. But Frederick Douglass (Document 36), the distinguished black antislavery leader, "abolitionized" the Constitution. He pointed out that the word *slavery* appears nowhere in the Constitution and that the basic purposes of the Union, announced in the preamble, as well as numerous provisions having to do with human rights, categorically rule out slavery. Who do you think was closer to the truth: Taney or Douglass? By 1857, the year of Taney's decision, the Democratic party was the only truly national party. What impact did his decision have on the unity of the party and on such Northern Democrats as Stephen A. Douglas?

DRED SCOTT v. SANFORD (1857)

The question is simply this: Can a negro, whose ancestors were imported into this country, and sold as slaves, become a member of the political community formed and brought into existence by the Constitution of the United States, and as such become entitled to all the rights, and privileges, and immunities, guaranteed by that instrument to the citizen? One of which rights is the privilege of suing in a court of the United States in the cases specified in the Constitution.

It will be observed, that the plea applies to that class of persons only whose ancestors were negroes of the African race, and imported into this country, and sold and held as slaves. The only matter in issue before the court, therefore, is, whether the descendants of such slaves, when they shall be emancipated, or who are born of parents who had become free before their birth, are citizens of a State, in the sense in which the word citizen is used in the Constitution of the United States. And this being the only matter in dispute on the pleadings, the court must be understood as speaking in this opinion of that class only, that is of persons who are the descendants of Africans who were imported into this country and sold as slaves. . . .

We proceed to examine the case as presented by the pleadings.

The words "people of the United States" and "citizens" are synonymous terms, and mean the same thing. They both describe the political body who, according to our republican institutions, form the sovereignty, and who hold the power and conduct the government through their representatives. They are what we familiarly call the "sovereign people," and every citizen is one of this people, and a constituent member of this sovereignty. The question before us is, whether the class of persons described in the plea in abatement compose a portion of this people, and are constituent members of this sovereignty? We think they are not, and that they are not included, and were not intended to be included, under the word "citizens" in the Constitution, and can, therefore, claim none of the rights and privileges which that instrument provides for and secures to citizens of the United States. On the contrary, they were at that time considered as a subordinate and inferior class of beings, who had been subjugated by the dominant race, and whether emancipated or not, yet remained subject to their authority, and had no rights or privileges but such as those who held the power and the government might choose to grant them. . . .

In discussing this question, we must not confound the rights of citizenship which a state may confer within its own limits, and the rights of citizenship as a member of the Union. It does not by any means follow, because he has all the rights and privileges of a citizen of a State, that he must be a citizen of the United States. He may have all of the rights and privileges of a State, and yet not be entitled to the rights and privileges of a citizen in any other State. For, previous to the adoption of the Constitution of the United States, every State had the undoubted right to confer on whomsoever it pleased the character of a citizen, and to endow him with all its rights. But this character, of course, was confined to the boundaries of the State, and gave him no rights or privileges in other States beyond those secured to him by the laws of nations and the comity

19 Howard 393 (1857).

of States. Nor have the several States surrendered the power of conferring these rights and privileges by adopting the Constitution of the United States. Each State may still confer them upon an alien, or any one it thinks proper, or upon any class or description of persons; yet he would not be a citizen in the sense in which that word is used in the Constitution of the United States, nor entitled to sue as such in one of its courts, nor to the privileges and immunities of a citizen in the other States. The rights which he would acquire would be restricted to the State which gave them. . . .

The question then arises, whether the provisions of the Constitution, in relation to the personal rights and privileges to which the citizen of a State should be entitled, embraced the negro African race, at that time in this country, or who might afterwards be imported, who had then or should afterwards be made free in any State; and to put it in the power of a single State to make him a citizen of the United States, and endue him with the full rights of citizenship in every other State without their consent. Does the Constitution of the United States act upon him whenever he shall be made free under the laws of a State, and raised there to the rank of a citizen, and immediately clothe him with all the privileges of a citizen in every other State, and in its own courts?

The court think the affirmative of these propositions cannot be maintained. And if it cannot, the plaintiff in error could not be a citizen of the State of Missouri, within the meaning of the Constitution of the United States, and, consequently, was not entitled to sue in its courts. . . .

It is difficult at this day to realize the state of public opinion in relation to that unfortunate race, which prevailed in the civilized and enlightened portions of the world at the time of the Declaration of Independence, and when the Constitution of the United States was framed and adopted. . . .

They had for more than a century before been regarded as beings of an inferior order; and altogether unfit to associate with the white race, either in social or political relations; and so far inferior that they had no rights which the white man was bound to respect; and that the negro might justly and lawfully be reduced to slavery for his benefit. . . . This opinion was at that time fixed and universal in the civilized portion of the white race. It was regarded as an axiom in morals as well as in politics, which no one thought of disputing, or supposed to be open to dispute; and men in every grade and position in society daily and habitually acted upon it in their private pursuits, as well as in matters of public concern, without doubting for a moment the correctness of this opinion. . . .

But there are two clauses in the Constitution which point directly and specifically to the negro race as a separate class of persons, and show clearly that they were not regarded as a portion of the people or citizens of the Government then formed.

One of these clauses reserves to each of the thirteen States the right to import slaves until the year 1808, if he thinks it proper. And the importation which it thus sanctions was unquestionably of persons of the race of which we are speaking, as the traffic in slaves in the United States had always been confined to them. And by the other provision the States pledge themselves to each other to maintain the right of property of the master, by delivering up to him any slave who may have escaped from his service, and be found within their respective territories. . . . And these two provisions show, conclusively, that neither the description of persons therein referred to, nor their descendants, were embraced in any of the other provisions of the Constitution; for certainly these two clauses were not intended to confer on them or their posterity the blessings of liberty, or any of the personal rights so carefully provided for the citizen. . . .

Indeed, when we look to the condition of this race in the several States at the time, it is impossible to believe that these rights and privileges were intended to be extended to them. . . .

The Act of Congress, upon which the plaintiff relies, declares that slavery and involuntary servitude, except as a punishment for crime, shall be forever prohibited in all that part of the territory ceded by France, under the name of Louisiana, which lies north of thirty-six degrees thirty minutes north latitude, and not included within the limits of Missouri. And the difficulty which meets us at the threshold of this part of the inquiry is, whether Congress was authorized to pass this law under any of the powers granted to it by the Constitution; for if the authority is not given by that instrument, it is the duty of this court to declare it void and inoperative, and incapable of conferring freedom upon any one who is held as a slave under the laws of any one of the States.

The counsel for the plaintiff has laid much stress upon that article in the Constitution which confers on Congress the power "to dispose of and make all needful rules and regulations respecting the territory or other property belonging to the United States," but, in the judgment of the court, that provision has no bearing on the present controversy, and the power there given, whatever it may be, is confined, and was intended to be confined, to the territory which at that time belonged to, or was claimed by, the United States, and was within their boundaries as settled by the treaty with Great Britain, and can have no influence upon a territory afterwards acquired from a foreign Government. It was a special provision for a known and particular territory, and to meet a present emergency, and nothing more. . . .

If this clause is construed to extend to territory acquired by the present Government from a foreign nation, outside of the limits of any charter from the British Government to a colony, it would be difficult to say, why it was deemed necessary to give the Government the power to sell any vacant lands belonging to the sovereignty which might be found within it; and if this was necessary, why the grant of this power should precede the power to legislate over it and establish a Government there; and still more difficult to say, why it was deemed necessary so specially and particularly to grant the power to make needful rules and regulations in relation to any personal or movable property it might acquire there. For the words, *other property* necessarily, by every known rule of interpretation, must mean property of a different description from territory or land. And the difficulty would perhaps be insurmountable in endeavoring to account for the last member of the sentence, which provides that "nothing in this Constitution shall be so construed as to prejudice any claims of the United States or any particular State," or to say how any particular State could have claims in or to a territory ceded by a foreign

Government, or to account for associating this provision with the preceding provisions of the clause, with which it would appear to have no connection. . . .

But the power of Congress over the person or property of a citizen can never be a mere discretionary power under our Constitution and form of Government. The powers of the Government and the rights and privileges of the Citizen are regulated and plainly defined by the Constitution itself. And when the Territory becomes a part of the United States, the Federal Government enters into possession in the character impressed upon it by those who created it. It enters upon it with its powers over the citizen strictly defined, and limited by the Constitution, from which it derives its own existence, and by virtue of which alone it continues to exist and act as a Government and sovereignty. It has no power of any kind beyond it; and it cannot, when it enters a Territory of the United States, put off its character, and assume discretionary or despotic powers which the Constitution has denied to it. It cannot create for itself a new character separated from the citizens of the United States, and the duties it owes them under the provisions of the Constitution. The Territory being a part of the United States, the Government and the citizen both enter it under the authority of the Constitution, with their respective rights defined and marked out; and the Federal Government can exercise no power over his person or property, beyond what that instrument confers, nor lawfully deny any right which it has reserved. . . .

The rights of private property have been guarded with equal care. Thus the rights of property are united with the rights of person, and placed on the same ground by the fifth amendment to the Constitution. . . . An Act of Congress which deprives a person of the United States of his liberty or property merely because he came himself or brought his property into a particular Territory of the United States, and who had committed no offense against the laws, could hardly be dignified with the name of due process of law. . . .

And this prohibition is not confined to the States, but the words are general, and extend to the whole territory over which the Constitution gives it power to legislate, including those portions of it remaining under territorial government, as well as that covered by States. It is a total absence of power everywhere within the dominion of the United States, and places the citizen of a territory, so far as these rights are concerned, on the same footing with citizens of the States, and guards them as firmly and plainly against any inroads which the general government might attempt, under the plea of implied or incidental powers. And if Congress itself cannot do this—if it is beyond the powers conferred on the Federal Government—it will be admitted, we presume, that it could not authorize a territorial government to exercise them. It could confer no power on any local government, established by its authority, to violate the provisions of the Constitution.

It seems, however, to be supposed, that there is a difference between property in a slave and other property, and that different rules may be applied to it in expounding the Constitution of the United States. And the laws and usages of nations, and the writings of eminent jurists upon the relation of master and slave and their mutual rights and duties, and the powers which governments may exercise over it, have been dwelt upon in the argument.

But . . . if the Constitution recognizes the right of property of the master in a slave, and makes no distinction between that description of property and other property owned by a citizen, no tribunal, acting under the authority of the United States, whether it be legislative, executive, or judicial, has a right to draw such a distinction, or deny to it the benefit of the provisions and guarantees which have been provided for the protection of private property against the encroachments of the Government.

Now . . . the right of property in a slave is distinctly and expressly affirmed in the Constitution. The right to traffic in it, like an ordinary article of merchandise and property, was guaranteed to the citizens of the United States, in every State that might desire it, for twenty years. And the Government in express terms is pledged to protect it in all future time, if the slave escapes from his owner. . . . And no word can be found in the Constitution which gives Congress a greater power over slave property, or which entitles property of that kind to less protection than property of any other description. The only power conferred is the power coupled with the duty of guarding and protecting the owner in his rights.

Upon these considerations, it is the opinion of the court that the Act of Congress which prohibited a citizen from holding and owning property of this kind in the territory of the United States north of the line therein mentioned, is not warranted by the Constitution, and is therefore void; and that neither Dred Scott himself, nor any of his family, were made free by being carried into this territory; even if they had been carried there by the owner, with the intention of becoming a permanent resident.

29. Liberty and Union
THE REPUBLICAN PARTY PLATFORM OF 1860

The great vehicle for antislavery politics was the Republican party. Founded in Ripon, Wisconsin, in 1854, the new party rapidly absorbed members of earlier, smaller antislavery organizations by pledging itself to oppose the further extension of slavery in the United States. In the election of 1856 the Republicans showed amazing strength: their candidate, John C. Frémont, won 1,339,932 popular and 114 electoral votes to Democratic candidate James Buchanan's 1,832,955 popular and 174 electoral votes. During the next four years the party broadened its appeal so as to attract industrialists and workers as well as farmers, professional people, and religious leaders who were opposed to slavery. It also developed able party leaders and made impressive gains at the state and congressional level.

The Republican party's 1860 platform not only upheld the Union and reiterated its stand against the extension of slavery but also contained a number of economic planks that would appeal to industrialists in the Northeast and farmers in the West. It favored a protective tariff, the building of a transcontinental railroad, and a homestead act giving free land to settlers. Adopted in Chicago in May 1860, the platform conformed closely to the views of such moderates as William H. Seward and Horace Greeley of New York, Benjamin F. Wade and Salmon P. Chase of Ohio, and its standard-bearer, Abraham Lincoln of Illinois. Only when leading abolitionists threatened to walk out of the convention did Republican leaders incorporate a reaffirmation of the Declaration of Independence into their platform. But though the Republicans took a moderate position in their platform, the victory of Lincoln in the 1860 election triggered secession and civil war.

Questions to consider. To what did the Republican platform refer when it announced that events of the past four years had established the necessity of organizing a new party? Do you agree with the statement that the principles of the Declaration of Independence are "essential to the preservation of our Republican institutions"? And with the assertion that "threats of Disunion" are equivalent to "an avowal of contemplated treason"? In denouncing "the lawless invasion by armed force of the soil of any State or Territory" what did the platform makers have in mind? What did the platform say about Kansas? About the *Dred Scott* decision (Document 28)? What dominated the platform: the slavery issue or economic issues? On balance, to whom was the platform supposed to appeal? With which planks would Alexander Hamilton (Document 14) have agreed? Why?

THE REPUBLICAN PARTY PLATFORM OF 1860

Resolved, That we, the delegated representatives of the Republican electors of the United States, in Convention assembled, in discharge of the duty we owe to our constituents and our country, unite in the following declarations:

1. That the history of the nation, during the last four years, has fully established the propriety and necessity of the organization and perpetuation of the Republican party, and that the causes which called it into existence are permanent in their nature, and now, more than ever before, demand its peaceful and constitutional triumph.

2. That the maintenance of the principles promulgated in the Declaration of Independence and embodied in the Federal Constitution, "That all men are created equal; that they are endowed by their Creator with certain inalienable rights; that among these are life, liberty and the pursuit of happiness; that, to secure these rights, governments are instituted among men, deriving their just powers from the consent of the governed," is essential to the preservation of our Republican institutions, and that the Federal Constitution, the Rights of the States, and the Union of the States, must and shall be preserved.

3. That to the Union of the States this nation owes its unprecedented increase in population, its surprising development of material resources, its rapid augmentation of wealth, its happiness at home and its honor abroad; and we hold in abhorrence all schemes for Disunion, come from whatever source they may; And we congratulate the country that no Republican member of Congress has uttered or countenanced the threats of Disunion so often made by Democratic members, without rebuke and with applause from their political associates; and we denounce those threats of Disunion, in case of a popular overthrow of their ascendancy, as denying the vital principles of a free government, and as an avowal of contemplated treason, which it is the imperative duty of an indignant People sternly to rebuke and forever silence.

4. That the maintenance inviolate of the rights of the States, and especially the right of each State to order and control its own domestic institutions according to its own judgment exclusively, is essential to that balance of powers on which the perfection and endurance of our political fabric depends; and we denounce the lawless invasion by armed force of the soil of any State or Territory, no matter under what pretext, as among the gravest of crimes.

5. That the present Democratic Administration has far exceeded our worst apprehensions, in its measureless subserviency to the exactions of a sectional interest, as especially evinced in its desperate exertions to force the infamous Lecompton constitution* upon the protesting people of Kansas; in construing the personal relation between master and servant to involve an unqualified property in persons; in its attempted enforcement, everywhere, on

---

From Francis Curtis, *The Republican Party* (2 v., G. P. Putnam's Sons, New York, 1904), I: 355-358.

* A proslavery constitution adopted by a proslavery legislature in 1857 and not submitted to a popular vote—Eds.

Republican nominating convention, May 1860. The Republicans, meeting in a huge boxlike structure called the Wigwam in Chicago, adopted a platform opposing the extension of slavery into the federal territories and favoring a protective tariff, the building of a transcontinental railroad, and a homestead act giving free land to settlers. The chief contenders for the nomination were New York Senator William H. Seward and former Illinois Congressman Abraham Lincoln. Seward had long been prominent in national affairs and was far better known than Lincoln, but he had made many political enemies and, although a moderate, had made statements from time to time that made him sound like an outright abolitionist. Lincoln, a newcomer to national politics, had no political enemies and, although he was strongly opposed to the expansion of slavery, he was not an abolitionist. (Library of Congress)

land and sea, through the intervention of Congress and of the Federal Courts of the extreme pretensions of a purely local interest; and in its general and unvarying abuse of the power intrusted to it by a confiding people.

7. That the new dogma that the Constitution, of its own force, carries Slavery into any or all of the Territories of the United States, is a dangerous political heresy, at variance with the explicit provisions of that instrument itself, with contemporaneous exposition, and with legislative and judicial precedent; is revolutionary in its tendency, and subversive of the peace and harmony of the country.

8. That the normal condition of all the territory of the United States is that of freedom; That as our Republican fathers, when they had abolished slavery in all our national territory, ordained that "no person should be deprived of life, liberty, or property, without due process of law," it becomes our duty, by legislation, whenever such legislation is necessary, to maintain this provision of the Constitution against all attempts to violate it; and we deny the authority of Congress, of a territorial legislature, or of any individuals, to give legal existence to Slavery in any Territory of the United States.

9. That we brand the recent re-opening of the African slave-trade, under the cover of our national flag, aided by perversions of judicial power, as a crime against humanity and a burning shame to our country and age; and we call upon Congress to take prompt and efficient measures for the total and final suppression of that execrable traffic.

10. That in the recent vetoes, by their Federal Governors, of the acts of the Legislatures of Kansas and Nebraska, prohibiting Slavery in those territories, we find a practical illustration of the boasted Democratic principle of Non-Intervention and Popular Sovereignty embodied in the Kansas-Nebraska bill, and a demonstration of the deception and fraud involved therein.

11. That Kansas should, of right, be immediately admitted as a State under the Constitution recently formed and adopted by her people, and accepted by the House of Representatives.

12. That, while providing revenue for the support of the General Government by duties upon imports, sound policy requires such an adjustment of these imposts as to encourage the development of the industrial interests of the whole country; and we commend that policy of national exchanges which secures to the working men liberal wages, to agriculture remunerating prices, to mechanics and manufacturers an adequate reward for their skill, labor and enterprise, and to the nation commercial prosperity and independence.

13. That we protest against any sale or alienation to others of the Public Lands held by actual settlers, and against any view of the Homestead policy which regards the settlers as paupers or supplicants for public bounty; and we demand the passage by Congress of the complete and satisfactory Homestead measure which has already passed the house.

14. That the Republican Party is opposed to any change in our Naturalization Laws or any State legislation by which the rights of our citizenship hitherto accorded to immigrants from foreign lands shall be abridged or impaired; and in favor of giving a full and efficient protection to the rights of all classes of citizens, whether native or naturalized, both at home and abroad.

15. That appropriations by Congress for River and Harbor improvements of a National character, required for the accommodation and security of an existing commerce, are authorized by the Constitution, and justified by the obligations of Government to protect the lives and property of its citizens.

16. That a Railroad to the Pacific Ocean is imperatively demanded by the interests of the whole country; that the Federal Government ought to render immediate and efficient aid in its construction; and that, as preliminary thereto, a daily Overland Mail should be promptly established. . . .

COUNTERPOINT
Education in the Shaping of the Nation

From its colonial beginnings, New England showed a keen interest in education: the Puritans of Massachusetts Bay enacted the first compulsory education laws in the colonies, the "common school revival" of the 1830s began in Massachusetts and Connecticut, and the colonists established some of the nation's most prestigious institutions of higher learning early in their history. Although the Puritans were concerned that one be able to read the Bible, New England educators later recognized also that schooling is power. Peter Hall has explored the implications of this realization by compiling data on the graduates of important New England colleges from college archives and classbooks.

Table 4.1 illustrates career choices at the most prestigious of the new nation's colleges. The figures reveal the consistently high attraction of law and also a marked shift toward business by mid-century. Can you list some of the social and economic changes that prompted the increasing interest in business? What traditional occupations declined as a consequence of these changes? Should Hall have included data on how medicine and the ministry fared during the period?

Table 4.2 indicates the location of colleges (excluding their own) where New England college graduates took positions before 1850. It also underscores their role in spreading higher education throughout the country. In doing so, what values do you suppose they disseminated? Would the most important of these have been cultural, occupational, or perhaps even organizational? Which region appears to have been most resistant to the educational influences of New England college graduates?

Table 4.3 shows the Union army service of New England collegians and demonstrates their high contribution to the crusade for the Union. Can you think of any reasons why these young men were so motivated? Do the tables suggest any?

Together, the tables suggest the vital role of the New England colleges in providing professional and commercial leaders, in exporting cultural values and institutions and thus establishing national (as opposed to regional) cultural standards, and in fighting to impose leadership and standards on the one great region that resisted them—the South. The implication is that the defense of a common culture bound the Western and Middle Atlantic states to New England in supporting the Union cause. Can you think of other shared interests that linked the regions together in the fight against slavery? How might a comparable study of Southern collegians during the period differ in its findings?

TABLE 4.1 Career Choices of Harvard and Yale Graduates, 1821-1870

Years of graduation	Law		Business	
	Harvard	Yale	Harvard	Yale
1821-1825	18%	32%	5%	8%
1826-1830	35	25	12	9
1831-1835	32	32	13	5
1836-1840	28	28	7	11
1841-1845	36	33	9	12
1846-1850	32	34	14	15
1851-1855	33	31	15	18
1856-1860	34	26	22	20
1861-1865	24	28	29	24
1866-1870	31	35	28	22

Source: Reprinted by permission of New York University Press from Peter Dobkin Hall, *The Organization of American Culture, 1700-1900: Private Institutions, Elites, and the Origins of American Nationality.* Copyright © 1982 by New York University.

TABLE 4.2 Location of College Professors and Administrators from New England Colleges Before 1850

College	New England	Middle States (N.Y., N.J., Pa., Md., Del., D.C.)	South (Va., N.C., Ga., Tenn., La., Ala., Tex.)	West	Total
Harvard	29	23	3	6	61
Yale	39	62	28	53	182
Dartmouth	28	21	12	37	98
Brown	14	15	4	12	45
Bowdoin	16	12	4	10	42
Williams	3	7	1	3	14
Amherst	3	2	2	11	18
Middlebury	3	14	19	35	68
Colby	1	3	2	3	9

Source: Reprinted by permission of New York University Press from Peter Dobkin Hall, *The Organization of American Culture, 1700-1900: Private Institutions, Elites, and the Origins of American Nationality.* Copyright © 1982 by New York University.

TABLE 4.3   Harvard, Yale, Dartmouth, and Brown Graduates, 1841-1861, Who Served in the Union Armies

Class year	Harvard	Yale	Dartmouth	Brown
1841	15%	4%	12%	32%
1842	6	6	10	—
1843	13	11	14	4
1844	13	14	12	5
1845	18	10	10	13
1846	14	7	10	14
1847	14	18	2	18
1848	15	12	9	8
1849	8	13	21	8
1850	15	15	14	14
1851	25	18	11	11
1852	26	28	15	18
1853	17	28	18	17
1854	21	22	17	16
1855	25	33	18	14
1856	29	25	19	13
1857	34	32	30	13
1858	35	35	30	28
1859	41	37	30	33
1860	44	49	32	34
1861	56	42	35	50

Source: From Bailey B. Burritt, *Professional Distribution of College and University Graduates* (Government Printing Office, Washington, D.C., 1912).

The surrender at Appomattox. General Robert E. Lee surrendering to General Ulysses S. Grant on April 9, 1865. (National Archives)

CHAPTER FIVE

Rebels, Yankees, and Freedmen

30. Flight from Union
MISSISSIPPI RESOLUTIONS ON SECESSION (1860)

The election of 1860 centered on slavery and the Union. The Republicans ran Abraham Lincoln for president on a platform opposing the further extension of slavery. The Democrats split over the issue. The Northern Democrats ran Illinois Senator Stephen A. Douglas on a platform calling for "popular sovereignty," that is, the right of people in the federal territories to decide for themselves whether they wanted slavery. The Southern Democrats ran Kentucky's John C. Breckinridge on a frankly proslavery platform demanding federal protection of slavery in the territories. A fourth party, the Constitutional Union party, which ran John Bell of Tennessee, tried to play down the slavery issue by emphasizing the preservation of the Union. This division of Lincoln's opponents made his victory an almost foregone conclusion. Though Lincoln did not win the majority of popular votes cast in the election, he won more popular votes than any of his three opponents and he also took the majority of electoral votes. But he received not one electoral vote in the South.

Even before Lincoln's election, Mississippi had contemplated withdrawing from the Union if the Republicans won. When Lincoln did win, Governor John J. Pettus issued a proclamation denouncing the "Black Republicans," held a conference with the state's congressional delegation, including Jefferson Davis, and recommended a state convention to take action on secession. Late in November 1860, the Mississippi legislature met in Jackson, received the governor's recommendation, and passed a bill providing for elections the following month for a convention to meet on January 7 "to consider the then existing relations between the government of the United States and the government and people of the State of Mississippi." It also passed a series of resolutions outlining the reasons for adopting secession as "the proper remedy" for the state's grievances.

On December 20, South Carolina seceded from the Union. Shortly afterward ten other states joined South Carolina in breaking away from the United States: Mississippi, Florida, Alabama, Georgia, Louisiana, Texas, Virginia, Arkansas, Tennessee, and North Carolina. In February 1861, delegates from the seceding states met in Montgomery, Alabama, to adopt a constitution for the Confederate States of America. They chose Mississippi's Jefferson Davis as president. On April 12, the Civil War began.

Questions to consider. The Mississippi resolutions contained a succinct summary of the outlook of Southern secessionists. To what extent did they depend on John C. Calhoun's "compact" theory of the Union? Were the resolutions correct in stating that the Northern states had "assumed a revolutionary position" toward the Southern states? Was the charge that the Northern states had violated the Constitution in their behavior toward the South valid? Was it accurate to say that Northerners sought an abolitionist amendment to the Constitution? To what "incendiary publications" do the resolutions refer? What "hostile invasion of a Southern State" did the drafters of the resolutions have in mind? The resolutions concluded by stating that the election of Lincoln meant that the North intended to use the powers of the federal government for the "overthrow of the Southern Section of this great Confederacy." How much truth was there in this belief? Do you see any similarities between the arguments advanced here and those appearing in the Declaration of Independence (Document 11)?

MISSISSIPPI RESOLUTIONS ON SECESSION (1860)

Whereas, The Constitutional Union was formed by the several States in their separate sovereign capacity for the purpose of mutual advantage and protection;

That the several States are distinct sovereignties, whose supremacy is limited so far only as the same has been delegated by voluntary compact to a Federal Government, and when it fails to accomplish the ends for which it was established, the parties to the compact have the right to resume, each State for itself, such delegated powers;

That the institution of slavery existed prior to the formation of the Federal Constitution, and is recognized by its letter, and all efforts to impair its value or lessen its duration by Congress, or any of the free States, is a violation of the compact of Union and is destructive of the ends for which it was ordained, but in defiance of the principles of the Union thus established, the people of the Northern States have assumed a revolutionary position towards the Southern States;

That they have set at defiance that provision of the Constitution which was intended to secure domestic tranquillity among the States and promote their general welfare, namely: "No person held to service or labor in one State, under the laws thereof, escaping into another, shall, in consequence of any law or regulation therein, be discharged from such service or labor, but shall be delivered up on claim of the party to whom such service or labor may be due;"

That they have by voluntary associations, individual agencies and State legislation interfered with slavery as it prevails in the slave-holding States;

That they have enticed our slaves from us, and by State intervention obstructed and prevented their rendition under the fugitive slave law;

That they continue their system of agitation obviously for the purpose of encouraging other slaves to escape from service, to weaken the institution in the slave-holding States by rendering the holding of such property insecure, and as a consequence its ultimate abolition certain;

Reprinted by permission of Louisiana State University Press from *Mississippi in the Confederacy,* edited by John K. Bettersworth, copyright ©1961, pp. 22-24.

Lincoln campaign poster. The election of 1860, the most fateful ever held in this country, was a four-cornered race. The Republicans ran Abraham Lincoln of Illinois and Hannibal Hamlin of Maine on a platform calling for the containment of slavery within the states where it already existed. The Republican campaign was a lively one, replete with songs, slogans, posters, torchlight parades, barbecues, picnics, and pole-raisings. The Republicans scoffed at warnings by Southerners that the South would leave the Union if Lincoln won. But Lincoln's victory in November was followed by secession and Civil War. (Library of Congress)

That they claim the right and demand its execution by Congress to exclude slavery from the Territories, but claim the right of protection for every species of property owned by themselves;

That they declare in every manner in which public opinion is expressed their unalterable determination to exclude from admittance into the Union any new State that tolerates slavery in its Constitution, and thereby force Congress to a condemnation of that species of property;

That they thus seek by an increase of abolition States "to acquire two-thirds of both houses" for the purpose of preparing an amendment to the Constitution of the United States, abolishing slavery in the States, and so continue the agitation that the proposed amendment shall be ratifed by the Legislatures of three-fourths of the States;

That they have in violation of the comity of all civilized nations, and in violation of the comity established by the Constitution of the United States, insulted and outraged our citizens when travelling among them for pleasure, health or business, by taking their servants and liberating the same, under the forms of State laws, and subjecting their owners to degrading and ignominious punishment;

That to encourage the stealing of our property they have put at defiance that provision of the Constitution which declares that fugitives from justice (escaping) into another State, on demand of the Executive authority of that State from which he fled, shall be delivered up;

That they have sought to create domestic discord in the Southern States by incendiary publications;

That they encouraged a hostile invasion of a Southern State to excite insurrection, murder and rapine;

That they have deprived Southern citizens of their property and continue an unfriendly agitation of their domestic institutions, claiming for themselves perfect immunity from external interference with their domestic policy. . . .

That they have elected a majority of Electors for President and Vice-President on the ground that there exists an irreconcilable conflict between the two sections of the Confederacy in reference to their respective systems of labor and in pursuance of their hostility to us and our institutions, thus declaring to the civilized world that the powers of this Government are to be used for the dishonor and overthrow of the Southern Section of this great Confederacy. Therefore,

Be it resolved by the Legislature of the State of Mississippi, That in the opinion of those who now constitute the said Legislature, the secession of each aggrieved State is the proper remedy for these injuries.

31. A Declaration of Freedom
Abraham Lincoln,
THE EMANCIPATION PROCLAMATION (1863)

From the outset, the abolitionists urged Abraham Lincoln to make freeing the slaves the major objective of the war. But Lincoln declared: "My paramount object in this struggle is to save the Union." The Republican platform had promised to check the extension of slavery, but it also pledged not to interfere with slavery where it legally existed. Four border slave states—Maryland, Kentucky, Missouri, and Delaware—had remained in the Union, and Lincoln was afraid that an abolitionist policy would drive them into the Confederacy, with disastrous results for the Union cause. He was not convinced at first, moreover, that the majority of Northerners favored abolition.

As the Civil War progressed, Northern public opinion moved slowly in the direction of emancipation. At the same time it was becoming clear that a Union victory would mean the end of slavery. Whenever Union troops occupied any part of the Confederacy, the slaves promptly left the plantations and became camp followers of the Northern armies. Union generals began asking what policy to adopt toward slavery in the occupied parts of the South. In addition, the European public was becoming critical of the North for its failure to emancipate the blacks. Lincoln finally decided that the time had come to take action.

At a secret cabinet meeting on July 22, 1862, Lincoln presented a proclamation abolishing slavery, on which he had been working nearly a month. Secretary of State William H. Seward urged him not to issue it until after a Union victory. Then, on September 17, came the battle of Antietam, at which the Union armies of General George B. McClellan halted the advance of General Robert E. Lee's troops. On September 22, Lincoln officially proclaimed emancipation. In his capacity as commander in chief he announced that, "on the first day of January, A.D. 1863, all persons held as slaves within any state or designated part of a state the people whereof shall then be in rebellion against the United States shall be then, thenceforward and forever free."

The Emancipation Proclamation did not immediately end slavery. It did not apply to the border states because they were not in rebellion. Nor did it apply to those parts of the Confederacy then held by Union troops. Nevertheless, in all Confederate territories subsequently occupied by Northern troops, the slaves became free by the terms of Lincoln's proclamation. Furthermore, the proclamation led to the voluntary freeing of slaves in many places where it did not apply; Missouri and Maryland freed their slaves in 1863 and 1864. But it was the Thirteenth Amendment that ended slavery everywhere in the United States for all time. Introduced in

Congress in December 1863 and adopted with Lincoln's energetic support in January 1865, it became part of the Constitution the following December when the necessary three-fourths of the states had ratified it.

Born to poverty in Kentucky in 1809, Abraham Lincoln grew up in Indiana and Illinois. As a young man he worked as a farmer, rail-splitter, boatsman, and storekeeper before turning to law and politics. He became enormously successful as a lawyer and served several years in the Illinois legislature and one term in the House of Representatives. Lincoln was largely self-educated; he read and reread such books as the Bible, Aesop's *Fables,* the works of Shakespeare, and the poems of Robert Burns and developed great skill as a writer. In 1858 his debates with Stephen Douglas over slavery brought him national prominence and helped win him the Republican nomination for president in 1860. During the Civil War he made restoration of the Union his primary objective, but he also made it clear it must be a Union without slavery. On April 14, while attending a performance at Ford's Theatre in Washington, he was shot by actor John Wilkes Booth, a Confederate sympathizer. He died the next morning, and the nation was plunged into grief.

Questions to consider. The Emancipation Proclamation has been called as prosaic as a bill of lading. Do you think this is a fair appraisal? Do you think a statement more like the preamble to the Declaration of Independence would have been better? Why do you think Lincoln, a great prose master, avoided exalted language in writing the proclamation? On what constitutional powers as president did he depend in announcing his policy? In what ways does the proclamation demonstrate that Lincoln was a practical man? Reactions to the proclamation were varied. The London *Spectator* made fun of it. "The principle," sneered the editor, "is not that a human being cannot justly own another, but that he cannot own him unless he is loyal to the United States." Was the editor's comment justified? Not everyone agreed with the *Spectator.* Many abolitionists and most Southern blacks hailed the proclamation as a giant step on the road to freedom. To what extent were they correct? Did Lincoln deserve his reputation as the Great Emancipator?

THE EMANCIPATION PROCLAMATION (1863)

Whereas on the 22d day of September, A.D. 1862, a proclamation was issued by the President of the United States, containing among other things, the following, to wit:

"That on the 1st day of January, A.D. 1863, all persons held as slaves within any State or designated part of a State the people whereof shall then be

From John Nicolay and John Hay, eds., *Complete Works of Abraham Lincoln* (12 v., Lincoln Memorial University, n.p., 1894), VIII: 161-164.

The effects of the Emancipation Proclamation. Lincoln's grant of freedom on January 1, 1863, to slaves in the states then in rebellion against the United States was a momentous event. In the South it was denounced as the work of a fiend, and even in the North many people criticized it as an unconstitutional exercise of the presidential power. But antislavery Northerners hailed it as an important step toward emancipation of all the slaves, and some wished it had gone even further. Lincoln agreed with Secretary of State William Seward's estimate that about 200,000 slaves gained their freedom under the Proclamation. Thousands flocked to Union camps or joined federal armies as they marched southward, and it soon became necessary for the army to take measures to provide for their livelihood. For the majority of slaves, freedom came only with the defeat of the Confederacy and the end of the war. (Library of Congress)

in rebellion against the United States shall be then, thenceforward, and forever free; and the executive government of the United States, including the military and naval authority thereof, will recognize and maintain the freedom of such persons and will do no act or acts to repress such persons, or any of them, in any efforts they may make for their actual freedom.

"That the executive will on the 1st day of January aforesaid, by proclamation, designate the States and parts of States, if any, in which the people thereof, respectively, shall then be in rebellion against the United States; and the fact that any State or the people thereof shall on that day be in good faith represented in the Congress of the United States by members chosen thereto at elections wherein a majority of the qualified voters of such States shall have participated shall, in the absence of strong countervailing testimony, be deemed conclusive evidence that such State and the people thereof are not then in rebellion against the United States."

Now, therefore, I, Abraham Lincoln, President of the United States, by virtue of the power in me vested as Commander-in-Chief of the Army and Navy of the United States in time of actual armed rebellion against the authority and government of the United States, and as a fit and necessary war measure for suppressing said rebellion, do, on this 1st day of January, A.D. 1863, and in accordance with my purpose so to do, publicly proclaimed for the full period of one hundred days from the first day above mentioned, order and designate as the States and parts of States wherein the people thereof, respectively, are this day in rebellion against the United States the following, to wit:

Arkansas, Texas, Louisiana (except the parishes of St. Bernard, Plaquemines, Jefferson, St. John, St. Charles, St. James, Ascension, Assumption, Terrebonne, Lafourche, St. Mary, St. Martin, and Orleans, including the city of New Orleans), Mississippi, Alabama, Florida, Georgia, South Carolina, North Carolina, and Virginia (except the forty-eight counties designated as West Virginia, and also the counties of Berkeley, Accomac, Northhampton, Elizabeth City, York, Princess Anne, and Norfolk, including the cities of Norfolk and Portsmouth), and which excepted parts are for the present left precisely as if this proclamation were not issued.

And by virtue of the power and for the purpose aforesaid, I do order and declare that all persons held as slaves within said designated States and parts of States are, and henceforward shall be, free; and that the Executive Government of the United States, including the military and naval authorities thereof, will recognize and maintain the freedom of said persons.

And I hereby enjoin upon the people so declared to be free to abstain from all violence, unless in necessary self-defense; and I recommend to them that, in all cases when allowed, they labor faithfully for reasonable wages.

And I further declare and make known that such persons of suitable condition will be received into the armed service of the United States to garrison forts, positions, stations, and other places, and to man vessels of all sorts in said service.

And upon this act, sincerely believed to be an act of justice, warranted by the Constitution upon military necessity, I invoke the considerate judgment of mankind and the gracious favor of Almighty God.

32. People's Government
Abraham Lincoln,
THE GETTYSBURG ADDRESS (1863)

Late in June 1863, General Robert E. Lee crossed the Potomac River and moved his Confederate army rapidly through Maryland into Pennsylvania. On July 1 his troops met the Union army, commanded by General George G. Meade, at Gettysburg, Pennsylvania. After three days of fierce fighting, with thousands of casualties, Lee's greatly weakened army began to retreat. Lincoln was disappointed that Lee's army was able to escape, but he realized that the Confederates had suffered a decisive defeat. "I am very grateful to Meade," he said, "for the great service he did at Gettysburg." The Gettysburg battle marked the peak of the Confederate effort. Never again were the Confederates able to invade the North, and they never came close to winning the war after that time.

Four months after the bloody encounter—on November 19, 1863—when a national cemetery was dedicated on the Gettysburg battlefield, Lincoln delivered perhaps his most famous address. Edward Everett, famed for his oratory, spoke first, talking for almost two hours. Lincoln's address lasted only a couple of minutes. Afterward, it is said, Everett took Lincoln's hand and told him, "My speech will soon be forgotten; yours never will be. How gladly I would exchange my hundred pages for your twenty lines!" Everett was right. His own speech was soon forgotten, while Lincoln's brief address came to be regarded as one of the most powerful statements of the democratic outlook ever made.

Questions to consider. Why was Everett so impressed with Lincoln's address? Lincoln once said that his basic political ideas came from the Declaration of Independence. Do you think this influence appears in the Gettysburg Address? What in Lincoln's opinion was the basic meaning of the Civil War? To what extent was style, as well as substance, important in the address Lincoln wrote for the Gettysburg dedication?

Lincoln's inauguration. More than 10,000 people gathered to hear Abraham Lincoln's inaugural address on March 4, 1861, and many of them clapped and cheered when he took his place on the platform in front of the Capitol building. Lincoln put his cane in a corner of the platform but didn't seem to know what to do with his hat. Illinois Senator Stephen A. Douglas, his old political foe, reached out his hand, took it, and held it during the half-hour inaugural ceremony. (National Archives)

THE GETTYSBURG ADDRESS (1863)

Fourscore and seven years ago our fathers brought forth on this continent a new nation, conceived in liberty, and dedicated to the proposition that all men are created equal.

Now we are engaged in a great civil war, testing whether that nation, or any nation so conceived and so dedicated, can long endure. We are met on a great battle-field of that war. We have come to dedicate a portion of that field as a final resting-place for those who here gave their lives that that nation might live. It is altogether fitting and proper that we should do this.

But, in a larger sense, we cannot dedicate—we cannot consecrate—we cannot hallow—this ground. The brave men, living and dead, who struggled here, have consecrated it far above our poor power to add or detract. The world will little note nor long remember what we say here, but it can never forget what they did here. It is for us, the living, rather, to be dedicated here to the unfinished work which they who fought here have thus far so nobly advanced. It is rather for us to be here dedicated to the great task remaining before us—that from these honored dead we take increased devotion to that cause for which they gave the last full measure of devotion; that we here highly resolve that these dead shall not have died in vain; that this nation, under God, shall have a new birth of freedom; and that government of the people, by the people, for the people, shall not perish from the earth.

From John Nicolay and John Hay, eds., *Complete Works of Abraham Lincoln* (12 v., Lincoln Memorial University, n.p., 1894), IX: 209-210.

33. Binding Wounds
Abraham Lincoln,
SECOND INAUGURAL ADDRESS (1865)

In June 1864, when the Republicans nominated Abraham Lincoln for a second term, the end of the war seemed as far away as ever. Northerners were shocked at the heavy casualties reported from battlefields in Virginia, and criticism of the administration had become so harsh that in mid-August Lincoln was convinced he would not be re-elected. The Radical Republicans, who spoke for the antislavery faction of the party, condemned him as "politically, militarily, and financially a failure" and for a time backed John C. Frémont for the presidency. The Northern Democrats nominated General George B. McClellan, a former federal commander, and adopted a platform calling for the immediate cessation of hostilities and the restoration of the Union by a negotiated peace. Lincoln was so sure McClellan would beat him that he wrote a secret memorandum explaining how he would co-operate with the new president after the election in order to save the Union.

But a series of federal victories—the closing of Mobile Bay, the capture of Atlanta, and the routing of Southern forces in the Shenandoah Valley—led public opinion to swing back rapidly to Lincoln: Republican newspapers began ridiculing the "war-is-a-failure" platform of the Democrats, and Frémont decided to drop out of the campaign. Lincoln's prediction that he would not be re-elected proved wrong. On election day he won a plurality of nearly half a million votes and carried every state in the Union except Kentucky, Delaware, and New Jersey.

In his second inaugural address on March 4, 1865, Lincoln singled out slavery as the cause of the Civil War and stated that its eradication was inevitable. He expressed hope for a speedy end to the conflict, called for "malice toward none" and "charity for all," and looked forward to the day when Americans would achieve a "just and lasting peace" among themselves and with all nations. On April 9, Lee surrendered to Grant at Appomattox; two days later Lincoln made his last public address, outlining his reconstruction policy. He had never considered the South to be outside of the Union and hoped for a speedy reconciliation. On April 14, at his last cabinet meeting, he urged the cabinet members to put aside all thoughts of hatred and revenge. That evening he was shot.

Questions to consider. Lincoln's second inaugural address is commonly regarded as one of the greatest addresses ever made by an American president. Why do you think this is so? Why might his second inaugural address have been shorter than the first? What did he regard as the basic issue of the Civil War? What irony did he see in the attitude of the contestants? What use of the Bible did he make? Do you think this was likely to appeal to Americans in 1865? Did the second inaugural address represent an advance in Lincoln's thinking about slavery since 1861?

SECOND INAUGURAL ADDRESS (1865)

FELLOW-COUNTRYMEN: —At this second appearing to take the oath of the presidential office there is less occasion for an extended address than there was at the first. Then a statement somewhat in detail of a course to be pursued seemed fitting and proper. Now, at the expiration of four years, during which public declarations have been constantly called forth on every point and phase of the great contest which still absorbs the attention and engrosses the energies of the nation, little that is new could be presented. The progress of our arms, upon which all else chiefly depends, is as well known to the public as to myself, and it is, I trust, reasonably satisfactory and encouraging to all. With high hope for the future, no prediction in regard to it is ventured.

On the occasion corresponding to this four years ago all thoughts were anxiously directed to an impending civil war. All dreaded it, all sought to avert it. While the inaugural address was being delivered from this place, devoted altogether to *saving* the Union without war, insurgent agents were in the city seeking to *destroy* it without war—seeking to dissolve the Union and divide effects by negotiation. Both parties deprecated war, but one of them would *make* war rather than let the nation survive, and the other would *accept* war rather than let it perish, and the war came.

One eighth of the whole population was colored slaves, not distributed generally over the Union, but localized in the southern part of it. These slaves constituted a peculiar and powerful interest. All knew that this interest was somehow the cause of the war. To strengthen, perpetuate, and extend this interest was the object for which the insurgents would rend the Union even by war, while the Government claimed no right to do more than to restrict the territorial enlargement of it. Neither party expected for the war the magnitude nor the duration which it has already attained. Neither anticipated that the *cause* of the conflict might cease with or even before the conflict itself should cease. Each looked for an easier triumph, and a result less fundamental and astounding. Both read the same Bible and pray to the same God, and each invokes His aid against the other. It may seem strange that any men should dare to ask a just God's assistance in wringing their bread from the sweat of other men's faces, but let us judge not, that we be not judged. The prayers of both could not be answered. That of neither has been answered fully. The Almighty has His own purposes. "Woe unto the world because of offenses; for it must needs be that offenses come, but woe to that man by whom the offense

From James D. Richardson, ed., *A Compilation of the Messages and Papers of the Presidents* (Government Printing Office, Washington, D.C., 1897-1907), II: 576-591.

cometh." If we shall suppose that American slavery is one of those offenses which, in the providence of God, must needs come, but which, having continued through His appointed time, He now wills to remove, and that He gives to both North and South this terrible war as the woe due to those by whom the offense came, shall we discern therein any departure from those divine attributes which the believers in a living God always ascribe to Him? Fondly do we hope, fervently do we pray, that this mighty scourge of war may speedily pass away. Yet, if God wills that it continue until all the wealth piled by the bondsman's two hundred and fifty years of unrequited toil shall be sunk, and until every drop of blood drawn with the lash shall be paid by another drawn with the sword, as was said three thousand years ago, so still it must be said, "The judgments of the Lord are true and righteous altogether."

With malice toward none, with charity for all, with firmness in the right as God gives us to see the right, let us strive on to finish the work we are in, to bind up the nation's wounds, to care for him who shall have borne the battle and for his widow and his orphan, to do all which may achieve and cherish a just and lasting peace among ourselves and with all nations.

34. Literacy for the Lowly
CONGRESSIONAL REPORT ON
THE FREEDMEN'S BUREAU (1868)

The Thirteenth Amendment, which became part of the Constitution in 1865, freed about four million former slaves in the South. But with freedom came uncertainty, insecurity, and perplexity. Unlike the peasants of France and Russia, who retained the land on which they had been working when they were freed from serfdom, the former American slaves were cast adrift at the end of the Civil War with no means of livelihood. They found themselves without property, legal rights, education, training, and any experience as independent farmers or laborers. Thousands began roaming the countryside looking for work and ways to survive. The first year of freedom meant hunger, disease, suffering, and death for many blacks. Thousands died of disease and starvation during 1865 and 1866.

The freedmen did receive some assistance from the federal government after the war. In March 1865, Congress established the Bureau of Refugees, Freedmen, and Abandoned Lands (commonly called the Freedmen's Bureau) to provide them with food, clothing, shelter, and medical aid. Under the direction of General Oliver O. Howard (the "Christian General"), the Freedmen's Bureau also established schools and colleges for young blacks, founded savings banks, set up courts to protect their civil rights, and tried to get them jobs and fair contracts of employment. During its seven years of existence (1865-1872), the bureau spent more than fifteen million dollars for food and other aid and over six million dollars on schools and educational work and gave medical attention to nearly half a million patients. Bureau agents also registered black voters and encouraged political participation. There is no doubt that the bureau did much to help Southern blacks during the Reconstruction period. When Reconstruction came to an end, however, the hostility of Southern whites and the growing indifference of whites in the North negated most of the bureau's work. Its permanent legacy became schools and colleges (like Hampton Institute, Fisk University, and Howard University) and the aspiration for full citizenship by former slaves.

Questions to consider. In February 1866 President Andrew Johnson vetoed a bill expanding the powers of the Freedmen's Bureau. Although Congress overrode his veto he continued to regard the bill as unconstitutional. He was especially critical of the authority it gave bureau agents to conduct courts to safeguard the freedmen's rights; he said it involved "military jurisdiction" in time of peace. Was there any merit in his opinion? According to the congressional report appearing below, how involved was the army in education for Southern blacks? What did the Freedmen's

Bureau accomplish in the field of education? From what sources did the bureau draw teachers and funds? How did J. W. Alvord explain the great "desire of the freedmen for knowledge"? What was the reaction of Southern whites to efforts to educate the former slaves? How would Benjamin Franklin (Document 10) have viewed the work of the bureau? Jefferson (Documents 11 and 16)? Calhoun (Document 19)? Lincoln (Documents 31-33)?

CONGRESSIONAL REPORT ON THE FREEDMEN'S BUREAU (1868)

When our armies entered the South two facts became apparent: first, a surprising thirst for knowledge among the negroes; second, a large volunteer force of teachers for their instruction.

Without delay schools were successfully established and the earliest efforts to impart knowledge found the freedmen ready for its reception. Teachers of character and culture were ready from the first. To some extent the army had carried its own instructors. Negro servants of officers studied at the camp-fires of fellow servants. Chaplains of colored troops became instructors. In the campaigns of 1864 and 1865 the Christian Commission employed 50 teachers in colored camps and regiments.

At the close of the war it is believed that 20,000 colored soldiers could read intelligently, and a much larger number were learning their first lessons.

Really wonderful results had been accomplished through the disinterested efforts of benevolent associations working in connection with the government. But arrangements were soon made to give, on a larger scale, systematic and impartial aid to all of them. This consisted in turning over for school use temporary government buildings no longer needed for military purposes, and buildings seized from disloyal owners; also transportation for teachers, books, and school furniture, with quarters and rations for teachers and superintendants when on duty.

Schools were taken in charge by the Bureau, and in some States carried on wholly (in connection with local efforts) by use of the "refugees and freemen's fund." Teachers came under the general direction of the assistant commissioners, and protection through the department commanders was given to all engaged in the work.

Superintendants of schools for each State were appointed July 12, 1865, whose duty it was "to work as much as possible in connection with State officers who may have had school matters in charge, and to take cognizance of all that was being done to educate refugees and freedmen, secure protection to schools and teachers, promote method and efficiency, and to correspond with the benevolent agencies which were supplying his field."

From *Report of the Joint Committee on Reconstruction*, 1st Session, 40th Congress (Government Printing Office, Washington, D.C., 1868), 369-388.

The total number of pupils January 1, 1866, in all the colored schools, as near as could be ascertained, was 90,589; teachers, 1,314; schools, 740.

Whenever our troops broke through the lines of the enemy, schools followed. At Hampton, Beaufort, North Carolina, Roanoke Island, and New Orleans, they were soon in operation. A very efficient system was instituted for Louisiana in the early part of 1864, by Major General Banks, then in command of that State. It was supported by a military tax upon the whole population. Schools were opened in Savannah, Georgia, on the entrance of General Sherman, in December, 1864, and 500 pupils were at once enrolled. Ten intelligent colored persons were the first teachers, and nearly $81,000 were immediately contributed by the negroes for their support. This work was organized by the Secretary of the American Tract Society, Boston. Two of the largest of these schools were in "Bryan's slave mart," where platforms occupied a few days before with bondmen for sale became crowded with children learning to read.

At the end of the school year, July 1, 1866, it was found that while complete organization had not been reached, the schools in nearly all the States were steadily gaining in numbers, attainment, and general influence.

The official reports of superintendants gave 975 schools, 1,405 teachers, and 90,778 pupils. But these figures were not a true exhibit of the actual increase. They did not include many schools which failed to report. It was estimated that in all the different methods of teaching there had been, during the preceding six months, 150,000 freedmen and their children earnestly and successfully occupied in study.

Some change of sentiment had, at this time, been observed among the better classes of the South; those of higher intelligence acknowledging that education must become universal. Still, multitudes bitterly opposed the schools. Teachers were proscribed and ill-treated; school-houses were burned; many schools could not be opened, and others, after a brief struggle, had to be closed. Nevertheless, the country began to feel the moral power of this movement. Commendations came from foreign lands, and the universal demand of good men was that the work should go on.

As showing the desire for education among the freedmen, we give the following facts: When the collection of the general tax for colored schools was suspended in Louisiana by military order, the consternation of the colored population was intense. Petitions began to pour in. I saw one from the plantations across the river, at least thirty feet in length, representing ten thousand negroes. It was affecting to examine it, and note the names and marks [X] of such a long list of parents, ignorant themselves, but begging that their children might be educated, promising that from beneath their present burdens, and out of their extreme poverty, they would pay for it.

In September, 1865, J. W. Alvord, the present general superintendant, was appointed "Inspector of Schools." He traveled through nearly all the States lately in insurrection, and made the first general report to the Bureau on the subject of education, January 1, 1866.

Extracts from this report give the condition of the freedmen throughout the whole South. He says, "The desire of the freedmen for knowledge has not been overstated. This comes from several causes.

"1. The natural thirst for knowledge common to all men.
"2. They have seen power and influence among white people always coupled with *learning;* it is the sign of that elevation to which they now aspire.
"3. Its mysteries, hitherto hidden from them in written literature, excite to the special study of *books.*
"4. Their freedom has given wonderful stimulus to *all effort,* indicating a vitality which augurs well for their whole future condition and character.
"5. But, especially, the practical business of life now upon their hands shows their immediate need of education.

"This they all feel and acknowledge; hence their unusual welcome of and attendance upon schools is confined to no one class or age. Those advanced in life throw up their hands at first in despair, but a little encouragement places *even these* as pupils at the alphabet.

"Such as are in middle life, the laboring classes, gladly avail themselves of evening and Sabbath-schools. They may be often seen during the intervals of toil, when off duty as servants, on steamboats, along the railroads, and when unemployed in the streets in the city, or on plantations, with some fragment of a spelling-book in their hands, earnestly at study.

"Regiments of colored soldiers have nearly all made improvement in learning. In some of them, where but few knew their letters at first, nearly every man can now read, and many of them write. In other regiments one-half or two-thirds can do this.

"Even in hospitals I discovered very commendable efforts at such elementary instruction.

"But the great movement is among *children of the usual school age.* Their parents, if at all intelligent, encourage them to study. Your officers add their influence, and it is a fact, not always true of children, that among those recently from bondage, the school-house, however rough and uncomfortable, is of all places the most attractive. A very common punishment for misdemeanor is the threat of being *kept at home for a day.* The threat, in most cases, is sufficient."

The report goes on to say, "Much opposition has been encountered from those who do not believe in the elevation of the negro. A multitude of facts might be given. It is the testimony of all superintendants that if military power should be withdrawn, our schools would cease to exist.

"This opposition is sometimes ludicrous as well as inhuman. A member of the legislature, in session while I was at New Orleans, was passing one of the schools with me, having at the time its recess, the grounds about the building being filled with children. He stopped and looked intently, then earnestly inquired 'Is this a school?' 'Yes,' I replied. *'What! of niggers?'* 'These are colored children, evidently,' I answered. 'Well! Well!' said he, and raising his hands, 'I have seen many an absurdity in my lifetime, but *this is the climax of absurdities!'* I am sure he did not speak from effect, but as he felt. He left me abruptly, and turned the next corner to take his seat with legislators similarly prejudiced."

The act of July 16, 1866, enlarged the powers of the Bureau in regard to education. It sanctioned co-operation with private benevolent associations, and with agents and teachers accredited by them. It directed the Commissioner

Issuing rations to the old and sick at the Freedmen's Bureau.
The Freedmen's Bureau, created by Congress in March 1865
to help the former slaves adjust to freedom, provided
emergency food and shelter at first. Later on it helped the
freedmen obtain work, conducted military courts to hear
complaints, established schools at both the elementary and
college level, and registered black voters. By 1872, when the
Bureau was abolished, it had spent more than $15 million
in aiding the freedmen and had established many schools
and colleges for educating blacks. (Library of Congress)

to "hire or provide, by lease, buildings for purposes of education whenever teachers and means of instruction, without cost to the government, should be provided." And, also, that he should "furnish such protection as might be required for the safe conduct of such schools."

The schools, on the passage of this act, assumed in all respects a more enlarged and permanent character. Schools in the cities and larger towns began to be graded. Normal or high schools were planned, and a few came into existence. The earliest of these were at Norfolk, Charleston, New Orleans and Nashville.

Industrial schools for girls, in which sewing, knitting, straw-braiding, etc., were taught, were encouraged. School buildings, by rent or construction, were largely provided, and new stimulus was given to every department.

The freedmen, in view of new civil rights, and what the Bureau had undertaken for them, had gained an advanced standing, with increasing self-respect and confidence that a vastly improved condition was within their reach.

Up to this time it had been questioned, whether colored children could advance rapidly into the higher branches, but it was found that 23,727 pupils were in writing, 12,970 in geography, 31,692 in arithmetic, and 1,573 in higher branches; and that out of 1,430 teachers of the day and night schools, 458 were colored persons.

The January report stated that "the actual results reached since these schools commenced, both in numbers and in advancement, were surprising." At the end of the school year, July 1, 1867, it could be said, "We look back with astonishment at the amount accomplished. Such progress as is seen under auspices admitted to be unfavorable; the permanency of the schools, scarcely one failing when once commenced; the rapid increase of general intelligence among the whole colored population, are matters of constant remark by every observer. Thus far this educational effort, considered as a whole, has been eminently successful. The country and the world are surprised to behold a depressed race, so lately and so long in bondage, springing to their feet and entering the lists in hopeful competition with every rival."

Reports from all the States show that there are 1,839 day and night schools, 2,087 teachers, and 111,442 pupils. By adding industrial schools, and those "within the knowledge of the superintendant," the number will be 2,207 schools, 2,442 teachers, and 130,735 pupils.

Sabbath-schools also show much larger numbers during the past year, the figures being 1,126 schools and 80,647 pupils; and if we add those "not regularly reported," the whole number of Sabbath-schools will be 1,468, with 105,786 pupils; totals, schools of all kinds, as reported, 3,695; pupils, 238,342. Of these schools, 1,086 are sustained wholly or in part by the freedmen, and 391 of the buildings in which these schools are held are owned by themselves; 699 of the teachers in the day and night schools are colored and 1,388 white; 28,068 colored pupils have paid tuition, the average amount per month being $12,720.96, or a fraction over 45 cents per scholar. Only 8,743 pupils were free before the war.

As showing the progress of the schools, it will be observed that 42,879 pupils are now in writing, 23,957 in geography, 40,454 in arithmetic, and 4,661 in higher branches. Twenty-one normal or high schools are in operation, with 1,821 pupils, the schools having doubled in number during the last year with three times the number of pupils. Of these schools not many are far advanced, but they are intended to be what their name implies.

There are now 35 industrial schools, giving instruction to 2,124 pupils in the various kinds of female labor, not including 4,185 in the day schools, who are taught needle-work. The average daily attendance in all the above schools has been nearly 75 per cent of the enrollment.

There are now connected with these schools 44 children's temperance societies, called the "Vanguard of Freedom," having, in the aggregate, 3,000 members. These societies are constantly increasing, and doing much to train children in correct moral habits.

Education in thrift and economy is effected through the influence of the "Freedmen's Savings and Trust Company," chartered by Congress, and placed under the protection of this Bureau. Twenty branches of this institution, located in as many of the central cities and larger towns of the Southern States, are now in operation. Six of these banks have, at this time (January 1, 1868), on deposit an average of over $50,000 each, the whole amount now due depositors at all the branches being $585,770.17. Four times this amount has been deposited and drawn out for use in important purchases, homesteads etc. Both the business and the influence of the banks are rapidly increasing. Multitudes of these people never before had the first idea of saving for future use. Their former industry was only a hard, profitless task, but under the instructions of the cashiers the value of money is learned, and they are stimulated to earn it.

35. The Great Retreat
Rutherford B. Hayes,
FIRST ANNUAL MESSAGE TO CONGRESS (1877)

During the election of 1876 both parties resorted to fraud. Two sets of electoral returns came in from Southern states still occupied by federal troops, and it was necessary for Congress to set up an electoral commission to decide whether Rutherford B. Hayes, the Republican candidate, or Samuel J. Tilden, the Democratic standard-bearer, had won. Seven commission members were Republicans and seven were Democrats. The fifteenth member was to have been an independent, but as it turned out, he voted with the Republicans. By a strict party vote of 8 to 7, the commission awarded all 20 of the disputed electoral votes to the Republicans, and Hayes became president with 185 votes to Tilden's 184. Most Democrats felt they had been cheated out of victory; some of them even talked of rejecting the commission's decision and trying to block Hayes's inauguration. Had they done so, the quarrel over the election would have continued far beyond Inauguration Day, with grave consequences for the nation.

In the end, Southern Democrats reached a compromise with Northern Republicans. At a series of secret meetings between party leaders the Southern Democrats agreed to accept the electoral commission's decision. In return, the Republicans promised that Hayes would withdraw the remaining federal troops from the South, appoint at least one Southerner to his cabinet, and see to it that the South received federal aid to promote industrialization. The Compromise of 1877 brought the crisis to an end, and Hayes became the new president. After his inauguration in March 1877, Hayes took prompt action to fulfil the promises made to the Southern Democrats: he appointed a Tennessee Democrat to his cabinet, he withdrew the last of the federal soldiers from the South, and he began supporting federal-aid bills to benefit the South. The withdrawal of federal troops from Louisiana and South Carolina in April 1877 led to the demise of Republican governments in the South and the end of Reconstruction.

In his first annual message to Congress in December 1877, Hayes recalled the 1876 crisis and expressed satisfaction that it had been peacefully resolved. He also reminded Congress of the plea he had made at his inauguration that love of country would mute the racial and sectional tensions agitating the nation. He went on to mention his efforts to reduce antagonisms between North and South and ventured the opinion that they had had "beneficent results." He was especially pleased with the consequences of ending military reconstruction. Returning the Southern states to local self-government had ended political turmoil and lawlessness there, he declared, and had produced a general restoration of order and "the orderly administration of justice." He did not mention the freedmen.

Hayes was born in Delaware, Ohio, in 1822. After he was graduated from Kenyon College, he studied law at Harvard and later established a successful law practice in Cincinnati. When the Civil War came, he joined a volunteer unit, rising to the rank of brevet major-general. He was wounded several times in action. After the war he served two terms in Congress, supporting Radical Reconstruction measures over President Johnson's veto and voting for Johnson's impeachment. He went on to serve as governor of Ohio and was elected to that office three times. In the Republican convention of 1876 he was a dark horse; he did not receive the presidential nomination until the seventh ballot. Though his presidency was generally undistinguished, he did please bankers by his sound money policies, and civil service reformers by his efforts to combat the spoils system. After leaving the White House he quickly disappeared into obscurity. He died in 1893.

Questions to consider. Some Northern Democrats bitterly resented the electoral commission's decision for Hayes. They called him His Fraudulency, the Usurper, and Ruther-fraud B. Hayes. Was Hayes's first annual message to Congress, reproduced here, likely to win them over? To what "recent amendments" to the Constitution was he referring? What actions to restore national harmony did he emphasize? What policies did he fail to mention? Was there any justification for charges by some Northerners that Hayes was being too kind to former rebels?

FIRST ANNUAL MESSAGE TO CONGRESS (1877)

To complete and make permanent the pacification of the country continues to be, and until it is fully accomplished must remain, the most important of all our national interests. The earnest purpose of good citizens generally to unite their efforts in this endeavor is evident. It found decided expression in the resolutions announced in 1876 by the national conventions of the leading political parties of the country. There was a widespread apprehension that the momentous results in our progress as a nation marked by the recent amendments to the Constitution were in imminent jeopardy; that the good understanding which prompted their adoption, in the interest of a loyal devotion to the general welfare, might prove a barren truce, and that the two sections of the country, once engaged in civil strife, might be again almost as widely severed and disunited as they were when arrayed in arms against each other.

The course to be pursued, which, in my judgment, seemed wisest in the presence of this emergency, was plainly indicated in my inaugural address. It

From James D. Richardson, ed., *A Compilation of the Messages and Papers of the Presidents* (Government Printing Office, Washington, D.C., 1897-1907), VII: 458-480.

"Great Acrobatic Feat of Rutherford B. Hayes." Hayes had
a difficult acrobatic act to perform if he was to succeed as
president. It had taken an Electoral Commission, set up by
Congress, to declare him a winner by one electoral vote
over Samuel J. Tilden, even though he won fewer popular
votes than Tilden. Even after his inauguration on March 4,
1877, some people continued to jeer at him as "His Fraudulency" and "Ruther-fraud B. Hayes." As president, Hayes
had to show people he was determined to end the kind of
graft and corruption that had discredited the Grant administration. He did reasonably well: he appointed reformers
to his cabinet, launched a cleanup of the civil service, and
removed several notorious spoilsmen from office. But while
he was president the Republican party for all practical
purposes abandoned the cause of civil rights for blacks.
(Library of Congress)

pointed to the time, which all our people desire to see, when a genuine love of our whole country and of all that concerns its true welfare shall supplant the destructive forces of the mutual animosity of races and of sectional hostility. Opinions have differed widely as to the measures best calculated to secure this great end. This was to be expected. The measures adopted by the Administration have been subjected to severe and varied criticism. Any course whatever which might have been entered upon would certainly have encountered distrust and opposition. These measures were, in my judgment, such as were most in harmony with the Constitution and with the genius of our people, and best adapted, under all the circumstances, to attain the end in view. Beneficent results, already apparent, prove that these endeavors are not to be regarded as a mere experiment, and should sustain and encourage us in our efforts. Already, in the brief period which has elapsed, the immediate effectiveness, no less than the justice, of the course pursued is demonstrated, and I have an abiding faith that time will furnish its ample vindication in the minds of the great majority of my fellow-citizens. The discontinuance of the use of the Army for the purpose of upholding local governments in two States of the Union was no less a constitutional duty and requirement, under the circumstances existing at the time, than it was a much-needed measure for the restoration of local self-government and the promotion of national harmony. The withdrawal of the troops from such employment was effected deliberately, and with solicitous care for the peace and good order of society and the protection of the property and persons and every right of all classes of citizens.

The results that have followed are indeed significant and encouraging. All apprehension of danger from remitting those States to local self-government is dispelled, and a most salutary change in the minds of the people has begun and is in progress in every part of that section of the country once the theater of unhappy civil strife, substituting for suspicion, distrust, and aversion, concord, friendship, and patriotic attachment to the Union. No unprejudiced mind will deny that the terrible and often fatal collisions which for several years have been of frequent occurrence and have agitated and alarmed the public mind have almost entirely ceased, and that a spirit of mutual forbearance and hearty national interest has succeeded. There has been a general reestablishment of order and of the orderly administration of justice. Instances of remaining lawlessness have become of rare occurrence; political turmoil and turbulence have disappeared; useful industries have been resumed; public credit in the Southern States has been greatly strengthened, and the encouraging benefits of a revival of commerce between the sections of the country lately embroiled in civil war are fully enjoyed. Such are some of the results already attained, upon which the country is to be congratulated. They are of such importance that we may with confidence patiently await the desired consummation that will surely come with the natural progress of events. . . .

36. Aftermath
Frederick Douglass,
ADDRESS TO THE
LOUISVILLE CONVENTION (1883)

Frederick Douglass regarded the Declaration of Independence as a "watchword of freedom." But he was tempted to turn it to the wall, he said, because its human rights principles were so shamelessly violated. A former slave himself, Douglass knew what he was talking about. Douglass thought that enslaving blacks fettered whites as well and that the United States would never be truly free until it ended chattel slavery. During the Civil War, he had several conversations with Lincoln, urging him to make emancipation his major aim. He also put unremitting pressure on the Union army to accept black volunteers, and after resistance to admitting blacks into the army gave way, he toured the country encouraging blacks to enlist and imploring the government to treat black and white soldiers equally in matters of pay and promotion.

Douglass had great hopes for his fellow blacks after the Civil War. He demanded they be given full rights—political, legal, educational, and economic—as citizens. He also wanted to see the wall of separation between the races crumble and see "the colored people of this country, enjoying the same freedom [as whites], voting at the same ballot-box, using the same cartridge-box, going to the same schools, attending the same churches, travelling in the same street cars, in the same railroad cars, on the same steam-boats, proud of the same country, fighting the same war, and enjoying the same peace and all its advantages." He regarded the Republican party as the "party of progress, justice and freedom" and at election time took to the stump and rallied black votes for the party. He was rewarded for his party services by appointment as marshal of the District of Columbia in 1877, as recorder of deeds for the District in 1881, and as minister to Haiti in 1889. But he was also asked to keep a low profile by Republican leaders, was omitted from White House guest lists, and was excluded from presidential receptions even though one duty of the District marshal was to introduce the guests at White House state occasions.

Douglass was puzzled and then upset by the increasing indifference of Republican leaders to conditions among blacks after the Civil War. In 1883 he attended a convention of blacks in Louisville, Kentucky, which met to discuss their plight and reaffirm their demand for full civil rights. In his keynote address, which is reprinted here, Douglass vividly portrayed the discrimination and persecution his people encountered; but he continued to believe that "prejudice, with all its malign accomplishments, may yet be removed by peaceful means."

Born into slavery in Maryland in 1817, Frederick Augustus Washington Bailey learned to read and write despite efforts to keep him illiterate. In 1838 he managed to escape to freedom and adopted the name Frederick Douglass. Shortly afterward he became associated with William Lloyd Garrison and developed into such an articulate spokesman for the anti-slavery cause that people doubted he had ever been a slave. In 1845 he published his *Narrative of the Life of Frederick Douglass, an American Slave*, naming names, places, dates, and precise events to convince people he had been born in bondage. Douglass continued to be an articulate spokesman for the black cause throughout his life. Shortly before his death in 1895 a college student asked him what a young black could do to help the cause. "Agitate! Agitate! Agitate!" Douglass is supposed to have told him.

Questions to consider. In the following address Douglass was speaking to a convention of blacks in Louisville, but his appeal was primarily to American whites. How did he try to convince them that blacks deserved the same rights and opportunities as all Americans? How powerful did he think the color line was? What outrages against his people did he report? What was his attitude toward the Republican party, which he had so faithfully served? Were the grievances he cited largely economic or were they social and political in nature? How would Douglass's address strike civil rights workers today?

ADDRESS TO THE
LOUISVILLE CONVENTION (1883)

Born on American soil in common with yourselves, deriving our bodies and our minds from its dust, centuries having passed away since our ancestors were torn from the shores of Africa, we, like yourselves, hold ourselves to be in every sense Americans, and that we may, therefore, venture to speak to you in a tone not lower than that which becomes earnest men and American citizens. Having watered your soil with our tears, enriched it with our blood, performed its roughest labor in time of peace, defended it against enemies in time of war, and at all times been loyal and true to its best interests, we deem it no arrogance or presumption to manifest now a common concern with you for its welfare, prosperity, honor and glory. . . .

It is our lot to live among a people whose laws, traditions, and prejudices have been against us for centuries, and from these they are not yet free. To assume that they are free from these evils simply because they have changed their laws is to assume what is utterly unreasonable and contrary to facts. Large bodies move slowly. Individuals may be converted on the instant and

From Philip Foner, ed., *The Life and Writings of Frederick Douglass* (4 v., International Publishers, New York, 1955), IV: 373-392. Reprinted by permission.

change their whole course of life. Nations never. Time and events are required for the conversion of nations. Not even the character of a great political organization can be changed by a new platform. It will be the same old snake though in a new skin. Though we have had war, reconstruction and abolition as a nation, we still linger in the shadow and blight of an extinct institution. Though the colored man is no longer subject to be bought and sold, he is still surrounded by an adverse sentiment which fetters all his movements. In his downward course he meets with no resistance, but his course upward is resented and resisted at every step of his progress. If he comes in ignorance, rags, and wretchedness, he conforms to the popular belief of his character, and in that character he is welcome. But if he shall come as a gentleman, a scholar, and a statesman, he is hailed as a contradiction to the national faith concerning his race, and his coming is resented as impudence. In the one case he may provoke contempt and derision, but in the other he is an affront to pride, and provokes malice. Let him do what he will, there is at present, therefore, no escape for him. The color line meets him everywhere, and in a measure shuts him out from all respectable and profitable trades and callings. In spite of all your religion and laws he is a rejected man.

He is rejected by trade unions, of every trade, and refused work while he lives, and burial when he dies, and yet he is asked to forget his color, and forget that which everybody else remembers. If he offers himself to a builder as a mechanic, to a client as a lawyer, to a patient as a physician, to a college as a professor, to a firm as a clerk, to a Government Department as an agent, or an officer, he is sternly met on the color line, and his claim to consideration in some way is disputed on the ground of color.

Not even our churches, whose members profess to follow the despised Nazarene, whose home, when on earth, was among the lowly and despised, have yet conquered this feeling of color madness, and what is true of our churches is also true of our courts of law. Neither is free from this all-pervading atmosphere of color hate. The one describes the Deity as impartial, no respecter of persons, and the other the Goddess of Justice as blindfolded, with sword by her side and scales in her hand held evenly between high and low, rich and low, white and black, but both are the images of American imagination, rather than American practices.

Taking advantage of the general disposition in this country to impute crime to color, white men *color* their faces to commit crime and wash off the hated color to escape punishment. In many places where the commission of crime is alleged against one of our color, the ordinary processes of the law are set aside as too slow for the impetuous justice of the infuriated populace. They take the law into their own bloody hands and proceed to whip, stab, shoot, hang, or burn the alleged culprit, without the intervention of courts, counsel, judges, juries, or witnesses. In such cases it is not the business of the accusers to prove guilt, but it is for the accused to prove his innocence, a thing hard for him to do in these infernal Lynch courts. A man accused, surprised, frightened and captured by a motley crowd, dragged with a rope about his neck in midnight-darkness to the nearest tree, and told in the coarsest terms of profanity to prepare for death, would be more than human if he did not, in his terror-stricken appearance, more confirm suspicion of guilt than the contrary.

Frederick Douglass receiving a salute of honor from the guns on Governor's Island, New York. Frederick Douglass's greatest work came before and during the Civil War. One of the most eloquent and magnetic of all the abolitionist leaders, he contributed enormously to the antislavery cause. During the Civil War he pressed hard for the enlistment of blacks to fight in the Union armies on an equal footing with whites. After the war he continued his efforts for civil rights, including black suffrage. For his services to the Republican party he received appointments as secretary to the Santo Domingo commission, marshal and recorder of deeds for the District of Columbia, and U.S. minister to Haiti. (Library of Congress)

Worse still, in the presence of such hell-black outrages, the pulpit is usually dumb, and the press in the neighborhood is silent or openly takes side with the mob. There are occasional cases in which white men are lynched, but one sparrow does not make a summer. Every one knows that what is called Lynch law is peculiarly the law for colored people and for nobody else. If there were no other grievance than this horrible and barbarous Lynch law custom, we should be justified in assembling, as we have now done, to expose and denounce it. But this is not all. Even now, after twenty years of so-called emancipation, we are subject to lawless raids of midnight riders, who, with blackened faces, invade our homes and perpetrate the foulest of crimes upon us and our families. This condition of things is too flagrant and notorious to require specifications or proof. Thus in all the relations of life and death we are met by the color line. We cannot ignore it if we would, and ought not if we could. It hunts us at midnight, it denies us accommodation in hotels and justice in the courts; excludes our children from schools, refuses our sons the chance to learn trades, and compels us to pursue only such labor as will bring the least reward. While we recognize the color line as a hurtful force, a mountain barrier to our progress, wounding our bleeding feet with its flinty rocks at every step, we do not despair. We are a hopeful people. This convention is a proof of our faith in you, in reason, in truth and justice—our belief that prejudice, with all its malign accomplishments, may yet be removed by peaceful means; that, assisted by time and events and the growing enlightenment of both races, the color line will ultimately become harmless. When this shall come it will then only be used, as it should be, to distinguish one variety of the human family from another. It will cease to have any civil, political, or moral significance, and colored conventions will then be dispensed with as anachronisms, wholly out of place, but not till then. Do not marvel that we are discouraged. The faith within us has a rational basis, and is confirmed by facts. When we consider how deep-seated this feeling against us is; the long centuries it has been forming; the forces of avarice which have been marshaled to sustain it; how the language and literature of the country have been pervaded with it; how the church, the press, the play-house, and other influences of the country have been arrayed in its support, the progress toward its extinction must be considered vast and wonderful. . . .

We do not believe, as we are often told, that the Negro is the ugly child of the national family, and the more he is kept out of sight the better it will be for him. You know that liberty given is never so precious as liberty sought for and fought for. The man outraged is the man to make the outcry. Depend upon it, men will not care much for a people who do not care for themselves. Our meeting here was opposed by some of our members, because it would disturb the peace of the Republican party. The suggestion came from coward lips and misapprehended the character of that party. If the Republican party cannot stand a demand for justice and fair play, it ought to go down. We were men before that party was born, and our manhood is more sacred than any party can be. Parties were made for men, not men for parties.

The colored people of the South are the laboring people of the South. The labor of a country is the source of its wealth; without the colored laborer to-day the South would be a howling wilderness, given up to bats, owls, wolves, and bears. He was the source of its wealth before the war, and has been the source of its prosperity since the war. He almost alone is visible in her fields, with implements of toil in his hands, and laboriously using them to-day.

Let us look candidly at the matter. While we see and hear that the South is more prosperous than it ever was before and rapidly recovering from the waste of war, while we read that it raises more cotton, sugar, rice, tobacco, corn, and other valuable products than it ever produced before, how happens it, we sternly ask, that the houses of its laborers are miserable huts, that their clothes are rags, and their food the coarsest and scantiest? How happens it that the land-owner is becoming richer and the laborer poorer?

The implication is irresistible—that where the landlord is prosperous the laborer ought to share his prosperity, and whenever and wherever we find this is not the case there is manifestly wrong somewhere. . . .

Flagrant as have been the outrages committed upon colored citizens in respect to their civil rights, more flagrant, shocking, and scandalous still have been the outrages committed upon our political rights by means of bull-dozing and Kukluxing, Mississippi plans, fraudulent courts, tissue ballots, and the like devices. Three States in which the colored people outnumber the white population are without colored representation and their political voice suppressed. The colored citizens in those States are virtually disfranchised, the Constitution held in utter contempt and its provisions nullified. This has been done in the face of the Republican party and successive Republican administrations. . . .

This is no question of party. It is a question of law and government. It is a question whether men shall be protected by law, or be left to the mercy of cyclones of anarchy and bloodshed. It is whether the Government or the mob shall rule this land; whether the promises solemnly made to us in the constitution be manfully kept or meanly and flagrantly broken. Upon this vital point we ask the whole people of the United States to take notice that whatever of political power we have shall be exerted for no man of any party who will not, in advance of election, promise to use every power given him by the Government, State or National, to make the black man's path to the ballot-box as straight, smooth and safe as that of any other American citizen. . . .

We hold it to be self-evident that no class or color should be the exclusive rulers of this country. If there is such a ruling class, there must of course be a subject class, and when this condition is once established this Government of the people, by the people, and for the people, will have perished from the earth.

COUNTERPOINT
After Slavery: Charleston Freedmen, 1870–1871

What did blacks do with their freedom following emancipation? Most remained on the land, but some tried to begin anew in Southern towns and cities, where they joined former urban slaves and a select group that had been freed prior to the Civil War. Carl Osthaus has depicted the main features of one such black community in the following tables, constructed from the manuscript records of the Charleston, South Carolina, branch of the Freedman's Savings Bank. The bank was chartered by Congress in 1865 in order to make saving attractive and possible for former slaves. With branches in towns across the South, it grew rapidly, attracting over 60,000 depositors and four million dollars in assets before failing in the 1870s from depression, bad loans, and graft at its headquarters.

Table 5.1 lists vital statistics on Charleston depositors in 1870 and 1871 and provides a view of the struggling black community in this one-time Confederate bastion. The portrait that emerges is at once discouraging and hopeful. Data on writing ability suggest that more than half the depositors were illiterate, yet historians estimate that, by comparison, no more than 10 percent of all slaves could read and write. Likewise, most depositors were unskilled workers, but the overall occupational structure speaks well of a people so recently out of bondage. The fact that so large a proportion of depositors were in their twenties raises some intriguing questions. Was this fact due to the ability of the young to adjust more readily to free society? Did the manual occupations at which most freedmen worked place such a premium on youth that earnings declined as one grew older? Can you think of some other explanations that might account for the age structure of depositors?

Table 5.2 portrays the rich associational life of the town's freedmen. The freedmen, like poor European immigrants at other times in the nation's history, displayed a strong fraternal impulse and established numerous benefit societies designed to provide security through mutual aid. Judging from the list, which institution figured most prominently in black life? The table also reminds us that although class distinctions in the black community were not as sharply drawn as in white society, they were very real nonetheless. The members of Laboring Union No. 2 (account 5911) undoubtedly had different interests than the aspiring contractors of the Charleston Joint Stock and Jobbing Company (account 7116), and it is not likely that many domestics or recent field hands belonged to the Ladies Historical Association (account 5710). Can you locate any other associations that might have served to differentiate Charleston blacks? Which societies tended to unite the entire black community? Given the freedmen's economic and social position in the post-bellum South, which tendency—uniting or differentiating—would you suppose was most prevalent?

In sum, the tables show an unexpectedly high propensity to save, among all ages and occupations, for a people who had not owned property before. The figures suggest, in fact, that saving might have been a fairly common practice even before emancipation. The data on occupations, however, indicate the weakness of the depositors: 27 percent, or almost a third, were unskilled laborers and children, who were on the low end of the earning scale. Presumably they would be the first to suffer during depression times. Which associations in Table 5.2 would have suffered most when the bank went under?

Table 5.1: From Carl R. Osthaus, *Freedmen, Philanthropy, and Fraud: A History of the Freedman's Savings Bank* (University of Illinois Press, Urbana, 1976), pp. 114-119. Copyright © 1976 by the Board of Trustees of the University of Illinois.

TABLE 5.1 Description of Every Tenth Charleston Depositor, July 1870–June 1871

Total descriptions of new accounts: 298
  92 were transfers or provided no information
206 provided substantial information
  19 of the above were societies or associations
187 total descriptions of new depositors

Characteristics	Number	Percent
Sex		
Male	126	67
Female	61	33
Ability to write name		
Signature	63	34
Weak signature	19	10
Signed with an "X"	97	52
Unknown	8	4
Race		
Negro	162	87
Caucasian	10	5
Unknown	15	8
Residence		
Charleston	135	72
Non-Charleston	42	23
Unknown	10	5
Age		
1-10	11	6
11-15	15	8
16-19	11	6
20-29	60	32
30-39	27	14
40-49	23	12
50-59	17	9
60-69	4	2
70-79	1	1
Unknown	18	10
Occupation		
Professional and white collar	9	5
Artisans (includes 12 carpenters)	30	16
Farmers (farming for others, 9; farming for selves, 12)	21	11
Cooks, washers, domestics (may include one or two cooks who worked for city restaurants and who, therefore, should be added to artisan class)	31	17
Waiters, butlers, porters, steward class	17	9
Laborers (unskilled)	39	21
School children	12	6
Unknown	28	15

TABLE 5.2   Charleston Societies and Businesses That
Opened Bank Accounts, July 1870–June 1871

Acct. no.	Organization
5038	Veterans Republican Brotherhood
5039	Daughters of Jerusalem (sickness and death benefits)
5087	Lincoln Branch (charitable society)
5088	Union Lodge No. 1
5113	Daughters of Emanuel Watchman (sickness and death benefits)
5137	Young Calvary Union No. 2 (sickness and death benefits)
5165	Zion's Watchman Society
5183	Emanuel Sabbath School
5200	St. Theresa Charitable Association
5219	Israel Branch Society (charitable society)
5221	Benevolent Sociable Society (charitable society)
5231	United Fire Company
5319	Angel March Branch No. 2
5326	Good Hope Society (charitable society)
5346	Baptist Faith Society
5354	Young Watchman of Charleston Neck No. 2
5381	Christian Professor Society
5391	Faith, Hope, and Love (sickness and death benefits)
5456	Benford and Masyck "Ethiopia Troop"
5460	Young Centenary Branch No. 2 (sickness and death benefits)
5463	United Benevolent Compact and Sisters
5466	Emanuel Branch (sickness and death benefits)
5496	Charitable Home Association
5497	Club of the Sons of Jacob
5551	Young Interested Branch No. 2
5581	Liberia Branch Society (sickness and death benefits)
5610	Leaders Board of the Methodist Protestant Church
5635	Union Society No. 1 of the A.M.E. Church (sickness and death benefits)
5666	Lincoln Republican Guard
5670	Delany Rifles—Military Company of the City of Charleston
5672	Sons and Daughers of Daniel
5685	Class Union No. 19 (sickness and death benefits)
5708	Class Union No. 8 of Emanuel Church
5710	Ladies Historical Association
5716	Longshore Cooperative Association
5804	Class Union No. 17
5843	Sons and Daughters of Waymond
5852	Ladies Benevolent Society
5880	Zion Presbyterian Union No. 3
5909	Lincoln Tabernacle No. 1
5911	Laboring Union No. 2
5922	Young Wesley Branch No. 1
5933	Ladies Companion
5943	Young Men's Christian Aid
6051	The Emanuel Branch
6087	Charleston Branch Joint Stock Company

TABLE 5.2 *(cont.)*

Acct. no.	Organization
6233	Wesley's Band
6243	Christian Social Nursery
6258	John Simmons Fish Company
6573	Sons and Daughters of Zareptha (sickness and death benefits)
6764	Class Union No. 9, Centenary M.E. Church
6778	Sons and Daughters of the Crops (sickness and death benefits)
6782	Ola Society of John the Baptist
6860	Lot Fund, Plymouth Church
6905	Class Union, Emanuel Church
6908	Class Union No. 9
6925	Lincoln Harp Society (sickness and death benefits)
6939	Protestant Gospel Society
6960	Beaufort Sons and Daughters of Love
7029	Plymouth Congregational Church
7059	Presbyterian Church, Wadisdo Island, S.C.
7065	Edisto Island Presbyterian Church
7111	Wesley Watchman Class No. 2
7116	Charleston Joint Stock and Jobbing Company (construction company)
7158	Spring Cart Association
7319	Charleston Land Company
7432	Good Samaritan Society
7440	Young Shebara Association
7500	Joshua Branch No. 2
7530	A.M.E. Church, Mt. Pleasant
7964	African M.E. Church, Edisto Island
8055	Mt. Olivet Independent Branch
8066	Union Star Fire Engine Company
8091	Enquiring Joshua Society
8181	Class Union No. 4

A Statistical Appendix

List of Appendix Tables

All the information in the appendix tables comes from *U.S. Historical Statistics from Colonial Times to 1970,* published by the U.S. Government Printing Office, Washington, D.C., 1975. In the tables a dash (—) means zero; the small letters *na* mean that figures are *not available.*

TABLE A.1   U.S. Population and Selected State Populations, 1790–1970

The population of the United States has grown steadily since the nation's founding, just as observers like Gottlieb Mittelberger (Vol. 1, Document 9) and James Madison (Vol. 1, Document 14) thought it would. It has grown faster in some periods than in others, however, and faster in some regions than in others, as shown by the figures for the six states below. Stemming chiefly from economics, immigration, and climate, this regional divergence has had profound political and social consequences—the early prominence of Massachusetts and Virginia statesmen, for example, and the election of two Californians and a Texan to the presidency since 1960.

	Population (in millions)						
Year	Mass.	N.Y.	Va.	Ill.	Tex.	Cal.	Total
1790	.4	.3	.7	—	—	—	3.9
1810	.5	1.0	.9	.01	—	—	7.2
1830	.6	1.9	1.0	.2	—	—	12.9
1850	1.0	3.1	1.1	.9	.2	.1	23.2
1870	1.5	4.4	1.2	2.5	.8	.6	39.8
1890	2.2	6.0	1.7	3.8	2.2	1.2	62.9
1910	3.4	9.1	2.1	5.6	3.9	2.4	91.9
1930	4.3	12.6	2.4	7.6	5.8	5.7	122.8
1950	4.7	14.8	3.3	8.7	7.7	10.6	150.7
1970	5.7	18.2	4.6	11.1	11.2	19.9	203.2

TABLE A.2   U.S. Population and Breakdown by
Urban Population Sizes, 1790–1970

The population of the United States grew rapidly from the start. But as the following figures show, towns and cities grew faster than rural areas even in the early decades of agricultural and frontier expansion. America seems to have been destined to be an urbanized society, which of course it largely was by the twentieth century.

Recently, almost all growth has been urban. But rapid urbanization has not always meant that big cities set the pace. For instance, the population in cities from 25,000–250,000 almost doubled from 27.2 million in 1950 to 48.8 million in 1970, while that in cities over 250,000 only went from 34.8 million to 42.2 million. During the same period, all towns of 2,500 and over grew from 96.5 million to 149.3 million in population. Cities of 250,000 and over grew most rapidly in population during 1850-1910, a period of great industrial growth.

	Population (in millions)				
Year	2,500 and over	2,500–25,000	25,000–250,000	250,000 and over	Total
1790	.2	.14	.06	—	3.9
1810	.5	.3	.2	—	7.2
1830	1.1	.6	.5	—	12.9
1850	3.5	1.3	1.6	.6	23.2
1870	9.9	4.2	2.6	3.1	39.8
1890	22.1	8.1	7.1	6.9	62.9
1910	42.0	13.6	13.0	15.4	91.9
1930	68.9	20.7	20.4	27.8	122.8
1950	96.5	34.5	27.2	34.8	150.7
1970	149.3	58.3	48.8	42.2	203.2

TABLE A.3   U.S. Immigrant Population by Origin, Occupation, Sex, and Age, 1820–1970

The United States has been called a nation of immigrants, and surely few nations were so influenced by newcomers as this one. Immigration, clearly a force behind the great surge in national population, also contributed to the development of cities, social classes, and ethnic and cultural diversity. The make-up of the immigrants themselves changed over time as well, not only in numbers but in nationality, occupational status, and even family structure (as suggested by the shifting proportions of males and of children). For example, in 1910 during industrial expansion, about 70 percent of the immigrants came from the eastern and southern European countries, with about 60 percent being laborers or servants. In 1970, the same area provided only 20 percent of the immigrants, while over 40 percent came from the Americas and about 25 percent from Asia; the occupational skills had also shifted, with only 10 percent in the laborer and servant categories, and over 30 percent being professionals or skilled workers.

Thus, not only do the totals below ebb and flow according to the coming of war or peace, prosperity or depression, tolerance or persecution, in both the country of origin and the United States, but later immigrants seldom possessed the same characteristics as their counterparts who came one, two, or three generations earlier. Here one may find, among other things, a context for James T. Farrell's portrait in the excerpt from *Studs Lonigan* (Vol. 2, Document 10), the Chinese Exclusion Act (Vol. 2, Document 6), and the current debate over further immigration restriction.

	1820	1850	1880	1910	1940	1970
Total*	10,311	324,098	457,257	1,041,570	70,756	373,326
Northern Europe†	7,467	307,044	310,213	202,198	37,520	35,375
Eastern and southern Europe	224	1,279	38,478	724,083	11,976	75,278
Asia	5	7	5,839	23,533	2,050	90,215
The Americas	387	15,768	101,692	89,534	17,822	161,727
Professional-commercial	1,038	7,318	9,699	36,639	18,578	68,497
Skilled workers and farmers	1,964	69,242	97,133	133,640	6,557	50,461
Laborers	334	46,640	105,012	505,654	2,372	18,480
Servants	139	3,203	18,580	105,735	3,940	19,751
None	6,836	188,931	217,446	260,002	39,409	216,137
Males	7,197	196,138	287,623	736,038	33,460	176,990
Under age 15	1,313	62,543	87,154	120,509	9,602	104,880

* Includes immigrants from Africa, Australasia, France, and the Low Countries as well as areas of origin listed below.

† Great Britain, Ireland, Scandinavia, and Germany.

TABLE A.4   U.S. Workers by Economic Sectors (Agriculture, Manufacturing, Construction, and Trade), 1810–1970

This table sorts American workers into four basic sectors of the economy. Here we see evidence of (among other things) the decline of farming after 1919, the growth of manufacturing before 1900 and its pre-eminence by 1950, the strong showing of construction for a hundred years and its subsequent flattening out to the same low level as agriculture, and the steady advance of the trade and finance sector to a place almost equal to manufacturing. We thus pass from the "farmer's age" to the "workshop of the world" to, at last, the "service economy." Observe how the rise of manufacturing and trade parallels the growth of cities (Table A.2) and how decline in agriculture and construction shows up in the occupations of the immigrants (Table A.3).

	Workers (in millions)				
Year	Agriculture	Manufacturing	Construction	Trade/finance	Total
1810	1.9	.08	na	na	2.3
1830	2.9	na	na	na	4.2
1850	4.5	1.2	.4	.5	8.3
1870	6.8	2.5	.8	1.3	12.9
1890	10.0	4.4	1.5	2.9	23.3
1910	11.8	8.3	1.9	5.3	37.5
1930	10.6	9.9	2.0	8.1	48.8
1950	7.9	15.7	3.0	12.2	65.5
1970	3.7	19.4	3.4	18.6	85.9

TABLE A.5 Growth of U.S. Transportation (Ship, Railroad, Airplane, and Automobile), 1790–1970

The following figures illustrate the evolution of transportation in the United States. Each new type of transportation has represented a technological advance—steam power, the internal combustion engine, heavier-than-air flight—and thus mirrors the progress of the Industrial Revolution. Each type has also coincided with a phase of national development: post-Revolutionary foreign trade, the winning of the West, suburbanization, and the modern aerospace era. The hugeness of the transportation system as a whole suggests both the size of the country and the frequency and speed with which Americans have tended to move themselves and their commodities. The individual columns show when each part of the system really took off—or, as in ship tonnage in the age of the supertanker, when it took off anew.

Year	Ship tonnage into U.S. ports (in millions)	Railroad track miles (in thousands)	Motor-vehicle registration (in millions)	Scheduled commercial air routes (in thousands of miles)
1790	.6	—	—	—
1810	1.0	—	—	—
1830	1.1	—	—	—
1850	3.7	9	—	—
1870	9.2	53	—	—
1890	18.1	200	—	—
1910	40.2	352	.5	—
1930	81.3	430	22.1	30
1950	86.6	396	49.2	77
1970	254.2	350	108.4	172

TABLE A.6   U.S. Production of Selected Commodities, 1870–1970

Whether industrialization advanced in a spurt after the Civil War, as Terence Powderly (Vol. 2, Document 12) and Upton Sinclair (Vol. 2, Document 15) believed, or steadily throughout the nineteenth century, as the occupational and transportation data in Tables A.4 and A.5 hint, there is no doubt that the process was very far along by the early twentieth century. The figures below show American gains in the production of a number of important commodities. All of them have gone up sharply over the past century. Yet the listing of the items in pairs highlights divergent growth rates of some interest. Production of sugar in 1970 is twenty times the amount produced in 1870, while that of flour is only three times what was produced a century ago. The rates of growth of rayon and cigarettes are extraordinarily high when compared with those for cotton and cigars. The number of pairs of shoes produced for women was less than that for men in 1910, but in 1970, women's shoes were more than double the number made for men. In most cases the difference in growth rates comes at a particular point in time rather than steadily. What causes the various differences? What does it say about American society that industry begins to produce typewriters and light bulbs? Does the speeding up or slowing down of production growth rates have to do more with technological change or with shifts in consumption habits?

Commodity	Production (in millions)					
	1870	1890	1910	1930	1950	1970
Flour (barrels)	48	83	107	120	115	129
Sugar (lbs.)	1.2	3.2	7.3	12	14.7	20.8
Bricks*	2.8	8	9.9	5.1	6.3	6.7
Steel (tons)	.08	4.8	28.3	44.6	96.8	131.5
Beer (barrels)	7	28	59.5	3.7	88.8	134.7
Liquor (gals.)	72	111	164	—	194	355
Cotton (bales)	3	8.6	11.6	13.9	10	10.2
Rayon (lbs.)	—	—	2	118	957	699
Cigars	1	4.2	6.8	5.9	5.5	8.0
Cigarettes	.02	2.5	9.8	124.2	392	562
Men's shoes (pairs)	na	na	98	77	103	100.
Women's shoes (pairs)	na	na	87	112	195	230
Typewriters	—	na	.2	.9	1.4	.1.4
Light bulbs	—	na	70	350	1,200	1,582

* Billions.

TABLE A.7   Growth of U.S. Commercial Banks
and U.S. Bank Assets, 1790–1970

The increase in the number of banks and in bank assets provides one measure of American economic growth, especially of growth as related to credit and money transactions—exactly the sort of thing that concerned Benjamin Franklin (Vol. 1, Document 10) and Andrew Jackson (Vol. 1, Document 20). Comparison of the two columns in the table below shows, too, that while bank assets grew steadily from 1790 to 1970, the number of banks shot up all through the era of territorial expansion (1830-1890) and early urbanization (1850-1910), then fell off after 1910 and especially after 1930. This of course reflects the ravages of the Great Depression, when so many banks failed that President Franklin Roosevelt declared a bank holiday. But the reduced number of banks in 1970 reflects a trend that this table does not fully encompass: a pattern of consolidation, takeover, and merger whereby fewer firms dominate *many* important sectors of the American economy.

Year	Number of commercial banks	Bank assets (in millions of dollars)
1790	na	na
1810	80	na
1830	330	350
1850	824	532
1870	1,937	1,781
1890	8,201	6,358
1910	25,151	22,922
1930	24,273	74,290
1950	14,676	179,165
1970	14,187	611,305

TABLE A.8   U.S. Consumer Price Index and Average Daily Wages of Construction, Manufacturing, and Unskilled Laborers, 1790–1970

The figures here provide a rough view of how ordinary laboring people fared under capitalism from 1790 to 1970. Although wages did not rise quickly for any group until well into the twentieth century, prices also remained fairly steady before that time, and therefore workers may have done better than first appears. The table shows the comparative advantage enjoyed by construction workers over other workers, and the smaller advantage of those in manufacturing over the unskilled. Observe that periods of steady or falling wages usually coincided with periods of heavy immigration (see Table A.3). Table A.8 does not reveal how the work day grew gradually shorter, particularly after 1890. But shown very clearly is the sharp wage rise after 1930, the handiwork in part of labor organizers such as John L. Lewis (Vol. 2, Document 19), whose successes were all the more important because of the tremendous recent growth of the manufacturing sector of the economy.

All the money figures, of course, must be viewed in light of changes in the cost of living over the decades. The consumer price index, which is based on the arbitrary assignment of the value 100 to 1967 prices, provides a rough measure of this cost-of-living change. Construction wages fell in the years from 1830 to 1850, for example. But the cost of living fell even more. Construction workers, therefore, fared better than might appear at first glance. Manufacturing workers made twice as much in 1930 as in 1910. But prices almost doubled, too, so that workers' gains were actually slight.

Year	Price index†	Daily wage (in current dollars)*		
		Construction	Manufacturing	Unskilled labor
1790	na	1.00	na	.50
1810	47	1.70	na	1.00
1830	32	1.75	na	1.00
1850	25	1.50	na	.90
1870	38	2.50	na	1.75
1890	27	3.00	2.00	1.50
1910	28	4.00	2.40	2.00
1930	50	5.00	5.50	na
1950	72	16.00	12.00	na
1970	116	42.00	27.00	na

* Wages for 1790–1830 are from the Philadelphia area, for 1850–1870 from the Erie Canal area, and for 1890–1970 from the entire nation. "Current dollars" means the actual wage, *not* adjusted for cost-of-living changes over the years.

† A price index assigns a base year (in this case 1967) a value of 100 to represent the price of important commodities (rent, food, clothing, and so forth), then assigns values to other years that relate to 100 as the prices of the same commodities in those years relate to prices in the base year. A glance at the index tells us instantly, therefore, that it cost approximately half as much to live in 1850 as it had in 1810, but about twice as much in 1970 as in 1930.

TABLE A.9   Selected Religious Affiliations of the U.S. Population (Methodist, Presbyterian, Southern Baptist, Episcopalian, and Roman Catholic), 1790–1970

Religious diversity became a hallmark of American society, just as Roger Williams (Vol. 1, Document 3) hoped it would. But the United States remained a broadly Christian land despite its diversity, and a heavily Protestant one despite its broad Christianity. The figures here show the growth of four important Protestant denominations and also of the Roman Catholic church.

Methodism and Presbyterianism, both intimately intertwined with the great reform movements of the nineteenth century, have grown steadily over the decades. Methodism tripled from 1850 to 1890 and tripled again from 1890 to 1970; the Presbyterians in this latter period quadrupled their numbers. The Southern Baptists, born partly in reaction to Northern anti-slavery agitation before the Civil War, tripled its membership from 1930 to 1970. Episcopalianism, initially prominent in the South and later attractive to wealthy industrialists, managed by contrast only a 50 percent increase after 1930.

Membership in the Roman Catholic church tripled from 1890 to 1930, but only doubled from 1930 to 1970. The great Catholic tide thus coincided with the great tide of immigration. Within a quarter-century, Catholics, though still a minority in the country, outnumbered the combined membership of all the four large Protestant denominations listed in Table A.9. Comparison with the totals for the United States population in Table A.1 will reveal, however, that all but one of these Protestant denominations grew at a pace faster than the population for the period from 1930 to 1970—perhaps a surprising development in what has often been called an age of materialism.

	Number of members (in thousands)				
Year	Methodist	Presbyterian	Southern Baptist	Episcopalian	Roman Catholic
1790	58	na	—	na	na
1810	175	na	—	na	na
1830	478	173	—	na	na
1850	1,186	207	400*	na	na
1870	1,822	445	na	na	na
1890	3,442	761	1,236	na	8,000*
1910	5,073	1,315	2,332	na	14,347
1930	7,319	1,937	3,850	1,939	20,204
1950	8,936	2,364	7,080	2,541	27,766
1970	10,672	3,096	11,629	3,475	47,872

* Estimate.

TABLE A.10 U.S. School Enrollments of School-Age Populations by Race and Sex, 1850–1970

Americans have always prized education, the Puritans, for example, to encourage Bible reading, Franklin and Jefferson to make good citizens. But modern public schools really began only after 1830 when reformers sought to use free schools to reduce social dislocations and foster unity. Enrollments grew rapidly, although mostly for Northern white males at this time. By 1890, however, about as many girls as boys went to school, a third of of the country's black children were in school, and the Southern educational system was growing. This expansion of Southern schools and black education was one positive result of the Reconstruction effort. The expansion of education generally is testimony to the strength of American local government.

Year	Whites only	Blacks only	Males only	Females only	Total*
1850	56%	2%	50%	45%	47%
1870	54	10	50	47	48
1890	58	33	55	54	54
1910	61	45	59	59	59
1930	71	60	70	70	70
1950	79	75	79	78	79
1970	88	85	89	87	88

* School-age has varied according to time and place over this period, but may generally be understood to mean from about six years old to the mid-teens.

TABLE A.11   U.S. Federal Civilian Employees (Total) and Numbers Employed by the U.S. Postal Service and the Department of Defense, 1816–1970

The growth of the federal government has been of great interest and concern to Americans recently. The following data show one reason why. In the early nineteenth century the central government employed only .5 percent of the nation's work force; in the early twentieth century, a full 1 percent; and by 1970, more than 3 percent. The figures show, too, the main sources of this rising federal percentage: the post office, which loomed large from the start and then grew with the country; and nonuniformed military personnel, who have been the dominant federal presence for several decades.

Year	Post office	Defense	Total government civilian employees
1816	3,341	190	4,837
1831	8,764	377	11,491
1851	21,391	403	26,274
1871	36,696	1,183	51,020
1891	95,449	20,561	157,442
1910	209,005	58,320	388,708
1930	297,895	103,462	601,319
1950	484,679	753,149	1,960,708
1970	741,216	1,219,125	2,981,574

TABLE A.12   U.S. Federal Expenditures (Total) and Selected Expenditure Categories (National Defense, Interest on the Public Debt, U.S. Postal Service, Veterans' Benefits, and Income Security Including General Retirement—Social Security and Medicare—and Public Assistance), 1791–1970

The federal government was an insignificant force in the economy of the nineteenth century, except perhaps directly after the Civil War, when interest on the war debt, veterans' pensions, postal spending, and outlays for military reconstruction and the Indian wars all drove the budget higher. Although the budget grew at a good clip between 1890 and 1930, the real leap came only after World War II.

Interest on the national debt was a key component of federal spending in the time of George Washington and remains so today: it is the third largest category, ahead of veterans' benefits and the post office combined. But interest payments pale in comparison with defense spending, which grew from 25 percent of the total in 1930 to 33 percent in 1950 to 40 percent in 1970. If one includes interest and veterans' benefits, both up mainly because of wars, the total military component of the budget suddenly rises to over one-half. And even defense has multiplied less rapidly than social security, now grown far beyond the expectations (if not the hopes) of Frances Perkins (Vol. 2, Document 18).

Remember that these figures must be modified for population growth (35 percent between 1950 and 1970) and inflation (70 percent for the same period). Even so, the federal government is clearly important as it never was before because of the unprecedented mix of welfare and warfare.

	Expenditures (in millions of current dollars)					
Year	Defense	Interest	Post office	Veterans' benefits	Social security	Total expenditures
1791	.6	2.3	.04	.2	—	4.3
1810	3.9	2.8	.6	.8	—	8.1
1830	8	1.9	1.9	1.4	—	15
1850	17	3.8	5.2	1.9	—	40
1870	79	129	24	28	—	310
1890	67	36	66	107	—	318
1910	313	21	230	161	—	694
1930	839	659	804	221	—	3,320
1950	13,440	5,750	2,223	2,223	784	39,544
1970	78,360	19,304	7,867	8,307	36,835	196,588

DATE DUE

The Library Store   #47-0103